Delivering Cancer and Palliative Care Education

Edited by

Lorna Foyle

and

Janis Hostad

Foreword by

Professor Karen Cox

Radcliffe Publishing
Oxford • San Francisco

Radcliffe Publishing Ltd
18 Marcham Road
Abingdon
Oxon OX14 1AA
United Kingdom

www.radcliffe-oxford.com
Electronic catalogue and worldwide online ordering facility.

_____

British Library Cataloguing in Publication Data

A catalogue record for this book is available from the British Library.

ISBN 1 85775 978 8

Typeset by Acorn Bookwork Ltd, Salisbury, Wiltshire
Printed and bound by TJ International Ltd, Padstow, Cornwall

Contents

Foreword

The education of the future healthcare workforce and the continuing professional development of the current workforce is the business of all those involved in health-care delivery. The level, scope, type and nature of education may vary from the formal setting of the university lecture theatre to the more informal mentor rela-tionships in practice, but the essence is the same – education is about encouraging, challenging and broadening horizons at the same time as preparing people to 'do the job'.

This book is designed for those who are involved in cancer and palliative care education. It seeks to examine cancer and palliative care education in context and explores issues of relevance to all those working in this field. But what is that context and what are the issues that are of current relevance to educators? What is it that is influencing the way educators are planning and designing their courses, engaging with their students, monitoring quality and assessing the outcomes of their teaching? A number of responses spring to mind.

In relation to the disciplines of cancer and palliative care there is a constant development of the knowledge base. New treatments are impacting on the manage-ment of cancer on a regular basis, the genetics revolution is affecting the way that cancer is screened for, diagnosed and treated; policy initiatives are constantly changing the way that services are organised and delivered and moral and ethical debates relating to palliative care are increasingly on the public and political agendas. To properly prepare those involved in the provision of cancer and pallia-tive care services educators have to be constantly horizon scanning and ensuring that their teaching is engaging with contemporary issues as well as critiqueing what is going on.

Not only is there ongoing development in the knowledge and practice base in cancer and palliative care, but also the modes of delivering, receiving and devel-oping that knowledge are constantly evolving. There is also something of a revolu-tion occurring in teaching and learning. Learning is no longer seen to be undertaken in the classroom. Work-based learning, e-learning and experiential learning are now important facets of the educational experience and, indeed, are demanded by managers in busy health services where freeing staff from clinical areas is increasingly difficult. This book highlights a number of innovative educa-tional techniques that can be employed to challenge learners to be enquiring, self-reflective and effective but which take place outside the formal classroom setting.

Another issue is the balance between, and the integration of, academic and practice aspects of the curricula. The challenge is getting a balance between the two and having skilled educators and practitioners working in partnership to enable students to integrate propositional knowledge with experiential learning. A further challenge is valuing both types of knowledge and recognising that we are seeking to educate our workforce not simply to be able to deliver the care required but to deliver it in a knowledgeable, thoughtful and questioning way.

Finally, educators also face the challenge of interprofessional education and learning. The field of cancer and palliative care would appear to be an ideal testing ground for such approaches as no one professional grouping can provide for the complex, physical and psychosocial needs of the individual with cancer as they move along the continuum from screening, diagnosis, treatment, survival, recurrence, palliative care and finally death.

Educators are important in facilitating active learning in their students, in whatever setting and at whatever level, which in turn enables them to be independent learners and critical thinkers. It is this active learning that we are striving for in education and I hope that within the pages of this book you find some inspiration, new knowledge or techniques to enable you to promote active learning, deliver excellent teaching, reflect on your own teaching practice and continue to contribute to the development of the workforce in cancer and palliative care.

Karen Cox
Professor in Cancer and Palliative Care
Head of School, School of Nursing
University of Nottingham,
Queen's Medical Centre, Nottingham
July 2004

Preface

The beginning of every journey begins with the first step. The road to this book started with the inception of the Yorkshire Palliative Care Education Interest Group (YPCEIG) in 1991. That first step was the product of numerous ideas which were generated at the YPCEIG meetings with the suggestion that such a group should capture the creativity and experiences of its members between the pages of a book. The journey faltered for a while until the inspiration for it was rekindled at a conference that both editors attended, entitled 'Death by Illumination'.

The theme of the book developed from discussions between the editors as they identified that although there was a plethora of books that had been written for clinicians in cancer and palliative care, there was a singular lack of literature available for educationalists or those for whom a significant part of their role involved delivering education. As the discussions intensified, a battery of ideas unfolded and a clear theme for this book emerged. The nature of education is multi-dimensional – hence the series title *Dimensions in Cancer and Palliative Care Education*, which also reflects the YPCEIG biannual conference title. Our intention is to complete a series of books to capture those dimensions. This book focuses on contextualising cancer and palliative care education, including current changes in healthcare practice. The main theme that emerged from all of the contributors without any prompting from the editors was that of holism. Without exception, every contributor discussed holism as a particular aspect of cancer and palliative care education while relating it to their specific topic area. This became the main theme throughout the book and was a major feature of most of the chapters. This reinforces the importance of holistic care not only within the specialties of cancer and palliative care, but also in relation to the very essence of education. Although this book is intended for those involved in the delivery of cancer and palliative care education, the content will have relevance for all those who care for individuals affected by a diagnosis of cancer or other life-limiting illness.

The opening chapter outlines the policy context of current cancer and palliative care education, against which the subsequent chapters explore a myriad educational strategies, methods, paradigms and approaches to delivering education. There is a rich vein of experience, creativity, knowledge and artistry reflected in the work of all of the contributors that will enhance the reader's learning. Indeed, one pair of contributors suggested that their chapter is an art form. As editors we would like to affirm that all of the chapters in this book *are in fact an art form* as well as being extremely informative and educational. The last chapter closes not only the book but also the loop in relation to the educational beginnings of palliative care – that of hospices. It provides information on the diversity of education that is delivered by hospices, and it outlines many of the qualities that are necessary to be an educator in this specialised field.

> Instruction begins when you, the teacher, learn from the learner; put yourself in his place so that you may understand what he learns and the way that he understands it.
>
> (Søren Kiekegaard, Danish philospher)

Lorna Foyle and Janis Hostad
July 2004

About the editors

Lorna Foyle M.Sc BA Hons Cert Ed. Dip HE Pall Care. NDN Cert. RGN Cert in Counselling. NLP Practitioner is a Lecturer in Cancer Care at the University of Leeds.

Janis Hostad M.Sc BA Hons Cert Ed. RGN Diploma in Counselling. NDN Cert. NLP Practitioner is Education and Development Co-ordinator in Cancer and Palliative Care at Hull Acute Trust and a Part-time Lecturer at the University of Lincoln.

The two editors' combined experience in cancer and palliative care adds up to over 40 years. The early part of their experience was firmly rooted in the clinical setting, while in latter years their focus has switched to education and research.

List of contributors

Robert Becker
Macmillan Senior Lecturer in Palliative Care
Staffordshire University School of Health and Shropshire and Mid Wales Hospice

Angela Brown
Senior Lecturer
School of Nursing and Midwifery
Northern General Hospital
Sheffield

Graham Farley
Lecturer in Cancer and Palliative Care
Marie Curie Cancer Centre
Bradford

Elizabeth Foster
Macmillan Clinical Nurse Specialist in Palliative Care
North East Lincolnshire Palliative Care Trust

Fiona Hicks
Consultant, Palliative Care Team
St James's University Hospital
Leeds

Jennifer Kwa Kwa
Director of Hospice Education
St Luke's Hospice
Plymouth

Dominic MacManus
Hospice Information and Education Manager
Dove House Hospice
Hull

Steve Morris
Macmillan Clinical Nurse Specialist in Palliative Care
Hull and East Yorkshire Hospitals NHS

Marie Nicoll
Macmillan Clinical Nurse Specialist in Palliative Care
Hull and East Yorkshire NHS Primary Healthcare Trust

Wendy Page
Charge Nurse
Oncology Unit
Hull and East Yorkshire Hospitals NHS Trust

Gill Scott
Lecturer Practitioner
University of Sheffield

Sally-Ann Spencer-Grey
Independent Lecturer and Consultant in Cancer and Palliative Care
Hull

Vanessa Taylor
Lecturer
University of Bradford

Ian Trueman
Lecturer
Lincoln Centre
University of Nottingham

Acknowledgements

The editors would like to acknowledge the support given to them during the production of this book both by contributors and by their families, and in particular they would like to dedicate the book to the memory of Frances Sheldon.

Frances was a dedicated and inspirational educationalist in the specialties of cancer and palliative care. Her presence and charisma illuminated her work and she has inspired many of us to continue in her footsteps.

To Frances, to let you know the light is still shining.

CHAPTER 1

The impact of health and social policy on cancer and palliative care education

Lorna Foyle

No great improvements in the lot of mankind are possible, until a great change takes place in the fundamental constitution of their modes of thought.

(John Stuart Mill, 1806–73, English philosopher and economist)

The aim of this chapter is to explore the impact of health and social policy on cancer and palliative care education.

Learning outcomes

By the end of this chapter the reader should be able to:

- understand the influence of current health and social policies on cancer and palliative care educational provision
- understand what influences the formulation of current health and social policy
- discuss the development of health and social policy
- identify sources for accessing specific policies relevant to cancer and palliative care education
- examine the dynamics of policy making and relate it to changes in cancer and palliative care healthcare education.

Introduction

Healthcare in the UK is continually being influenced by directions, goals and principles of Government and dominant groups in the policy-making process (Robinson *et al.* 1999, p.9). The world is changing rapidly – more than at any time since the

Industrial Revolution (Ham and Alberti 2002). This applies to the advancement of medical science and technology. In modern society, as a result of the Internet and the media, the public has become more knowledgeable about the latest medical discoveries and treatments. With this new-found knowledge, public expectations have risen with regard to all aspects of life. Healthcare provision is no exception, and the demand for improved healthcare is at the top of most people's agenda. Cancer and palliative healthcare provision is often the focus of public dissatisfaction with healthcare services. In recent years, health and social policy reform has been introduced as a response to adverse public opinion, along with other social and political pressures within these healthcare specialties. In the last ten years, a succession of wide-ranging policies related to cancer and palliative care has impacted deeply on healthcare professionals and educationalists in those settings. Extraordinary demands have been placed on them to educate and train qualified and non-qualified healthcare workers while maintaining other aspects of their roles that have been initiated by national or local policy makers.

Regardless of these demands, there is a commitment from healthcare professionals and educationalists alike to develop and deliver the appropriate educational programmes for those involved in the care of individuals who are affected by a diagnosis of cancer or require palliative care, while responding to recent policy developments. It is essential for those individuals who are delivering education or who have leadership roles in the clinical areas to be cognisant of the policy imperatives that are driving their professional development. In a twenty-first-century culture of instant and accessible information, many would argue that it is not enough simply to relate the contents of recent policies, but that responsibility should be taken for creating and co-ordinating appropriate responses to the needs of the complex health agendas that face society by becoming actively involved in the policy-making process (Fatchett 2002).

The involvement of cancer and palliative care professionals and educationalists in influencing future policy making is crucial, as is their ability to analyse health and social policy and interpret the pervading politics. The current delivery of cancer and palliative care education has unquestionably been driven by recent Government policies. Yet these policies are often implemented with only a limited knowledge of their formulation or limited evaluation of their impact. Knowledge and understanding of policy making and policy analysis can assist in the development of the appropriate curricula and training programmes delivered by clinicians and full-time educationalists in the specialties of cancer and palliative care. This knowledge and understanding can be used to predict potential policy developments in cancer and palliative care education, and to anticipate potential changes in the delivery of education.

Those educationalists with dual responsibilities to the clinical areas and academic institutions also need to ensure that they are familiar with the latest educational policies to balance the competing demands on their time.

This chapter will outline the study of policy formulation and analysis. Similarly, recent policies that are relevant to cancer and palliative care and their impact on education provision will be highlighted. The impact of policy on the future education of all healthcare workers will be discussed. However, reflecting this author's professional background, the focus of this section will predominantly be on nursing.

Therefore this chapter aims to look at the concepts of policy, to assist in developing skills of policy analysis, and to outline relevant policies that are applicable to cancer and palliative care education.

What is policy?

The concept of policy is rather difficult to define, and has generated a variety of interpretations and complex perspectives. As this chapter progresses the reader will identify how closely intertwined the study of policy and the study of politics truly are. *Polis* is the Greek root for the English words 'policy' and 'politics', which according to the *Shoter Oxford English Dictionary* is related to issues concerned with citizenship, Government and the State. Taken at face value, this definition would appear straightforward, it being implicit that Government, State and citizenship are either a part or a whole of the same paradigm in its organisation and administration. Yet policy is more likely to be encountered in a wide range of contexts, such as different fields of action, different times and circumstances, often making it impossible to cover them all (Colebatch 2002). This definition begins to introduce some of the complexities involved in the study of policy, and healthcare policy is no exception.

Policy studies can embrace the study of policy formulation, policy analysis and public administration, and these terms have been used interchangeably, often creating confusion amongst students of the subject. The study of policy and its definitions can be defined and represented from a range of unique stakeholder perspectives, such as economics, anthropology, psychology, sociology, history, medicine and nursing, to name just a few. Levin (1997, p.15) suggests that policy has a variety of uses that are espoused by politicians, but could be broadly categorised under four headings:

1 policy as a stated intention
2 policy as a current or past action
3 policy as an organisational practice
4 policy as an indicator of formal or claimed status of a past, present or proposed course of action.

For politicians, policy also has certain attributes, symbolising commitment, 'belongingness', status and specificity (Levin 1997, p.17). Politicians enact policy through the processes of legislative measures, decisions about public expenditure, organisational structuring and management activities (Clark and Seymour 1998).

Policy making is not just the remit of those who are formally identified as formulating and making policy, such as politicians and managers, but also involves those who have varied interests and expertise in different health policies promoting distinctive perspectives and interests (Fatchett 1998). In the UK, health service provision is not solely dependent on State provision. The UK healthcare system consists of multiple service providers, including the NHS and the voluntary and private sectors. Recent cancer and palliative care policy has been substantially influenced by the voluntary and charitable sector. The voluntary hospice movement began to provide unique and specialised care for the dying in the late 1960s and early 1970s. Often led by charismatic individuals, hospices began to fill a void of indifference to the care of the dying that had become prevalent in the NHS (Clark and Seymour 1998). This secured public support for their endeavours and indignation at the care provided by the NHS. At the same time, other charities with similar philosophies but different interpretations of service delivery were also emerging. These voluntary groups, although primarily involved in the provision of care, were and are active in campaigning and lobbying governments for improvements in service delivery. The main campaigners are independent hospices, Macmillan Cancer Relief and Marie Curie Cancer Care, along with other cancer charities. These voluntary groups united with NHS specialist palliative care providers to form the National Council for Hospice and Specialist Palliative Care Services (NCHSPCS). This group's purpose is to continue political activities with a more cohesive, co-ordinated and systematic approach, while representing nationally agreed perspectives. The voluntary sector has made a significant contribution both to policy development and to cancer and palliative care education.

For the purpose of this chapter, policies relevant to cancer and palliative care in the last 15 years and their impact on education will be discussed. More detail can be obtained by tracing the history of healthcare policy formulation and analysis in the UK over the last century (listed as further reading at the end of the chapter, as is the study of the policy process). Policies that have affected current educational approaches to cancer and palliative care will now be considered.

The Calman–Hine Report

In 1995, the Department of Health published the document *A Policy Framework for the Commissioning of Cancer Services*, known as the Calman–Hine Report (Department of Health 1995). Since its publication, this document has been influential in guiding the development of cancer services. It aimed:

> to create a network of care in England and Wales which will enable a patient, wherever he or she lives, to be sure that the treatment and care received is of a uniformly high standard.
>
> (Department of Health 1995)

When it published the Calman–Hine Report, the Expert Advisory Group on Cancer (Department of Health 1995) recommended that palliative care should be incorporated into the cancer care agenda. Consequently, it was recommended that the provision of specialist palliative care services should be an integral part of the cancer care pathway. The report highlighted the objective that primary care services, cancer-care-specific teams and specialist palliative care services were to combine to create a 'seamless service' (Richards 1997).

The Calman–Hine Report outlined a framework for the management of cancer patients, including the development of cancer units and centres, while recognising a need to expand the knowledge base and role of primary care and make the focus of care more patient centred (Baker 2002). The report precipitated organisational and structural changes that were fundamental to the development of future policies such as *The New NHS: Modern, Dependable* (Department of Health 1997) and *The NHS Cancer Plan* (Department of Health 2000a) when a new Labour Government came into power in 1997.

The New NHS: Modern, Dependable (Department of Health 1997)

The main themes running through this document were developing partnerships, improving financial efficiency, effectiveness of care and care delivery supported by evidence, and finally the promotion of excellence in all aspects of healthcare delivery. The intention was to improve access to services, reduce regional variations and devolve responsibility for care at local level while simultaneously establishing national evidence-based standards and guidelines. National standards were required via National Service Frameworks that would define generic and specific clinical standards for a range of services and conditions. In all parts of the UK, the NHS is required to organise its services to match the standards set in the frameworks and to ensure equity in provision and access. National standards were to be created through the establishment of the National Institute for Clinical Excellence (NICE). Clinical governance was the recommended process by which the quality of clinical services could be monitored, accompanied by programmes of lifelong learning and professional self-regulation.

The NHS Cancer Plan (Department of Health, 2000a)

This takes forward the principles of *The New NHS: Modern, Dependable* and applies them to cancer. The four key aims of the NHS Cancer Plan are:

1   to save lives through better detection, prevention and treatment of cancer
2   to improve quality of life by improvements in service provision and to foster a 'patient-centred' approach that treats cancer patients 'with humanity, with dignity and respect' (Department of Health 2000a, p.62)
3   to tackle the inequalities and variations in the incidence, treatment and outcomes of cancer

4   to build for the future through investment in the cancer workforce and also
    through research and development in order to meet the challenge of develop-
    ments, including the impact of advances in genetic science.

Although beyond the scope of this chapter, there are key factors within the Cancer
Plan that are pertinent to this topic and which have major influences on cancer
and palliative care education provision.

The inclusion of prevention and screening programmes within the Cancer Plan,
coupled with an emphasis on smoking cessation campaigns, was welcomed by
cancer-related professions (Hall *et al.* 2002). The implications for education are
clear in that a public education smoking cessation campaign, although primarily
the responsibility of health promotion teams, must necessarily fall within the remit
of all cancer and palliative care-related professions, which are not always cognisant
of the ways to achieve this and require further training to acquire these skills. Some
ways of providing public education are explained later in this book by Hostad,
MacManus and Foyle.

The national Cancer Plan (Department of Health 2000a) suggested that there
would be an increase in the numbers of staff involved in the delivery of cancer and
palliative care, but these figures merely reflected existing training schemes – with
the exception of nursing, where an increase in numbers was dependent on return
to nursing programmes or the employment of overseas nurses (Baker 2002). The
plan identified shortfalls in the numbers of healthcare professionals available to
provide specific cancer and palliative care. It outlined targets that should be met by
2006 with a minimal strategy with regard to the processes available to achieve
this. Some recognition and funding were given to radiotherapy and imaging
services to counteract the previous shortfall in staffing numbers (Baker 2002). By
the year 2006 there will be almost 1000 extra cancer specialists, 20 000 additional
nurses and 6500 additional allied healthcare professionals (Department of Health
2000a). The plan identified additional funds, rising in three annual increments to
£570 million by the year 2003, although naturally not all of this money was specifically designated for education purposes.

However, £6 million was earmarked over three years to fund additional education and support to over 10 000 district nurses (one in four) in the principles and
practice of palliative care. This project is currently being evaluated by researchers
at King's College London (Department of Health 2003a). Cancer networks were
invited to submit tenders for models of palliative care education delivery. One such
model adopted in West Yorkshire was that of the gold standards framework
(Thomas 2003).

There is a commitment in the NHS Cancer Plan for joint training to be undertaken in non-clinical generic skills such as teamworking and communication skills.
There are several initiatives under way throughout the UK.

These targets for increasing the cancer and palliative care workforce were and
still remain extremely ambitious.

National Cancer Guidance

Initiated by the NHS Executive following the publication of the Calman–Hine Report, the National Cancer Guidance aims to provide detailed recommendations for the management of specific cancers and to form the basis for establishing national standards for cancer care. *Improving Outcomes* guidance is now available for breast (NHS Executive 1996a, 1996b), lung (NHS Executive 1998), colorectal (NHS Executive 1997a, 1997b), gynaecological (NHS Executive 2000a) and upper gastrointestinal (NHS Executive 2000b) cancer. The programme for subsequent outcomes guidance was set out in the NHS Cancer Plan and commissioned by NICE. The guidance uses externally commissioned systematic reviews and multi-disciplinary consultation to produce evidence-based guidelines. Key issues shaping the guidance are caseload, outcomes, specialisation, staffing and audit. Guidance is produced in different formats (manual, research evidence and GP format). Patient versions of the guidelines are being produced. Johnson (2002) suggests that guidelines are based on the results of political pressure and clinical trials which are affected by the limitations of clinical research, and fail to provide individual quality holistic care. The successful implementation of a guideline is likely to lead to less variation in management, which may decrease the number of treatments that are given without an evidence base to support them (Howard 2001).

The educational implications of the formulation and implementation of guidelines are complex. Medicine has had substantially more training in guidance and guideline development than have other healthcare professions, where training has been limited and sporadic. Nurses and other healthcare professionals are now actively encouraged to collaborate in the development and audit of guidelines, with minimal knowledge, skills and experience to undertake this activity. From work within this author's university and experience, it takes time to develop an individual's skills in critically analysing evidence-based literature or grasping the four types of methodology used for their production (Woolf 1992). It takes time and patience on the part of the teacher before individuals are able to integrate the theories into their own practice and are sufficiently confident to feel competent to collaborate or lead in guideline production. Equally important is the development of a discerning expert practitioner (Benner 1984) who can challenge existing guidelines and deviate from those guidelines when appropriate in order to provide individualised care. Any deviation should be underpinned by an informed rationale, which requires the individual to articulate this well in order to obtain the collaboration of the rest of the healthcare team. The education of healthcare professionals, including those with a medical training, to acquire the necessary skills and level of expertise requires tenacity and a range of different teaching strategies.

The distinction between the guidance and clinical guidelines is important. Guidelines specify how clinical interventions should take place in order to assist clinicians in the management of patients. Clinical guidelines are intended to be advisory, although in the clinical setting there is an expectation that they will be followed. In contrast, the guidance recognises that local circumstances and priorities impact legitimately on implementation, and specifically enables this process to be conducted objectively (Haward and Eastwood 2001). The NICE cancer guidance incorporates clinical guidelines, technology appraisals, cancer service guidance, cancer referral and confidential inquiries such as review of cancer care in acute units.

Currently there is only limited evaluation of the cancer guidance. Howard (2001) postulates that guidelines will be produced for the foreseeable future and will form the basis for clinical governance and underpin assessments such as peer review.

Manual of Cancer Services: Standards (Department of Health 2001)

This contains national standards and performance indicators for cancer services. Ten topics that span the patient pathway are included:

1 Patient-centred care
2 Multidisciplinary team
3 Imaging and pathology services
4 Non-surgical oncology support to cancer units
5 Radiotherapy
6 Chemotherapy
7 Specialist palliative care
8 Education, training and continuing professional development
9 Communication between primary, secondary and tertiary sectors
10 Management and organisation of cancer services.

The manual of standards is to be reviewed and revised on an annual basis as new guidance and standards are developed. These standards are the major focus for the cancer and peer review process, where the standards are assessed during visits made to cancer centres and units. Many of these standards are relevant to the development of cancer care education and require urgent attention. One example of this is the development of courses specific to chemotherapy administration by nurses and intrathecal administration by physicians to meet the requirements set out in the *Manual of Cancer Services Standards* and subsequent policies (Department of Health 2003b). Running simultaneously with the development of cancer policies is the evolution of clinical governance as a constant quality process.

Clinical governance

Clinical governance has been defined as a framework through which NHS organisations are accountable for continuously improving the quality of their services and

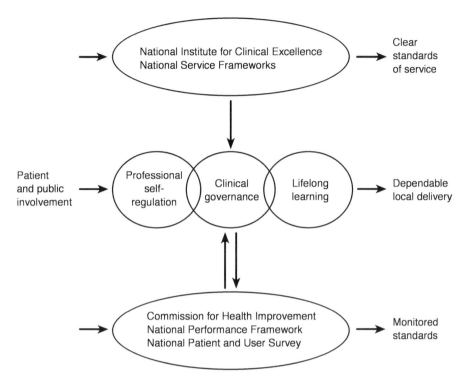

Figure 1.1   The NHS quality structure. Reproduced with the permission of the Department of Health.

safeguarding high standards of care by creating an environment in which excellence in clinical care can flourish (Department of Health 1998, p.33).

The boards of organisations now have a formal duty to ensure that quality of healthcare delivery is improved and statutory bodies established. The Commission for Health Improvement (CHI) and NICE are to assist this process. These initiatives combined ensure that NHS healthcare professionals audit the care that they delivered by evaluating, benchmarking and striving for continuous improvement.

This framework, although compulsory for all NHS services, including cancer and palliative care, is not legally binding for voluntary hospices and independent specialist palliative care services. The National Council for Hospice and Specialist Palliative Care Services encouraged the replication of the principles of clinical governance by voluntary hospices and independent specialist palliative care services in order to monitor quality while maintaining independence.

The National Council for Hospice and Specialist Palliative Care Services outlined the following definition for clinical governance:

An internal framework through which the voluntary sector providers of hospice and SPC (specialist palliative care) demonstrate accountability for and ensure continuous improvement in the quality of their services for patients and those who care for them and the safeguarding of standards of care by creating an environment in which clinical care will flourish.

(National Council for Hospice and Specialist Palliative Care Services 2000, p.9)

In this document, clinical governance was promoted as an opportunity for voluntary hospices and specialist palliative care teams to provide commissioners with much needed evidence of their effectiveness and quality of care.

The result of this was the initiation of several monitoring systems to measure quality in the voluntary sector using external audit tools such as health service review or *quality by peer review* (QPR) (Barker 2001), the latter originally being commissioned for development by a group of independent hospices in Yorkshire in the mid-1990s. The QPR audit tool extensively audits the quality of service provision within these hospices, but there is minimal evaluation of the quality of educational provision delivered within or externally to these hospices.

Clinical governance demands a cultural change towards openness, participation, staff empowerment, partnership and collaboration. It is an important goal to move away from a culture based on blame and towards one that emphasises learning from mistakes (Department of Health 1999).

Clinical governance can be viewed as a process of introducing health improvement measures over time which are capable of responding to change brought about by developments in science, medicine, nursing, other healthcare professions, management and healthcare funding agencies. NHS facilities must develop a culture of innovation, enterprise, efficiency and good customer services in order to create and sustain clinical governance arrangements (Deparment of Health 1999). The vision for clinical governance is that healthcare environments will move towards a culture of lifelong learning where examples of good practice are rapidly incorporated into everyday work, and a spirit of innovation, enterprise and a patient-centred approach to care is employed throughout individual organisations.

The concept of lifelong learning is attributed to the outcome of discussions during the United Nations International Education Year in 1970. The United Nations International Educational, Scientific and Cultural Organisation (UNESCO) adopted the notion in 1972 and presented it as a potential alternative to existing educational principles (Cross-Durant 1991). Lifelong learning places the onus of professional and self-development firmly on the individual, but within the healthcare setting there is an expectation of organisational support. This support is often provided initially, but as finances and resources dwindle, the offer of support becomes mere rhetoric as agreed study leave is withdrawn. This is particularly relevant to post-registration nurses.

It is important to have the right number of people with the right skills to deliver a quality agenda (Department of Health 1999). This should be achieved by integrating lifelong learning and continuing professional development into healthcare provision, by providing all healthcare staff with the knowledge and tools to enable them to offer the most modern, effective and high-quality care to patients and their families. Merging quality improvement plans, workforce training strategies, professional development planning and resource mechanisms is fundamental to the success of clinical governance. Local human resource strategies have been recommended to provide structure to the training and to address the educational needs of staff (both clinical and managerial).

Clinical governance is based on continuing professional development (lifelong learning), risk management and clinical effectiveness. Among these components, the following themes require constant attention:

1 national consistency
2 accountability
3 quality assurance improvement
4 management of poor performance
5 collaboration and teamwork.

The concept of shared governance embodies the very nature of these components, specifically collaboration and teamwork. Shared governance is an approach that can make the invisible processes visible and that can value the undervalued. It can transform organisations that lack a sense of purpose, and where professional morale is low it can give rise to highly motivated, accountable, efficient organisations. The outcome of shared governance will be the growth of an organisation where quality clinical activity is increased through enhanced clinical practice and individual job satisfaction improves though shared ownership of decision making.

Shared governance is internationally recognised as a tool directed towards facilitating the maturation of the healthcare professional (Porter O'Grady 1991). It is a creative approach to professional accountability that has its roots embedded in clinical effectiveness, clinical supervision and clinical governance.

As part of the clinical governance process, organisations are required to report monthly to local health authorities on their performance against *national clinical indicators*. In order to meet these targets and performance indicators, models of excellence that identify best practice, transfer across care settings and provide evidence to measure against national benchmarks have been recommended. One such initiative that demonstrates shared governance and best practice is the Liverpool Integrated Care Pathway (LCP). This care pathway was developed for the dying patient, and it simultaneously empowers generic workers in hospital and community settings to follow best practice and provides specialist palliative care teams with educational opportunities (Kinder and Ellershaw 2003).

The educational impact of the clinical governance agenda on clinicians, educationalists and trainers across healthcare settings is enormous. The examples cited in this section on clinical governance are only two instances of a range of educational imperatives required to meet this agenda. Murphy (2003) has outlined a 12-month educational programme to replicate the implementation of the LCP in other localities. Similarly, QPR requires that staff within hospices be trained to meet the organisational and clinical standards outlined in this audit tool. Both of these educational projects require a comprehensive approach to training, often with limited resources. Multiply the intensity and time-frame of these projects by all of the other educational activities required to meet the clinical governance agenda, and you will start to comprehend the enormity of the task facing clinicians and educationalists in the current healthcare climate.

The National Care Standards Commission

The regulation of private and voluntary healthcare was the main purpose of the National Care Standards Commission (NCSC), which was established after the publication of the National Care Standards Act (Department of Health 2000b). All inspections of independent care and the quality of that care, including hospices and other private healthcare providers, will be the responsibility of an amalgamation of the Commission for Health Improvement, the Audit Commission and the NCSC (Barker and Hawkett 2004). The Commission for Health Improvement and Audit (CHAI) became fully operational in 2004. The private and voluntary sector will be required to meet the inspectorate standards, and this includes private nursing companies. This may require that staff in some establishments are educated to minimal standards or above in order to meet the inspectorate requirements. As a consequence of this, staff from these institutions may develop their own in-service training, access the training programmes of other institutions or even undertake validated and recognised courses at academic institutions. The effect will inevitably be that educationalists and trainers are working to full capacity to meet the demands and expectations of all healthcare sectors which have been affected by a raft of healthcare policies that compel change in healthcare delivery.

Supportive and Palliative Care for People with Cancer

The final guidelines for *Supportive and Palliative Care for People with Cancer* were published in March 2004 and can be found on the NICE website.* The guidelines will become part of the *Manual of Cancer Service Standards* and will apply to all specialist palliative care services, regardless of setting (Barker and Hawkett 2004). These service guidelines concentrate on service configuration and how best to educate and facilitate information flow between clinicians and patients, but they do not give clinical guidance on best supportive care and treatments (Bosanquet and Tolley 2003). The aims, development and implementation of these guidelines are clearly outlined in the executive summary.

This guidance defines service models which are likely to ensure that patients with cancer, together with their families and carers, receive the necessary support and care to help them to cope with cancer and its treatment at all stages.

---

*National Institute for Clinical Excellence; www.nice.org.uk

The guidelines make 20 recommendations, many of which are critically dependent on workforce development, the appointment of additional staff and the enhancement of the knowledge and skills of existing staff. Frontline staff will require more training in the assessment of patients' problems, concerns and needs, in information giving and in communication skills. Additional specialist skills will be needed in roles related to information delivery, psychological support, rehabilitation, palliative care and support for families and carers. The educational implications are highlighted in Key Recommendations 19 and 20.

> Key Recommendation 19:
> Cancer Networks should work closely with Workforce Development Confederations (the Workforce Development Steering Group in Wales) to determine and meet workforce requirements and to ensure education and training programmes are available.

> Key Recommendation 20:
> Provider organisations should identify staff who may benefit from training, and should facilitate their participation in training and ongoing development. Individual practitioners should ensure they have the knowledge and skills required for the roles they undertake.

These particular recommendations are explicit and laudable, but the whole concept raises concerns about resources not so much in terms of financial constraints, but in human terms. The demand for all types of education in healthcare provision is often hard to meet. Most clinicians in cancer and palliative care are dedicated to education and training, although they are often hampered by other priorities encroaching on their time. The numbers of dedicated and appropriately trained teachers in these specialties reflect the current shortages in healthcare provision.

The guidance for *Supportive and Palliative Care for People with Cancer* is likely to have far-reaching consequences for all those working with individuals affected by cancer and who require palliative care. Service activities must cross all healthcare settings, and inter-agency collaboration will be obligatory. The potential educational implications appear at face value to be limitless and daunting. Yet the possibility of major achievements in improving quality is implicit. Stepping back from the recent publication of this guidance there is a need to take stock of what already exists or is at an educational planning stage before we hurtle into another round of unstructured responses to meet the recommendations.

The Nursing Contribution to Cancer Care (Department of Health 2000c)

This document, which was published in June 2000, outlines a 'strategic programme of action' for senior cancer nurses in support of the national cancer programme, and was later detailed within the NHS Cancer Plan. Five areas of action are identified and expanded upon:

1 organising and delivering services
2 workforce planning
3 education, training and continuing professional development
4 recruitment, retention and career pathways
5 leadership.

Four categories of nursing competency categories outlined in *The Nursing Contribution to Cancer Care* are currently being drafted into specific competencies by a National Cancer Nurses Working Party, as are palliative nursing competencies. These categories are as follows:

1 healthcare support worker
2 registered practitioner
3 senior registered practitioner (degree level)
4 consultant practitioner (masters level).

The competency framework has been designed to reflect the clinical skills/competencies required by all nurses involved in the provision of care to cancer patients and their families, irrespective of the care setting. The cancer framework will be piloted in selected areas of the country. Other professions, such as pharmacy and medicine, are developing competency frameworks in cancer and specialist palliative care. Team competencies frameworks for evaluation of team inputs, processes and outcomes are being cascaded. The standardisation of profession-focused competencies has the potential to raise quality of care and level the existing inequalities in care delivery nationally, while truly embedding learning in the clinical area.

User involvement policies

As user involvement has become more important in the healthcare delivery agenda, it warrants a section of its own. Its implementation has educational consequences both for educationalists and for clinicians.

User involvement has received increasing priority in successive policy publications. The notion was first introduced by the Calman–Hine Report by establishing the ideal of patient-centred cancer services, (Department of Health 1995). This approach was supported by the NHS Cancer Plan (Department of Health 2000a):

> At a local level, cancer networks will be expected to take account of the views of patients and carers when planning services.
>
> (Department of Health 2000a: 7.19)

These principles became firmly fixed in the recent Health and Social Care Act
(2001):

> It is the duty of every body to which this section applies to make arrangements
> with a view to securing, as respects health services for which it is responsible,
> that persons to whom those services are being or may be provided are, directly
> or through representatives, involved in and consulted on (a) the planning of
> the provision of those services, (b) the development and consideration of
> proposals for changes in the way those services are provided, and (c) decisions
> to be made by that body affecting the operation of those services.
>   This section applies to (a) health authorities, (b) primary care trusts and (c)
> NHS trusts.

User involvement is unlikely to develop effectively without specialist education and
training for both health professionals and users (Tritter *et al.* 2004). This requires
an educational strategy that involves creative and realistic approaches which will
cross professional boundaries and institutions. Inter-professional education is one
such approach that can improve collaboration between professionals as well as
enhancing user involvement, and it has proved to be successful in the West
Country (Tritter *et al.* 2004). The resource implications may not be vast, but the
selection of individuals who are committed to delivering such an education
programme is crucial.

   Programmes may involve formal approaches or mentoring. Professionals have
not for many years engaged in discussions with patients about quality of service
delivery, and they often lack the skill to facilitate such discussions. Some professionals may not want to acquire these skills, but so long as their support for these
projects is assured there should be no obvious barriers. The participation of users in
service delivery is essential, but they need to be equally involved in the formulation
of formal education programmes. During the recent development of a cancer degree
pathway at this author's university, users were encouraged to give written and
verbal feedback on the proposed programme. The outcome of this feedback was that
the contents and delivery of the programme were positively altered to meet the
users' recommendations. Time will decide whether there will be more extensive
effects on cancer and palliative care education as a result of user involvement
programmes.

Voluntary sector educational contributions

As was mentioned earlier in this chapter, voluntary organisations have a major
impact on policy. This is equally true of their contribution to educational developments in cancer and palliative care. The contribution of hospices is discussed in
greater detail at the end of this chapter. Macmillan Cancer Relief (MCR) has a
thriving educational strategy that not only supports post holders but also permeates

into all aspects of cancer and palliative care education. There is a Macmillan National Education Institute which is accommodated at five regional universities that employ specialist lecturers. These lecturers profile Macmillan post holders, identify their training needs, and will often recommend specific courses that are tailored to those needs. These may be accredited courses at universities or subject-specific courses delivered by other institutions. Macmillan lecturers also deliver educational sessions that are consistent with MCR philosophy, aims and objectives. The aim of this education is to ensure that a high standard of care will be delivered in the post holder's clinical setting, and to maintain close contact between Macmillan and front-line services.

Marie Curie Cancer Care has had a major influence on education. It currently delivers accredited degree programmes through Thames Valley University at its cancer care centres throughout the UK. These centres deliver courses on specialised aspects of cancer and palliative care. A major programme developed by Marie Curie Cancer Care, namely communication skills for the patient with advanced cancer, has been adopted and rolled out by the National Health Services University.

It is evident that there have been considerable changes in education as a result of the range of policies reviewed above. Many of the changes have had positive benefits, but other changes pose challenges.

The challenges

The level and range of policies introduced over the last ten years has created a health service of many departments, and confusion can arise as to which department is responsible for monitoring particular aspects of policy implementation. The demand for reports and statistical information has increased the pressure on clinicians and educationalists by reducing the time available to be spent in the clinical and educational settings. Policy often becomes merely a paper exercise, as exemplified by the essence of care benchmarking documents which arrived in clinical areas in folders. Many areas were unable to implement them due to staff shortages or inadequate training in their relevance and implementation. A shortage of appropriately qualified clinicians and educationalists, increases the workload for those who are in post. There are limited resources to fund the delivery of a variety of educational projects. Commissioners are compelled to prioritise and fund projects at the expense of other equally worthwhile initiatives. Beacons of excellence have been identified, but other areas have been unable to replicate best practice due to a lack of resources and appropriate expertise. Educationalists appear proactive and industrious while cancer networks are busy developing a global approach to cancer and palliative care education. This global approach to planning educational strategies will reach senior healthcare professionals but still sometimes fails to reach front-line workers, where the motivation to deliver is most urgently required.

The benefits

Conversely, there are several positive benefits that have accrued from recent policy developments in cancer and palliative care. The formulation of national standards that allow local interpretation has been welcomed. This flexibility allows local delivery of education to be tailored to the needs of local trusts and workforce.

The current cancer care workforce is being mapped at national and local levels by cancer networks in order to provide valuable information for the formulation of network educational strategies. Workforce Development Confederations have acknowledged the current cancer workforce problems, and are drawing together new and innovative ways of filling the gaps, both in recruitment and in extending existing workforce skills. Despite the inability to disseminate information to all healthcare workers, educational activities are becoming more transparent, with the inevitable outcome that this information is more accessible to the appropriate stake-holders, thus promoting cross-agency collaboration.

Inter-disciplinary education is developing, and there is evidence (although as yet limited) that these multi-professional educational programmes are benefiting patients and their families (Koffman 2001).

The new and creative ways of educating the cancer workforce are being developed and shared, as is evidenced throughout the chapters of this book. The future of health policy is tenuous in nature, as its formulation rests with the Government and the prevailing influences of the day. Currently, cancer and palliative care education is favoured in the healthcare agenda and is attracting additional resources. However, this could all change in response to either public opinion or an impending general election.

Conclusion

The quality of cancer and palliative care is going through unprecedented changes and developments as a result of policy imperatives. Likewise, the impact of these policies on education is unparalleled. It is essential that clinicians and educationalists are aware of the policy formation process and contemporary educational strategies to meet the demands of these changing times. As the cancer workforce is encouraged to implement these changes, it is crucial that they understand their responsibility in contributing to the consultation processes of future policy developments. It is no longer acceptable to deny knowledge of these processes. Part of educationalists' responsibilities are that practitioners are made aware of policy issues and their potential contribution to the policy process.

Change is inevitable in a progressive country. Change is constant.
(Benjamin Disraeli, speech in Edinburgh, 29 October 1867)

Key points to consider
- Policy and politics impact on healthcare education.
- Policy development is shaped by many sources.
- Cancer and palliative care education is responding to policy imperatives.
- Practitioners and educationalists need to engage in policy-shaping processes.
- Educationalists are developing new and creative approaches to delivering education.
- Standards of cancer and palliative care delivery are improving.

Implications for the reader's own practice
1. In what ways do the above-mentioned guidelines and policies affect your clinical and educational practice?
2. In your role, how do you ensure that you adhere to current policies and guidelines?
3. How can you evaluate implementation of policy and guidelines in your clinical area?
4. In what ways are you currently involved in policy development?
5. What measures could you undertake to ensure involvement in policy development?

References

Baker M (2002) Introduction: Cancer – a suitable case for treatment. In: M Baker (ed.) *Modernising Cancer Services*. Radcliffe Medical Press, Oxford.

Barker E (2001) *Quality Peer Review*. Presentation to the Conference on Interpreting the Challenges for Specialist Palliative Care Services, October, Harrogate.

Barker L and Hawkett S (2004) Policy, audit, evaluation and clinical governance. In: S Payne, J Seymour and C Ingleton (eds) *Palliative Care Nursing Principles and Evidence for Practice*, Open University Press, Buckingham.

Benner P (1984) *From Novice to Expert: excellence and power in clinical nursing practice*. Addison-Wesley, Menlo Park, CA.

Bosanquet N and Tolley K (2003) Treatment of anaemia in cancer patients: implications for supportive care in the National Health Service Plan. *Curr Med Res Opin.* **19**: 643–50.

Clark D and Seymour J (1998) *Reflections in Palliative Care*. Open University Press, Buckingham.

Colebatch HK (2002) *Policy* (2e). Open University Press, Buckingham.

Cross-Durant PA (1991) Basil Yeaxlee and the origins of lifelong learning. In P Jarvis (ed.) *Twentieth-Century Thinkers in Adult Education*. Routledge, New York.

Department of Health (1995) *Improving Quality of Cancer Services: a Report by the Expert Advisory Group on Cancer to the Chief Medical Officers of England and Wales*. HMSO, London.

Department of Health (1997) *The New NHS: modern, dependable.* The Stationery Office, London.

Department of Health (1998) *A First-Class service: quality in the new NHS.* The Stationery Office, London.

Department of Health (1999) *Clinical Governance: quality in the new NHS.* The Stationery Office, London.

Department of Health (2000a) *The NHS Cancer Plan: a plan for investment, a plan for reform.* The Stationery Office, London.

Department of Health (2000b) *The National Care Standards Act 2000.* The Stationery Office, London.

Department of Health (2000c) *The Nursing Contribution to Cancer Care.* The Stationery Office, London.

Department of Health (2001) *Manual of Cancer Services: Standards.* The Stationery Office, London.

Department of Health (2003a) *The NHS Cancer Plan Three-Year Progress Report: maintaining the momentum.* The Stationery Office, London.

Department of Health (2003b) *Updated National Guidance on the Safe Administration of Intrathecal Chemotherapy.* The Stationery Office, London.

Fatchett A (1998) *Nursing in the New NHS: modern, dependable?* Bailliere Tindall, London.

Fatchett A (2002) The influence of policy. In D Clarke, J Flanagan and K Kendrick (eds) *Advancing Nursing Practice in Cancer and Palliative Care.* Palgrave Macmillan, London.

Hall G, Perren T and Selby P (2002) Calman Hine and after. In: M Baker (ed.) *Modernising Cancer Services.* Radcliffe Medical Press, Oxford.

Ham C and Alberti K (2002) The medical profession, the public, and the government. *BMJ.* **324**: 838–42.

Haward R and Eastwood A (2001) The background, nature and role of the national guidance. *Clin Onco.* **13**: 322–5.

Howard G (2001) Cancer guidelines. *Clin Onco.* **13**: 320–21.

Johnson N (2002) Guidelines on using guidelines. *Br J Obstet Gynaecol.* **109**: 495–7.

Kinder C and Ellershaw J (2003) How to use the Liverpool pathway for the dying patient: In: J Ellershaw and S Wilkinson (eds) *Care of the Dying. A pathway to excellence.* Oxford University Press, Oxford.

Koffman J (2001) Multiprofessional palliative care education: past challenges, future issues. *J Palliat Care.* **17**: 86–92.

Levin P (1997) *Making Social Policy.* Open University Press, Buckingham.

Murphy J (2003) The education strategy to implement the Liverpool care pathway for the dying. In: J Ellershaw and S Wilkinson (eds) *Care of the Dying. A pathway to excellence.* Oxford University Press, Oxford.

National Council for Hospice and Specialist Palliative Care services (NCHSPCS) (2000) *Raising the Standard: clinical governance for voluntary hospices.* Occasional Paper No.18. NCHSPCS, London.

NHS Executive (1996a) *Guidance for Purchasers: improving outcomes in breast cancer (the manual).* Department of Health, London.

NHS Executive (1996b) *Guidance for Purchasers: improving outcomes in breast cancer (the research evidence).* Department of Health, London.

NHS Executive (1997a) *Guidance on Commissioning Services: improving outcomes in colorectal cancer (the manual)*. Department of Health, London.

NHS Executive (1997b) *Guidance on Commissioning Services: improving outcomes in colorectal cancer (the research evidence)*. Department of Health, London.

NHS Executive (1998) *Guidance on Commissioning Cancer Services: improving outcomes in lung cancer (the rersearch evidence)*. Department of Health, London.

NHS Executive (2000a) *Guidance on Commissioning Services: improving outcomes in gynaecological cancers (the manual)*. Department of Health, London; www.doh.gov.uk/cancer

NHS Executive (2000b) *Guidance on Commissioning Services: improving outcomes in upper gastrointestinal cancers (the manual)*. Department of Health, London; www.doh.gov.uk/cancer

Porter O'Grady T (1991) Shared governance for nursing. Part I. Creating the new organisation. *AORN J.* **53**: 458–66.

Richards M (1997) Calman–Hine: two years on. *Palliat Med.* **11**: 433–34.

Robinson J, Latimer J, Avis M and Traynor M (1999) *Competing Interests: insights into health care and policy*. Churchill Livingstone, London.

Thomas K (2003) The gold standards framework. *Eur J Palliat Care.* **10**: 113–15.

Tritter J, Daykin N, Evans S and Sandidos M (2004) *Improving Cancer Services Through Patient Involvement*. Radcliffe Medical Press, Oxford.

Woolf SH (1992) Practices guidelines – a new reality in medicine. II. Methods of developing guidelines. *Arch Intern Med.* **152**: 946–52.

Further Reading

Barker C (1996) *The Policy Process*. Sage Publications, London.

Clark D and Seymour J (1998). *Reflections in Palliative Care*. Open University Press, Buckingham.

Levin P (1997*) Making Social Policy*. Open University Press, Buckingham.

Robinson J, Latimer J, Avis M and Traynor M (1999) *Competing Interests: insights into health care and policy*. Churchill Livingstone, London.

Wall A and Owen B (1999) *Health Policy*. The Gildridge Press Limited, Routledge, London.

CHAPTER 2

Clinical governance in 'face-to-face' and 'online space' palliative care education

Jennifer Kwa Kwa

One looks back with appreciation to the brilliant teachers, but with gratitude to those who touched our human feelings. The curriculum is so much necessary raw material, but warmth is the vital element for the growing plant and the soul of the child.

(Carl Jung)

It's teaching, Jim ... but not as we know it.

(Star Trek)

The aim of this chapter is to provide the reader with an overall understanding of clinical governance and the utilisation of information technology.

Learning outcomes

By the end of this chapter the reader should be able to:

- appreciate the mutual relationship between education and clinical governance that impacts on evidence-based clinical care
- be aware of the increased teaching strategies and tools that both Web- and information-based technologies offer
- be aware of the specific issues of integrating these into palliative care education
- identify the future challenges facing palliative care educators in ensuring that quality of education is maintained.

Introduction

As a *Star Trek* fan of many years, I have included phrases that 'trekkies' will be familiar with and are synonymous with the programme.

The title of the first draft of this chapter used the term 'cyberspace' instead of 'online space', which was certainly an attention grabber, but does lean towards an interpretation of computer-game technology. However, it is interesting that the term 'cyberspace' engenders fear of the unknown – 'going into places where we have never gone before'. This is both common and has a horror dimension all of its own in information technology literacy. In its use of the World Wide Web for palliative care education, research and clinical searching, the UK compared with, say, North America (Pereira *et al.* (2001) is 'backward'. This merely reflects the telephony-access infrastructure, which in the UK is not as advanced, fast, readily available or cheap as in some other major business zones on this planet. For example, some American schools email parents to inform them of changes to the curriculum, assignment dates, and so on, but this practice is generally unheard of in the UK.

By now it should be evident to the reader that a large section of the brain neocortex purporting to be that of the author, a purportedly serious palliative care academic, is in fact a mass of wireless access protocols (WAPs) tuned to technology and the future. The situation is changing as Broadband is becoming more accessible to the general public. In 1992 the UK 'Teaching and Learning Technology Programme' (TLTP) drove at impulse speed to establish widespread computer learning. The universities subsequently bought up their sections of bandwidths from satellites, so speeding up information access for the student. The Dearing Report (National Committee for the Inquiry into Higher Education 1997) has ensured that university students can access computers, so for many, huge learning curves are vaporising the fear and opening global doorways to unforeseen opportunities in education.

The digital divide

Improvements in hardware, software and communication links have enhanced clinical and educational opportunities in palliative care (Regnard 2000). However, pockets of education still remain where online access is not so readily available – for example, in the home, in some NHS clinical areas and to an even greater extent in clinical areas such as hospices where investment in information technology means a shift of funds from direct patient care. Although hospices are a 'shared-care' provider for NHS patients, there are still force fields that block the sharing of common information technology systems and equity of access with their NHS partners' information technology systems for accessing educational opportunities and clinical data. Private care areas are also a long way from offering every healthcare professional access to information technology-based information.

This is a picture of a 'digital divide', which has been discussed by Philip Barker

(2002), where the inequity of access, understanding and resources blocks the peaceful exploration of the unknown for all. So where does this fit with clinical governance in education? And how does this specifically relate to palliative care education, which by its very nature includes small group teaching and face-to-face delivery with the main focus being psychosocial development?

In 1998, the Department of Health identified in *A First-Class Service: Quality in the New NHS* the wide variation in the provision of evidence-based healthcare and service efficacy, and in 1999 the Commission for Health Improvement was set up for England and Wales (Scotland has its own regulatory body, namely the Clinical Standards Board). 'Turbolifts' of governance were identified, each of which impacted on the whole organisation at all levels (also known as 'pillars' in UK governance dialect). One of these is 'Education, Training and Continuing Professional Development'. This is summed up as:

> A commitment to education ... that involves partners ... multi-disciplinary teams ... and supports continuing professional development ... in order to put into practice what they have learnt.
>
> (Commission for Health Improvement 2000)

With the launches of the Commission for Health Improvement and the NHS plan, in 1997 the National Council for Hospice and Specialist Palliative Care Services identified 'Staff Development' as one of their six key service 'Quality Policies'. This reaffirmed the importance of continuing education and training for *all* staff (National Council for Hospice and Specialist Palliative Care Services 1997). The turbolift to continuing professional development has a commitment to reach all staff within the overall dimension of 'learning effectiveness' (National Council for Hospice and Specialist Palliative Care Services 2002). I use the term 'turbolift' in preference to 'pillar' (Commission for Health Improvement 2000a) since it promotes a dynamic, status-free, accessible route for all. The turbolift is an accessible educational route-finder for all who work in an organisation, be they clinicians, administrative or other services staff, permanent or agency/bank, paid or unpaid. In an ideal 'cyberworld', turbolift doors would open a rich variety of learning sources, including:

- personal development courses linked to specific performance review
- experiential opportunities
- continuing professional development
- schemes to obtain further qualifications
- work-based mandatory training (e.g. basic food hygiene, health and safety).

To achieve this effectively a clear committee structure with specific staff responsible for education, training and continuing professional development would be needed to ensure that continual development is embedded in every service area and the turbolift doors are opening educational opportunities in order to meet the specialist palliative care prime directive:

> To enhance the living time left, to each and all those dying, to achieve a 'good death' and to help the carers (both family/friends and health professionals) to cope during the dying stages and for the future.

Clinical governance extends beyond each clinical area, with the bringing together of service partners, the public, carers and users, and a sharing of the successes, failures, problem-solving strategies and costs (Commission for Health Improvement 2002b). The whole subject of integration of all the aspects of clinical governance (see below) effectively into a hospice and any other specialist palliative care area is beyond the scope of this chapter, which will focus solely on the educational components.

The turbolifts (also known as pillars) of clinical governance can be summarised as follows (Commission for Health Improvement 2000b):

1 use of information to support clinical governance and health care delivery
2 patient/service user and public involvement
3 risk management
4 clinical audit
5 clinical effectiveness programmes
6 staffing and staff management
7 education, training and continuing personal and professional development.

However, it would be wrong to divorce the educational turbolift from the other six, as education is integral to each. For example, it has a critical role to play in facilitating the dissemination and application of evidence-based clinical care as well as fostering effective working with external partners in care, such as social services, the NHS, Macmillan and Marie Curie services, universities, schools and local colleges. It is a supportive turbolift to all service areas to incorporate patient and carer involvement in care and service planning, utilise information to support healthcare delivery, and underpin staffing and staff management processes.

An often missed or understated power of education is its vast potential to disseminate and promote challenging effective practice to a wide range of multidisciplinary health professionals and lay healthcare workers. In palliative care more than in any other field, there are significant numbers of individuals in this last group, which also includes the service of multi-skilled volunteers and family carers. To truly meet the prime directive for each patient, their experiences of repeatedly 'dipping in and out of' service care should be tweaked to optimum care. For example, in addition to specialist palliative care services, they may also seek support from GPs, receptionists, Nurse Direct, car drivers, social services, benefits advisers, complementary therapists, diagnostic units and treatment centres, to name just a few. The life-limiting journey may encounter inconsistency, duplication, conflicting information, ineffective treatment and sheer bureaucratic force fields. Given that an individual and their family during their trajectory from life-limiting diagnosis through to bereavement may come into contact with numerous services (Robbins 1999), education can really make a difference here. However, to have that kind of immeasurable impact it must be evidence-based, challenging, problem solving, supportive and generalisable to other clinical areas – in other words, it has to be 'effective teaching'.

Approaches to effective teaching

Two bodies procedurally check the quality of teaching, namely the Higher Education Funding Council (HEFC) and the Quality Assurance Agency (QAA). Teaching and learning excellence is currently rewarded in the UK through the National Teaching Fellowship Scheme. The Institute for Learning and Teaching (ILT) was the fourteenth recommendation of the Dearing Report (National Committee for the Inquiry into Higher Education 1997) to promote higher education in the UK so that it would be a 'world leader in the practice of teaching at higher levels'. The ILT is responsible for the management of the National Teaching Fellowship Scheme (NTFS), which clearly identifies excellence as innovation in the design, organisation and delivery of teaching, as well as inspiring, supporting and valuing the diversity of student life forms.

Whatever the subject area, there are a number of core areas to effective teaching:

- feedback to the student which is critical to the effectiveness of learning (Gibbs 1992)
- utilisation of evaluated teaching methodologies – for example, whether e-learning or conventional learning, ensuring that the design of the chosen learning activities is constructively aligned to the learning outcomes (Biggs 1999)
- technological skills and expertise in whatever methodology is utilised – for example, problem-based learning (Juwah 2002) or e-learning (Salmon 2000a)
- reliable and equitable access to technology, books, journals, handouts, extended resources lists (e.g. websites, further reading guidance)
- Special Education Needs and Disability Act (SENDA) compliance for those with disabilities (see Box 2.1, which details one example of good teaching practice, with the use of bold instead of underlining and an appropriate font type to make skim reading easier for all; this is good teaching practice for all teaching materials, e.g. presentations and handouts)
- a teaching facilitator who maintains up-to-date subject awareness and actively motivates students to link theory and practice throughout
- teachers and students alike assimilate knowledge and understanding from the process of teachers keeping up to date.

Box 2.1   Reading equity (1 is easiest to read and 4 is the hardest)

1   To know analgesic
2   To know analgesic
3   To know analgesic
4   <u>To know analgesic</u>

1   Arial font (note that this is recommended as the easiest common font to read)
2   Times New Roman – has extra character recognition processing involved for each letter; look at the 'T' before the whole word is recognised as part of skim reading the whole sentence
3   Black on white – difficult for individuals with scotopic sensitivity syndrome to read
4   <u>Underlining</u> – confusing if there are any perceptual problems

---

Core effective teaching areas that are more common to palliative care

These include the following:

- small group teaching to ensure that the holistic 'depth' of discussions is promoted; a central core disassembling of all the psychosocial, biomedical and service issues that the patient and family encounter, in order to enhance awareness and step outside the 'professional' role of competence
- within online teaching, ensure that there is a private tutorial area in the *managed learning environment* (MLE), since the core subject is emotive and it is not uncommon for personal issues to take precedence and, just as in 'face-to-face' teaching, this may be better managed outside group teaching
- a toolbox of strategies to utilise sensitively and tactfully when dealing with the strong emotions that can be engendered when teasing out ethical and cultural issues in order to foster memorable constructive debate.

A cyberview of innovative teaching technologies that promote effective learning

The web (also known as the World Wide Web) is a warp-speed global communications medium that offers accessible healthcare information to whole populations, including some previously inaccessible Third World countries with serious palliative care issues. This is an unprecedented 'where others have not gone before' form of communication equity. Second only to email, the Web is the most widely used element of the Internet. Educationally it offers a distributed hypermedia system of links to vast library facilities, research papers, graphs, three-dimensional disassembling rotating models that allow one to look beneath the skin, the fascia, etc., video links and many potential multimodal interactive learning opportunities.

Computer-mediated communication (CMC) can be asynchronous (one-way) (e.g. email and bulletin boards) or synchronous (two-way), with all online at the same time and an icon indicating when a student leaves the discussion (e.g. first-class conferencing, satellite seminars, Microsoft Messaging or other NetMeeting forums. Synchronous computer-mediated communication allows the creation of electronic 'areas' where learning can be nurtured, and learners can both discuss issues privately with the tutor and participate in the group discussions, sharing issues, tasks, resources, insight and analysis.

As discussions can be threaded or linked thematically (Juwah 2002) (e.g. a discussion on living wills can be an offshoot to a discussion on euthanasia), meaningful debates are recorded for student reaccess and rethinking as well as for scrutiny by later cohorts. The 'slowed up' response caused by typing instead of speaking has been found to encourage deeper reflection and cognitive learning development (Bayne 2001).

Real-time conferencing is a multi-modal approach that uses telecommunications and/or computer equipment to offer a number of teaching modes that all link more than two sites. There are three different types.

1   Video conferencing enables on-screen people to be present, with pictures linking different sites and presenting a virtual 'presence'. This has been successfully used in palliative care clinical practice (Regnard 2000).
2   Audio conferencing also enables more than two sites to link up with higher-quality audio than that of conventional telephones.
3   Data conferencing involves sharing virtual workspace on a desktop PC (e.g. a shared whiteboard for combining ideas and importing pictures and text in real time). Electronic whiteboards can also be Internet-linked, and the Learning Technology Support Service suggests that this is a 'very powerful teaching tool'. In the conventional classroom both teachers and learners can use write-on digitising tablets to brainstorm and explore topics. Similar to putting up sheets of paper on walls, this has the advantage of being downloadable into a handout/overhead projector (OHP) to refresh learning.

However, all technologies are far from perfect, and quality issues such as demands on resources (e.g. time, staff, expertise, equipment) and online fragility can lead to 'de-learning' if frustration is promoted, resulting in poor educational delivery.

Teachers also need to adapt to new teaching contexts, methods and audiences by developing online communication and e-moderating skills (Salmon and Giles 1998). In palliative care teaching it is particularly important that they are able to:

1   provide support and academic counselling via email
2   fire off ethical debates with thought-provoking online questions
3   learn when to control groups and when to let go and sit back as the students drive the discussion.

Such engaged learning, where 'all students' activities involve cognitive processes such as creating, problem solving, reasoning, decision making and evaluation' (Kearsley and Shneiderman 1998), clearly enhances learning effectiveness. The danger is that time, exhaustion and frustration will result in stress if the focus is on the technology rather than on supporting the online teacher in developing e-moderating skills. *Managed learning environment* (MLE) skills are necessary to utilise online software effectively in order to track, guide and monitor students' progress (Jeffries 2001).

A new era of educational systems has evolved, including *Content management*, *Integrated learning* and *Managed learning environment* systems. Early pedagogical educational approaches were in danger of didactically transmitting information as if the learner was awaiting reprogramming, but *communication and information technologies* (C and IT) have evolved to build on the rich experiences of practitioners and incorporate problem solving into experiential methods of learning, as this has long been recognised to be a key principle of adult education (Jeffrey 2002). There has been a huge expansion in educational software such as Web Course Tools (WebCT) and Blackboard software for the management of World-Wide-Web-based educational environments. Both support the creation of entire online courses, or simply posting up supplementary materials to existing courses. Such software offers bulletin boards, online chat facilities, threaded discussions, online quizzes, calendars, assessments and workshops.

Wireless Wide Area Networks (WWANs) are the colleges of the future. Waverider, Lucent and Ionic Companies have established these at a fraction of the costs involved previously, to the remotest places on earth.

Evidence for the use of computer-mediated technologies (communication management technologies) in teaching

A number of studies have indicated that online learning is more effective than conventional learning (Jeffries 2001; Malloy and de Natale 2001; Ross and Touvinen 2001; Wharrad *et al.* 2001). However, none of these studies dispute the value of face-to-face teaching, and Rouse (2000) and Mehta *et al.* (1998) are just two of a number of researchers who have found that learning effectiveness is enhanced by assimilating communication management technologies with conventional face-to-face teaching methods.

Pereira *et al.* (2001) conducted a World Wide Web survey to explore Internet use by palliative care professionals. Interestingly, they found (as might be expected in my 'cyberworld') growing interest in the use of communication management technologies in palliative care internationally. In every clinical educational course the synergy of applying theory to practice examples and bringing practice innovations and issues into theory discussion can only enhance the ability to address practice failures and to support and share good practice. Those educators who believed that most learning takes place in the classroom have beamed out to practice, bringing back clinical experts as an integral part of evidence-based teaching.

As Marsick and Watkins (1992) have identified, learning in the workplace is continuous. Problem-based learning has supported this process, and there is a wealth of literature to recommend this teaching methodology for enhancing learning effectiveness in the workplace (Heliker 1994; Engel 1997; Biggs 1999; Maudsley and Strivens 2000). The use of online technology has been shown to be effective in furthering problem-based learning (Engel 1997; Juwah 2002).

The sharp learning curve for such technology has resulted in the growth of distributed multimedia technologies to enhance communication and learning (Curran 2001). The increase in software such as that discussed above is market-driven – both by testimonies of its effectiveness and by the decreases in cost of both hardware and software.

A comparison of the learning effectiveness of online and face-to-face teaching methodologies

Strengths of online technologies in teaching

These include the following:

- conferencing – everyone has equal access to material which they can take away and read at their own set pace (Wilson and Whitelock 1997)
- a question posted up, together with the reply, is seen by all and remains as a record for later access/revision (this allows 'lurking') (Bayne 2000 and Smith 2001)
- in an online conference, several discussions can take place at the same time, unlike linear conversations in face-to-face teaching. The 'moment' does not get lost for any of these, since the recorded message feature of online conferencing enables students to revisit points they may have missed or incompletely understood. Online teaching has no time or space boundaries (Smith 2001)
- the process of formulating the question in written form demands reflection, which adds to learning and memory recall
- tutors can present fully prepared answers instead of 'off-the-cuff' ones which it is hoped are correct (Wilson and Whitelock 1997)
- misunderstandings are avoided and the playing field is levelled for those struggling to keep up, because they can revisit the discussion
- students have the opportunity to think through the various discussion points and make their contribution in their own time
- there are useful additional features such as links (can be hypertext) to course material, particular references, to save library searching, to handouts, handbooks, forms and also logs of previous courses.

Strengths of face to face teaching

- Face-to-face contact is more personal, no matter how many 'smiley' emoticons are used! It has been claimed that 75% of human communication takes place through non-verbal actions (Berger *et al.* 1977).
- Face-to-face teaching supports 'in-depth' work (e.g. exploring difficult conceptual issues such as soul pain, utilising problem-based learning to clinically develop theory and practice alongside each other).
- This approach has *Immediacy*, allowing one to identify the troubled, confused, daydreaming student and respond by flexibly changing direction or expanding on a point (Wilson and Whitelock 1997).
- Social interaction reduces the social isolation of study and can potentially increase confidence and enjoyment.
- Early studies have shown that engagement is more likely to occur with face-to-face teaching than with computer-assisted teaching (Haile 1986, cited in Harasim 1987; Wilson and Whitelock 1997) but this was when the technology was relatively unsophisticated. More recent studies suggest that learning effectiveness can be equal to if not actually better with online teaching (Jeffries 2001; Malloy and de Natale 2001; Ross and Touvinen 2001; Wharrad *et al.* 2001).

The answers to the common questions below aim to provide a balanced picture to support the educator in their choice of effective online and face-to-face teaching.

1   I like to have paper-based books to hand so that I can pick them up and browse through them. How can a computer be better than books and magazines?
    Answer: Really? Think of your back! And finding the pages that only discuss what you are looking for can be difficult.
    Computer-mediated communication offers immediate access anytime and anywhere. This is convenient for the student in that learning can take place from home with a rich virtual store of multimedia resources to access. Online conferencing software can level out access to material from the home so that learners with young children, mobility problems or long distances to commute can browse archivable discussions between tutor and learner about course learning outcomes, and can obtain the resources placed in folders by students and tutors as well as those archived by previous cohorts.
    Yet being engrossed in a book is a lot nicer than using a computer, and there is always the serendipity factor – coming across something interesting unexpectedly. Computer-mediated communication tends to steer you to a tightly focused subject area, whereas clinical practice spans a broad spectrum of care issues.
2   I struggle with computers, trying to type fast and spending all the time getting them to do what I want. They are supposed to save time, but they can take ages (and years off my life!). What advantage is there in that?

Answer: Your computer never gets sick, and when you are, you can still switch it on even though sometimes you may want to throw something at it when it is frustratingly slow! And it does seem to be deliberately laughing at you losing or overwriting files.

However, even on a Sunday, when all self-respecting teachers are not around and the library is closed, it is still there for you ... and of course your information technology learning curve has its advantages in other areas (shopping, online banking, route planning etc.).

3   I think I like the face-to-face and group approach more. Where is the quality in online stuff?

Answer: Not everyone conscientiously stays with the discussion, and this can be distracting ... but then again you cannot obtain tactile support online (yet!), ... nor can you really see who is actively listening. Reading body language is a crucial part of communication.

However, in face-to-face teaching, group dynamics and personalities can detract from learning ... and online video conferencing can reach larger remote audiences.

Overall, then, although face-to-face teaching will always have a strong role in palliative care education where the teaching of multi-disciplinary communication skills is effectively assimilated (Dowell 2002), online technologies can support deep as well as surface learning to take back into the clinical arena. With appropriate e-moderating skills, the online teaching environment can encourage critical reflection on practice (Baker and Lund 1997) in order to identify and resolve problems, thereby enhancing the overall quality of care.

However, the following are necessary if online teaching is to be utilised effectively.

1   Buffers need to be built in to prevent work overload for tutors!
2   Online teachers (also known as e-moderators) (Salmon 2002b) required specific training to make full use of all the opportunities and effectively manage the learning environment.
3   Students need to have strict guidelines about how much email tutorial time is permitted.
4   Material can be made available in stages online ready for the next block of learning.
5   There should be read-only access to certain material!
6   Frequently asked questions (FAQs) and built-in helplines are essential.
7   It is important to keep to manageable numbers online (e.g. six for net meetings).

Key points to consider
- The use of technologies in teaching should effectively meet all learners' needs.
- Teachers should keep abreast of the latest evidence for selecting teaching methods and materials.

- The two-way flow between theory and practice should be maintained and developed.
- Palliative care education should be actively offered in service areas of need.

Conclusion

Learning effectiveness is a vital turbolift of clinical governance, and the ability of new technologies integrated into new teaching methodologies to promote effective learning is a crucial development area for all teachers. The shift in the burden of illness from acute to chronic conditions has created a generation of people living with long-term illness, disability and life-limiting conditions. These patients are also undergoing the *computer-mediated communication* learning curve, albeit as 'expert' patients. NHS Direct is increasing the opportunities for fast access and choice through the development of a multi-channel service using 24-hour telephone call centres, the Web, digital interactive television and public touchscreen kiosks. What was once the exclusive preserve of professionals is now accessible and supporting the potential of patient and carer involvement in care, service planning, research and essentially education. The opportunities are available to go where no man has gone before ...

'Dream. Believe. Dare. Do.' The only limit to our development is our imagination

Walt Disney

Implications for the reader's own practice:
1   How do you utilise the various information technology systems in your present teaching?
2   How do your students learn best? Is the teaching:
   - face to face?
   - online and/or computer-based?
   - a combination of the above?
3   How does the above choice affect your preparation, teaching methods and delivery?
4   How can you facilitate your patients/carers/students to learn effectively from the various information technology systems and resources?
5   What learning do you need to ensure that your learners' needs are met in this technological culture?

References

Baker M and Lund K (1997) Promoting reflective interactions in a CSCL Environment. *J Comput Assist Learning.* **13**: 163–74

Barker P (2002) *Enhanced Learning Opportunities Through the Appropriate Use of CIT.* University of Teeside; www.ilt.ac.uk/portal/

Bayne S (2000) *Computer-Mediated Conferencing* Napier University, Edinburgh.

Bayne S (2001) *An Introduction to Learning Technology.* Learning Technology Support Services, Bristol University, Bristol.

Berger J (1977) *Status Characteristics and Social Interaction.* Elsevier, New York.

Biggs J (1999) *Teaching for Quality Learning at University.* Society for Research into Higher Education and Open University Press, Buckingham.

Commission for Health Improvement (2000a) *A Guide to Clinical Governance Reviews.* Commission for Health Improvement, London.

Commission for Health Improvement (2002b); www.chi.nhs.uk/eng/about/whatischi.shtml

Curran K (2001) *Web-Based Distance Learning in Educational Organisations.* University of Ulster; www.ilt.ac.uk/portal/

Department of Health (1998) *A First-Class Service: quality in the new NHS.* Department of Health, London.

Dowell L (2002) Multiprofessional palliative care in a general hospital: education and training needs. *Int J Palliat Nurs.* **8**: 294–303.

Engel C (1997) Not just a method but a way of learning. In: D Boud and G Feletti (eds) *The Challenge of Problem-Based Learning* (2e). Kogan Page, London.

Gibbs G (1992) *Improving the Quality of Student Learning.* Technical and Educational Services, Bristol.

Harasim L (1989) *On-line education: a new domain.* In: R Mason and AR Kaye (eds) *Mindweave: communication, computers and communication.* Pergamon, Oxford.

Heliker D (1994) Meeting the challenge of the curriculum revolution: problem-based learning in nursing education. *J Nurs Educ.* **33**: 45–7.

Hillier Y (2001) *The Quest for Competence, Good Practice and Excellence.* City University; www.ilt.ac.uk/portal/

Jeffrey D (2002) *Teaching Palliative Care: a practical guide.* Radcliffe Medical Press, Oxford.

Jeffries PR (2001) Computer versus lecture: a comparison of two methods of teaching oral medication administration in a nursing skills laboratory. *J Nurs Educ.* **40**: 323-9.

Juwah C (2002) *Using Communication and Information Technologies to Support Problem-Based Learning.* Robert Gordon University; www.ilt.ac.uk/portal/

Kearsley G and Shneiderman B (1998) Engagement theory: a framework for technology-based teaching and learning. *Educ Technol.* **3**: 20–37.

Malloy SE and de Natale ML (2001) Online critical thinking: a case study analysis. *Nurse Educator.* **26**: 191–7.

Marsick V and Watkins KE (1992) Continuous learning in the workplace. *Reflect Practitioner.* **12**: 9–12.

Maudsley G and Strivens J (2000) Promoting professional knowledge, experiential learning and critical thinking for medical students. *Med Educ.* **34**: 535–44

Mehta MP, Sinha P, Kanwar K, Inman A, Albanese M and Fahl W (1998) Evaluation of Internet-based oncologic teaching for medical students. *J Cancer Educ.* **13**: 197–202.

National Committee for the Inquiry into Higher Education (NCIHE) (1997) *Higher Education in the Learning Society.* NCIHE: Norwich.

National Council for Hospice and Specialist Palliative Care Services (NCHSPCS) (1997) *Making Palliative Care Better: quality improvement, multiprofessional audit and standards.* Occasional Paper 12. NCHSPCS, London.

National Council for Hospice and Specialist Palliative Care Services (NCHSPCS) (2002) *Turning Theory into Practice: practical clinical governance for voluntary hospices.* NCHSPCS, London.

Pereira J, Bruera E and Quan H (2001) Palliative care on the Net: an online survey of health care professionals. *J Palliat Care.* **17**: 41-5.

Regnard C (2000) Videoconferencing and palliative care. *Eur J Palliat Care.* **7**: 168–71.

Robbins M (1999) *Evaluating Palliative Care: establishing the evidence base.* Oxford University Press, Oxford.

Ross GC and Touvinen JE (2001) Deep versus surface learning with multimedia in nursing education: development and evaluation of WoundCare. *Comput Nurs.* **19**: 213–23.

Rouse DP (2000) The effectiveness of computer-assisted instruction in teaching nursing students about congenital heart disease. *Comput Nurs.* **18**: 282–7.

Salmon G (2000a) *E-moderating: the key to teaching and learning online.* Kogan Page, London.

Salmon G (2002b) *E-tivities: a key to online learning.* Kogan Page, Open University Business School, Milton Keynes.

Salmon G and Giles K (1998) *Creating and Implementing Successful Online Learning Environments: a practitioner perspective.* Open University Business School, Milton Keynes.

Smith B (2001) *Teaching Online: new or transferable skills?* Open University, London; www.ilt.ac.uk/portal/

Wharrad HJ, Kent C, Allcock N and Wood B (2001) A comparison of CAL with a conventional method of delivery of cell biology to undergraduate nursing students using an experimental design. Computer-assisted learning. *Nurse Educ Today.* **21**: 579–88.

Wilson T and Whitelock D (1997) *Changing Roles: comparing face-to-face and online teaching in the light of new technologies.* Centre for Educational Software, Institute of Educational Technology, Open University, Milton Keynes.

Web sources

http://flexiblelearning.net.au/nw2000/talkback/n42.htm – Avatars and Intelligent Tutoring Systems.

http://archive.uwaterloo.ca/~vkeller/litreview.html – a literature review of computer-mediated communication.

www.blackboard.com/ – offers a complete suite of enterprise software products and services that power a total 'e-Education Infrastructure' for schools, colleges, universities and other education providers.

www.chi.nhs.uk/ – the Commission for Health Improvement, whose purpose is to help the NHS in England and Wales to assure, monitor and improve the quality of clinical care.

http://coe.cedu.niu.edu/~bailey/leit535/computer.htm – research and issues in distance education and computer-mediated communication.

www.ilt.ac.uk/criteria_2002.htm – the Institute for Learning and Teaching in Higher Education (ILT) (good-practice-sharing section).

www.learningtechnologies.ac.uk/ – the Learning and Skills Development Agency (LSDA) is the managing agent for the new sector ILT staff development programme.

http://materials.netskills.ac.uk/info/module52.html – Module Information Online Assessment using the Web.

http://oubs.open.ac.uk/gilly – Open University Business School (plenty of resources).

www.tact.fse.ulaval.ca/ang/html/collabu/catherine/teachingvc/conferencing.html – computer conferencing

www.webct.com – provider of e-learning solutions for the higher education market.

www.qaa.ac.uk/crntwork/benchmark/phase2consult.htm – academic benchmarking standards.

www.techdis.ac.uk – this service aims to make the technological learning environment accessible to learners with disabilities.

www.bton.ac.uk/adc-ltsn/issues_disab3.htm – Disability website links, including Senda Compliance.

Websites of interest

www.ncteam.ac.uk/ – the Teaching Quality Enhancement Fund National Co-ordination Team (also known as the National Co-ordination Team).

www.icbl.hw.ac.uk/itdi/ – the Learning Technology Dissemination Initiative.

www.jisc.ac.uk/jtap – the JISC Technology Applications Programme.

www.toolcit.scotcit.ac.uk/about.htm – TOOLCIT supports lecturers by providing tools and materials that will help them to select and use communication and information technology more effectively in their work as teachers.

http://iet.open.ac.uk/coursesonline/ – the Institute of Educational Technology (IET) at the Open University offers teaching, research and development of educational technologies in the service of effective learning.

www.ukoln.ac.uk/services/elib – the Electronic Libraries Programme.

www.seda.ac.uk/ – the professional association for staff and educational developers in the UK, which promotes innovation and good practice in higher education.

CHAPTER 3

Public information and education in palliative care

Janis Hostad, Dominic MacManus and Lorna Foyle

Man is not disturbed by events but by the view he takes of them.
(Epictetus, stoic philosopher)

The aim of this chapter is to provide the reader with an understanding of the importance of public education to palliative care – it is an essential and integral dimension. Due to the embryonic nature of public education in palliative care there is a dearth of literature on the topic. As a result, the format of this chapter takes a more descriptive, informative approach with the intention that this will inspire the reader to increase their awareness of and involvement in public education.

Learning outcomes
By the end of this chapter the reader should be able to:
- consider the core concepts of public education in palliative care
- gain knowledge of a model that may be utilised to underpin public education
- appreciate the diversity and challenges of public education in palliative care
- reflect on specific projects and ideas, formulating ways in which these could be adapted or applied in practice.

It may be argued that all health professionals working in palliative care are involved in public education at some level. This is often implicit rather than explicit, and in some cases the individuals concerned may not even be aware that this is what they are involved in. How many times do we help someone to cope or understand by reframing their point of view of death, dying, cancer or life-limiting illness? The opening quote implies that it is more likely that our imagination, fears and anxieties create our view of life and information. Rigid beliefs and attitudes may adversely affect individuals with life-limiting illnesses. The general avoidance and denial of the issue of death in our society makes public education a very important but very challenging aspect of care. The authors believe that the only way to give this subject the credence it deserves is to ensure that it is explicit and recognised as a topic in its own right.

At present it is accepted that many professionals are busy devising and producing leaflets, posters, information folders, websites, etc. for their patients and those patients' families. Money and resources are seldom available to support these ventures, and much of this hard work often goes unnoticed.

Public education has been on the agenda for some time, although it has not always been at the top of the healthcare professional's agenda. Public education was the approach that Dame Cicely Saunders, the founder of the modern-day hospice movement, used when she began her work.

Right from the start, Saunders set herself a punishing itinerary of lectures and public speaking engagements. She also produced numerous pamphlets and short articles for the public (Clark 1997). Her motivation was the need for the public to understand about palliative care. To this end, much of her time in the early days was spent going out and spreading the word. Her work, alongside that of others such as the Voluntary Euthanasia Society (VES), was a response to poor-quality care for cancer patients evidenced, for example, in the Marie Curie Report in 1952. It can be argued that they both had the same aims, namely the reduction of suffering by using public education as a means of trying to achieve this goal. Accepting this premise, their solutions were very different. The VES argued for the legalisation of voluntary active euthanasia, whereas Saunders, utilising her own experiences, advocated a *quality-of-life* approach (James and Field 1992).

Over time, public education seemed to lose its impetus as the need for bricks and mortar, in the form of bedded units, took precedence. The Wilkes Report warned of the outcome of this approach, namely concentrating time and resources wholly on inpatient care at the expense of a broader approach specifically educating others about such topics as pain and symptom control (Wilkes 1980).

The very nature of a specialised palliative care service means that it will tend to cater for the minority. Specialised inpatient units are accessed by only a small number of all those with life-limiting illness. The majority of patients with palliative care needs are cared for in the wider community.

The lack of public education may have added to the inequality of the development of palliative care services across the UK. For example, there is clear evidence to suggest that ethnic minorities are reluctant to access palliative care services (Tebbit 2000; Firth 2001; Gatrad and Sheikh 2002). If there had been more public education in the past, this might have helped to raise awareness among these marginalised groups so that they were provided with an opportunity to access the services available. Little notice was taken of Wilkes (1980), even though he continued to advocate the need for education, not beds. In the late 1990s, eminent palliative care authors identified the fact that this aspect of palliative care had been neglected. Clark (1997) argues that palliative care had lost a golden opportunity by not providing more public education. Doyle (1997) supported this view, saying that 'Palliative care education should be expanded to meet the wider needs of the community working toward equity of care for all'. The authors recognised that public education in palliative care had the potential to raise public awareness.

If we are to understand why public education is so important, there needs to be an adequate definition. The authors suggest that the following definition encompasses the core facets of public education in palliative care:

> Public education is providing the public with information and knowledge in order to promote understanding and awareness, thus developing skills so that they may adapt more effectively when faced with life-limiting illness.

Education allows vulnerable patients to adapt more effectively so that positive outcomes for themselves, their families and society may be more widely achieved (Walker *et al.* 2003).

Such difficulties and problems may arise from diagnosis onward, so it is vital to obtain full information from an early stage. Public education can therefore help in many ways. Listed below are a number of different examples of ways in which this may be achieved.

- Pre-bereavement work, in the form of specific information and education related to the loss process as well as to the loved one's illness, has been shown to be important in reducing morbidity in the relatives of the deceased.
- Public education at an early stage in diagnosis can empower patients and carers to function more autonomously. This could mean that patients and relatives need less support later (this has positive cost-effect implications).
- Public education at the terminal stage can provide the information which allows the patient to die comfortably in the most appropriate place for them and their family. The need to improve these elements of care has already been identified and documented (Northern and Yorkshire Cancer Registry Information Services 2000). Surely such an opportunity to actively change these inadequacies in current services cannot be missed.

The model shown in Figure 3.1 is an attempt to capture in diagrammatic form the numerous facets of Public Information and Education (the 'PIE' model). The outer circle represents the 'PIE' but also the holistic nature of the topic. The circle encompasses the inherent principles of public education (coping, empowerment and autonomy), also implicitly symbolising holism.

Within the circle is a triangle to identify the processes that are required to deliver public education, namely those of health promotion, health and social policy and community commitment. The triangle in the diagram is deliberately represented as an equilateral triangle to demonstrate that each of the above processes is of equal importance. Each of these processes will be considered in turn below.

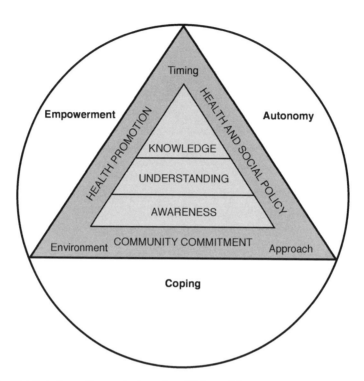

Figure 3.1   Public information and education (PIE) model

Health promotion

At first glance it may seem surprising that health promotion is one of the key components of the model. Indeed there has been much debate about the relevance of health promotion to palliative care.

At a recent conference, Spencer-Grey (2002) emphasised the importance of health promotion to palliative care, advocating further collaboration and partnerships, and suggesting that the two make 'good bedfellows'.

Although health promotion will include an element of improving health to increase life expectancy, essentially they both have the same aim, namely to enhance quality of life.

There is no reason why health promoters and hospices should not work together on smoking cessation campaigns, with such collaboration potentially having a greater impact on the smoking population. Equally, preparing people for bereavement by raising these issues at an early age (e.g. at school) could be undertaken with all parties, sharing their expertise.

Likewise, Kellerhear (1999) had earlier suggested that it is a common misunderstanding that health promotion and palliative care are opposite initiatives, when in fact they can and should enjoy a complementary relationship. There are more similarities than differences between health promotion and palliative care, as the following definition illustrates:

> Health promotion is the process of enabling people to increase control over, and to improve, their health.
>
> (World Health Organization 1984)

The resemblance to palliative care is evident, focusing on an approach that encompasses care of the dying person and those who matter to that person, patient autonomy and choice, with an emphasis on open and sensitive communication (National Council for Hospice and Specialist Palliative Care Services 1996).

The amalgamation of health promotion and palliative care paradigms holds the promise not only of streamlining resources but also of developing more imaginative and creative modes of delivery that will inevitably assist lifestyle changes.

> Lifestyle changes can be facilitated through a combination of efforts to enhance awareness, change behaviour and create environments that support good health practices.

These components, namely increased awareness, promotion of behavioural change and the creation of a supportive environment, are priorities in palliative care. Both increased awareness and behavioural change are facilitated by open and sensitive communication, allowing both the patient and their family to adapt to their new situation which has been brought about by life-limiting illness.

The interface and similarities between the two disciplines are best seen in the following definitions, one of which is relevant to each discipline.

> Health promotion is about enhancing quality of life. Its goal is to help people achieve optimal health.
>
> (O'Donnell 2000)

> The goal of palliative care is the achievement of the best possible quality of life for patients and their families.
>
> (World Health Organization 1990)

These definitions are almost interchangeable, providing some of the more obvious parallels to palliative care and health promotion. In Chapter 6 of this book, Graham Farley emphasises the importance of death education to healthcare promotion, which is equally applicable to public education. The core concerns of health promotion in palliative care are health education, death education, social supports, interpersonal reorientation, and environmental and policy development (Kellerhear 1999).

Health promotion as an aspect of public education in palliative care enables both earlier and tailored intervention via a variety of activities. These activies provide different sectors or individuals within a community with the most appropriate levels of 'education' utilising this approach. Examples include public awareness events that attempt to dispel the myths surrounding cancer, dying and treatments (death education and health education), or teaching a group of patients about treatments such as radiotherapy or chemotherapy (health education), or developing an information and drop-in centre where the public can obtain information on life-limiting illness and bereavement (health education, death education and social supports).

It is hoped that, in the future, health promotion will be seen as an integral part of palliative care public education, and that there will be further collaboration between professionals and agencies.

The next component of the PIE model is health and social policy.

Health and social policy

The importance of health and social policy to palliative care education is detailed much more comprehensively in Chapter 1 by Lorna Foyle. Health and social policy provides a platform for us to focus on specific issues, such as the reinforcement of the need for the public to be involved.

Health and social policies may have both negative and positive effects on public education in palliative care. Many policies and Government agency documents emphasise the importance of prevention and cure of diseases. The emphasis within these documents tends to be on cancer as opposed to some of the other life-limiting illnesses. In general, the policies tend to be death-denying. However, health and social policies can be used effectively to enhance public education. For example, many of the recent Government papers have highlighted issues such as the lack of patient and carer activities, but also reinforce previous and ongoing work by palliative care specialists (Department of Health 1999, 2000). Work undertaken with the public in two different parts of the country has illustrated the need for an increase in information for both the patient and the carer (Clark *et al.* 1996; MacManus *et al.* 2001; Syrett 2001).

Clark *et al.* (1996) cited one individual who felt that patients 'need as much help as possible'. In another study, an informal carer asked the question, 'Why weren't they given more information automatically?' (MacManus *et al.* 2001).

Facilitators of public education should exert their influence towards policy makers, as some of the language and focus in current official documentation reflects death-denying societal attitudes.

There needs to be a change in the cultural attitude towards a perspective where death is perceived to be a natural part of life. Currently, the opportunities to write policies that encompass issues related to death, dying, bereavement and palliative care while giving them the credence that they deserve are missed. There are many creative ways of doing this, including enhancing public awareness by using a variety of resources. For example, schools should include loss in their curriculum, as well as the production of information packs on death and dying, and raised awareness of the work of hospices and palliative care services.

Public education policy should ensure that people receive quality information about funerals so that informed choices can be made. The providers of palliative care education would contend that this type of information should be included in policy development, and that it is just as relevant as, for example, information on vaccination for children!

The Government set standards in healthcare for hip replacements, so why should there not be national standards for funeral directors and crematoria? Part of the standard could be to ensure that the bereaved are adequately supported and given appropriate information which would help the bereavement process.

The third important component of the PIE model is ensuring that there is community commitment to the awareness of palliative care and issues relating to death and dying.

Community commitment and involvement is both a discrete and a symbiotic component of the model. Health and social policy development along with health promotion can assist the process of community commitment.

Community commitment

The really exciting challenge of this aspect of public education is that it encourages creativity in matching the approach to the needs of the specific community or community 'subgroups'. The importance of reaching the margins of society as well as the mainstream is well documented (Douglas 1991; Higginson 1997; Oliviere *et al.* 1998).

Community involvement is vital for breaking down death-denying attitudes and raising awareness of palliative care issues. Gorer (1965) described death as a 'taboo' subject in our society. He suggests that throughout our lives we have been learning cultural rules that tell us to avoid, repress and perhaps even deny the fact of death. Furthermore, the mass media avoids talking about natural death (death from natural causes such as disease and ageing), but has a fascination with violent death.

To overcome some of these attitudes, a community approach is required so that we are able to feel comfortable discussing death in an honest and open way. More direct methods should be adopted (e.g. public awareness days at supermarkets, rural community education roadshows, etc.) (Hostad and MacManus 2002).

Clark *et al.* (1996) suggest that 'In a society that demands information, a dynamic approach to information giving must be developed, taking full advantage of new media and technologies'.

Active participation in the media is a powerful way of reaching the general public. This may be through local radio, local newspapers, the Internet and television. Utilising topical issues that are discussed or portrayed in the broadsheet newspapers, documentaries, tabloids or soaps can be a way of focusing attention on important and often neglected palliative care issues.

An example of this is the television soap opera *Coronation Street*, in which one of the characters died of cervical cancer. The number of smears performed in the Lancashire and Greater Manchester zones of the North-West Region of the NHS increased quite dramatically after the storyline had been broadcast. There was also a large increase in the number attending 'on time' (Howe *et al.* 2003).

By forging relationships with local reporters and television representatives, it is possible to address issues in a form to which the public can relate. A regular slot in the local newspaper or local radio station is another way of gaining community commitment. The other advantage of this approach is that on the whole it is relatively low in cost, as the overheads for most of these are minimal.

The widely read paper from Trent Palliative Care Centre entitled 'Assessing palliative care needs in Southern Derbyshire' (Clark *et al.* 1996) emphasises the importance of community commitment. This involves a much more proactive approach, and requires a high level of co-ordination and liaison which incorporates all aspects of Government policy, the support of health professionals and involvement of users.

This approach encourages the view that potential service users and all community groups should have a voice. It is also consistent with the virtuous objective of a 'seamless service' which has so far proved somewhat elusive. For it to work, it is crucial that all health professionals and other members of the multi-disciplinary team work together.

The Public information and education ('PIE') model indicates three phases in which public education can be provided, namely awareness, understanding and knowledge (*see* Figure 3.1). They do not necessarily take place in a hierarchical or linear fashion.

Awareness raising may simply involve, for example, providing a leaflet on motor neuron disease or lung cancer at an awareness morning at a local hospital, or providing information on access to local services (via a website address, local newspaper, local library, etc.). It may involve someone walking past a 'stall' in the local supermarket or a noticeboard. They have seen it and they now know where the information is, but they do not necessarily want to access it immediately.

Understanding, on the other hand, may be facilitated by providing talks and seminars at public education roadshows delivered by professionals on issues recognised as important to the general public. This should be delivered at a level which may be understood by everyone attending or modified to the group's or individual's specific or intellectual needs. The following two examples illustrate how understanding can be achieved.

All of the women attending meetings on breast cancer held at a local hospice, as well as having a 'formal' presentation of the possible treatments and investigations available to them, were also encouraged individually to share any thoughts or questions with the group regarding their own specific disease and treatment pathway. One-to-one discussion with the tutors was available to check out full understanding.

Another example was when a group of students with learning disability required information on bereavement as part of their studies. A 'formal' session was set up, but it became clear over a short period of time that artwork was a medium with which all participants felt comfortable, having used it for other parts of their course, where it had enhanced their learning experience.

Consequently, the medium of art in the form of painting was used both to stimulate participation and to develop understanding. A major discussion with the group opened up, and there was 'in-depth' conversation about life, death, hospice care and bereavement. The outcome of this session was particularly poignant as the group posted their completed pictures together with explanations which demonstrated their understanding of issues surrounding death and dying. This was further reinforced by one young participant's response which was overheard by a member of staff. A carer who was collecting this individual expressed the view that the hospice was the place where you go to die. His response was 'Oh no, it's not just that – lots of people go there to make things better for a while'.

Knowledge provides a further step in the process. The client, patient and members of the public will use awareness and understanding as a foundation for changing behaviour and attitudes and empowering them to cope more effectively with their illness. There are a range of circumstances where gaining knowledge will change individuals' behaviours.

Consider the following examples.

> A non-compliant patient with cancer who did not know about the disease process and its management was given the appropriate information related to his disease. His attitude towards taking medication changed and he used his new-found knowledge of morphine to overcome his fears associated with the drug. Subsequently he complied with recommended increased doses, achieving pain relief and a better quality of life.

Similarly, a carer's behaviour changed as a result of knowledge.

> A carer gains an understanding of how her husband's terminal illness is likely to progress and how he might be feeling and coping. Through this knowledge of the disease trajectory she is able to help her husband more appropriately and this empowers her to cope more effectively. Previously she had stopped her husband discussing his funeral arrangements as she thought there was plenty of time and discussing this subject would be 'bad for him'.

> Knowledge gained by schoolteachers from bereavement workshops on the likely emotions shown by children who are in their care and are going through bereavement will ensure that both teachers and children are better able to cope with this situation. To a certain extent this has a domino effect, since as teachers become more informed about this topic they may become the new educators.

At each corner of the triangle is a vital aspect of the process of public information and education which needs to be considered in order to provide an appropriate comprehensive and high-quality service (*see* Figure 3.1).

Environment

Public education can be provided in a variety of environments. For example, it may be in a local church hall, drop-in centre, mobile bus (roadshow), local hospital, community, school, hospice, support group, Internet chatroom, etc. It is vitally important that the environment reflects the needs and comfort of the specific group or individual as far as resources will allow.

For example, a group of day hospice patients looked forward to their weekly input on a six-week course. The group was already feeling at ease with their surroundings and fellow learners by building on relationships that had been developed on a weekly basis.

A hospice may be a good environment for public education, but equally it may be less appropriate. For example, an individual may only associate hospices with death and may be very reluctant to attend, reinforcing the need for public education in other settings.

The environment also needs to reflect where necessary the way in which the interventions and information are to be delivered.

Approach

It is of paramount importance that the approach also reflects the type of intervention and the specific form of education. For example, an individual who has telephoned for specific information on services available may not want detailed information about the disease trajectory, whereas a casual drop-in visitor may require explicit information. The provider of the information should be trained to elicit the individual's specific needs.

The following case illustrates this point.

A woman telephoned a centre for information specifically on bowel cancer. However, through discussion with a qualified, experienced nurse it became clear that what she actually required was advice on how to obtain physical help in caring for her father, who had been discharged from hospital and was deteriorating rapidly. Towards the close of the conversation she said 'Thank you for not "palming me off" with yet more information on bowel cancer,' which was very interesting given that this was exactly what she had asked for at the outset! Therefore the professional should not only be a knowledgeable resource, but also be skilled in communication and psychosocial aspects of care. This ensures that the information/education meets the specific needs of the individual, and the approach is therefore adapted to suit each person and their particular situation.

Timing

Timing and approach are inexorably linked. The woman mentioned on the previous page visited the centre several months after the telephone call. Sadly, her father had died, but interestingly, her information needs had changed as she was now seeking information about the bowel cancer, which had not been a priority previously. She felt the need to understand her father's illness because she now had time to reflect on her concerns. She felt that this information had given her peace of mind.

> While a public education project was on location at a local supermarket, where information on services and life-limiting illnesses was available, a couple passed the 'stall' several times, giving a cursory glance at our information on AIDS and HIV. Eventually one of them approached us. He asked 'Does the local hospice care for people with AIDS?' We informed the man that the hospice does indeed care for patients with all life-limiting illnesses, including AIDS, and we explained that should he require any further information on the hospice or on AIDS, we would be happy to provide this. However, he said very firmly 'That is all we need for now.'

The above examples highlight the fact that in public education timing is axiomatic to a successful outcome. The elements of environment and approach can to a certain extent be 'controlled' and prepared by the professional, in contrast to timing, where to a greater degree control lies with the individual who requires information. However, the professional has the control of delivery, in ensuring that the information/education is available and accessible at many different levels and venues using different approaches. Where public education involves specific events (e.g. stalls at supermarkets, hospital awareness days), these must be repeated and offered in different formats in order to provide the service user with this choice and control.

Empowerment, autonomy and coping

The outer periphery of the model shown in Figure 3.1 has the outcomes of empowerment, autonomy and coping. It is anticipated that if the processes are followed then the outcome will be an informed and empowered individual. These outcomes are reached by providing the service user with choices, coping mechanisms and control. By working towards equity for all, in partnership with individuals, public education will empower the individuals at whom the service is targeted and achieve success.

The authors felt that it would be useful to provide evidence of public education in practice. Therefore the last part of this chapter will provide information about their work. In their conclusion they provide guidelines which may be helpful when setting up any similar project.

It is important to recognise that, as stated at the beginning of this chapter, most health professionals who are working in both specialist palliative care and more generic settings are already involved in public education. Due to lack of space, just one activity will be considered of which the authors have some experience (e.g. the Hull Project).

The Hull Project was developed in order to emphasise and increase the public education elements of the hospice's educational provision.

The Hull Project is loosely based on the results of previous research (Meredith *et al.* 1996; Slevin *et al.* 1996; Shingler *et al.* 1997). For example, Shingler reported that in a study of 210 cancer patients and carers it was found that 100% sought information about sources outside the healthcare team, and 38% sought information from media sources. Research has also been carried out during the project (e.g. research into carers' information and educational needs) (MacManus *et al.* 2001). A grant from the National Lottery Charities Board provided the funds to employ an individual to lead the project and ensure that many of the public's educational requirements would be met. These requirements included setting up a drop-in/information centre, public awareness days, roadshows, patient and carer courses, a schools project, study days, courses for the public and health professionals, media information (newspapers and radio), and working with minority groups (details of these activities and the project may be obtained from the authors).

Key points to consider

This chapter hopefully raises awareness of how important the topic of public education is within palliative care. The challenge for palliative care practitioners and educators is to find innovative ways to educate members of the public that are appropriate to their collective and ultimately their individual needs. As already stated, current Government policy and guidelines focus on services that reflect and respond to consumer preferences (Department of Health 2000). How this is to be achieved can only be decided by the professionals and the public within their locality.

However, for those planning to set up such projects or activities in the future, the following list offers simple but helpful points to consider.

1 *Needs analysis.* Are such projects needed locally? Does anything similar exist? What are the specific local needs?

2 *Policies and protocols.* Have you developed a business plan for the project? Do you have a local strategy for public education? Can you develop protocols and standards?

3 *Funding.* Can funding be sought for this project from local, regional or national sources?

4 *Collaborative working.* Can you work together with other members of the multi-disciplinary team? Are there other organisations or an NHS trust that could form part of a management group for the project?

5 *Environment and location.* Are these suitable for the activity/service? Is it the most appropriate location? Is it accessible to those members of the public for whom it is designed? Are there a number of different settings and locations appropriate to the activity?

6 *Activities.* What are the most appropriate activities for your locality and client groups? Where should these activities be delivered? For how long? How often?

7 *Delivery.* Who will be involved? Are they skilled in teaching and communication? How large a group should it be? Is there provision to see individuals/families on a one-to-one basis if required or necessary? Can you target specific groups?

8 *Media response.* Can you respond to current topical issues related to palliative care presented in newspapers, on the radio, etc.? Could you secure a regular slot in the local newspaper or on the local radio?

9 *Research.* Have you completed any research on your activities? What areas would lend themselves to effective research and useful outcomes?

10 *Audit, evaluation and feedback.* Did you complete a baseline audit? Can you evaluate all of the different activities? Do you collect data for who accesses your service? Could a detailed annual report of all activities, their successes and recommendations be circulated widely?

Collaborative working

This is vitally important within such projects planned for the future. A management group that incorporates local stakeholders, minority groups and a patient involvement representative, and which encourages inter-professional working, will do much to support the project. Partnerships between the National Health Service, hospices, universities, cancer network and local charities all help to promote public education endeavours, and indeed the seamless service for which everyone continues to strive. The power of working together cannot be underestimated, as Norton, the founder of the creative Missoula project in Montana in the USA, illustrated when they successfully changed the way in which many members of the local community responded to death, dying and bereavement. He stated:

'The end result will be a stronger network of professional and voluntary providers, linking dying persons and their families with appropriate information and services – if we focus all that energy we can move mountains.

Conclusion

This chapter has looked at the importance of public education to palliative care, recognising that health professionals working in palliative care are already involved in public education at some level. We set out to make it clear that public education is an essential and integral dimension of palliative care.

We suggest that public education should be 'formalised' and that it should be given the credence it deserves. Public education implemented appropriately will ensure that it achieves its overall aim of empowering the public so that they are able to adapt to their new situation in whatever form this takes.

Working towards reframing individuals' and societies' negative perspectives of life-limiting illness, as the opening quote stated: 'Man is not disturbed by events but by the view he takes of them'.

Implications for the reader's own practice

1   How do you integrate public education into your current practice?
2   As a result of reading this chapter, do you consider that there are aspects of your role that you could adapt to include public education?
3   In what way can you develop health promotion in your clinical setting?
4   Can you identify ways in which you can work collaboratively with others both locally and nationally to raise awareness of this important area of education?
5   Would you be interested in belonging to a national public education forum that the authors of this chapter may set up? (if so, please contact one of the authors).

References

Clark D (1997) Public education: a missed opportunity? *Prog Palliat Care.* **5**: 189–90.

Clark D, Heslop J, Malson H and Craig B (1996) *As Much Help as Possible. Assessing palliative care needs in southern Derbyshire.* Occasional paper no. 19. Trent Palliative Care Centre, Sheffield.

Department of Health (1999) *Making a Difference: strengthening the nursing, midwifery and health visiting contribution to health and health care.* The Stationery Office, London.

Department of Health (2000) *The NHS Plan: a plan for investment, a plan for reform.* The Stationery Office, London.

Douglas C (1991) For all the saints. *BMJ.* **304**: 579.

Doyle D (1997) *The way forward for effective palliative care education.* Inaugural Lecture, Dove House Hospice, Hull.

Firth S (2001) *Wider Horizons.* National Council for Hospice and Specialist Palliative Care Services, London.

Gatrad AR and Sheikh A (2002) Palliative care for Muslims and issues before death. *Int J Palliat Nurs.* **8**: 526–53.

Gorer G (1965) *Death, Grief and Mourning.* Cresset, London.

Higginson I (1997) Palliative and terminal care. In: A Stevens and J Raftery (eds) *Health Care Needs Assessment.* Radcliffe Medical Press, Oxford.

Hostad J and MacManus D (2002) Public Education in Palliative Care, Is it Pie in the Sky? Paper given at Fourth National Conference on Dimensions in Palliative Care Education, Yorkshire Palliative Care Education Interest Group, July.

Howe A, Owen-Smith V and Richardson J (2003) The impact of a television soap opera on the NHS cervical screening programme in the North West of England. *J Public Health Med.* **25**: 183.

James N and Field D (1992) The routinization of hospice: charisma and bureaucratisation. *Soc Sci Med.* **34**: 1363–75.

Kellerhear A (1999) *Health-Promoting Palliative Care.* Oxford University Press, Oxford.

MacManus D, MacDonald J, Hostad J and Heslop J (2001) *Informal carers' satisfaction with information and education received whilst their relative was receiving in-patient care at a hospice.* Unpublished paper.

Meredith C, Symonds P, Webster L *et al.* (1996) Information needs of cancer patients in west Scotland: cross-sectional survey of patients views. *BMJ.* **313**: 724–6.

Norton A (1997) Missoula Demonstration Project (1997) www.missouldemonstration.org/

National Council for Hospice and Specialist Palliative Care Services (NCHSPCS) (1996) *Education in Palliative Care.* Occasional paper no. 9. NCHSPCS, London.

Northern and Yorkshire Cancer Registration Information Services (NYCRIS) (2000) *The Provision of Bereavement Support Services. Clinical Outcomes Monitoring.* NYCRIS

O'Donnell MP (2000) www.healthpromotionjournal.com

Oliviere D, Hargreaves R and Monroe B (1998) *Good Practices in Palliative Care: a psychosocial perspective.* Ashgate Publishing Ltd., Aldershot.

Shingler CT, Balusu R and Thomas R (1997) Where do patients seek additional information after a diagnosis of cancer? A multi-centre survey. *Eur J Cancer.* **33** (**Suppl. 8**): S321.

Slevin ML, Nichols SE, Downer SM *et al.* (1996) Emotional support for cancer patients: what do patients really want? *Br J Cancer.* **74**: 1275–9.

Spencer-Grey SA (2002) *Do palliative care and health promotion make good bed fellows?* Health Promotion in Palliative Care Conference, 8 March 2002, Dove House Hospice, Hull.

Syrett J (2001) *Evaluating the public's perception of hospice and hospice care.* Unpublished MSc dissertation.

Tebbit P (2000) *Palliative Care 2000. Communicating through partnership.* NCHSPCS, London.

Walker L, Walker M and Sharp D (2003) Current provision of psychosocial care within palliative care. In: M Lloyd-Williams (ed.) *Psychosocial Issues in Palliative Care.* Oxford University Press, Oxford.

Wilkes E (1980) *Report of the Working Group on Terminal Care.* Standing Medical Advisory Committee, Department of Health and Social Security, London.

World Health Organization (WHO) (1984) *Health Promotion: a discussion document on the concept and principles.* WHO Regional Office for Europe, Copenhagen.

World Health Organization (1990) *Cancer Palliative Care.* Technical Report Series 804. World Health Organization, Geneva.

CHAPTER 4

Specialist and advanced nursing practice

Vanessa Taylor

Introduction

> The recent proliferation of new job titles for nurses practising at a higher level has caused confusion among professionals and consumers. There is a need for clarification of the roles and responsibilities of higher-level practice to maintain public confidence.
>
> (Jeyasingham *et al.* 1999, p.311)

Recent Government publications (Department of Health 1997, Department of Health 1999, Department of Health 2000a, 2000b, 2000c) reveal a radical agenda for change within healthcare and encourage the development of innovative nursing roles to support the Government's agenda of patient-centred healthcare provision. *The New NHS: modern, dependable* (Department of Health 1997) identified the role of the expert nurse and the influence that nurses could have in improving the quality and effectiveness of clinical care. Subsequently, building on the opportunities offered by *The Scope of Professional Practice* (United Kingdom Central Council for Nursing, Midwifery and Health Visiting 1992) for nurses to expand and develop specialist roles, the Department of Health's nursing strategy, *Making a Difference* (Department of Health 1999) endorsed the creation of new nursing roles and the potential for a clinical career pathway for expert nurses. For nurses providing cancer and palliative care, *The Nursing Contribution to Cancer Care* (Department of Health 2000a) identified the need for specialist nurses to lead in ensuring high standards of patient care based on evidence. These publications therefore endorse the value of nursing and offer challenges and opportunities to nurses within clinical practice to develop nursing practice and nursing roles to meet the demands of contemporary healthcare.

In response, the last decade has seen the emergence of a plethora of specialist nursing roles, including nurse specialist, nurse practitioner and nurse consultant. Within cancer and palliative care, specialist roles include the site-specific roles (e.g.

breast or lung cancer), treatment-focused roles (e.g. chemotherapy or radiotherapy) and generic oncology and palliative specialist roles. However, the expansion in specialist nursing roles may be described as rapid and un-coordinated, with varying titles, responsibilities and educational requirements apparent both within and between organisations. In addition, the lack of a nationally agreed standard for these roles has caused confusion among employers, the public (Jeyasingham *et al.* 1999) and other professional groups. Furthermore, nurses working at higher levels of practice are only partially regulated through the recording of specialist practitioner qualifications and adherence to the principles within *The Scope of Professional Practice* (Humphris and Masterson 1998). The need for verification and clarity of higher-level practice continues, with assessment of this level of practice demonstrated through practice competence rather than completion of an educational course (Humphris and Masterson 1998) in order to protect the nurse, the employer and the public. Calls for the standardisation of titles and the level of experience expected from nurses using the specialist title are increasingly being made, and such standardisation is seen as essential for public confidence (Jeyasingham *et al.* 1999).

Focusing on the work previously undertaken by the United Kingdom Central Council for Nursing, Midwifery and Health Visiting (UKCC) and recent publications from Government and the Nursing and Midwifery Council (NMC), this chapter aims to review the interpretations of specialist and advanced practice and encourage nurses working in cancer and palliative care to consider the implications of the debate surrounding specialist practice for their career development.

Learning outcomes

By the end of this chapter the reader should be able to:

- provide an overview of the development of the concepts of specialist and advanced nursing practice by the UKCC and NMC within the UK
- consider the implications for nurses wishing to develop their careers or working within cancer and palliative care.

Background

> It would be clearer to purchasers and less confusing for practitioners and patients/clients if the framework for professional practice beyond registration was integrated, coherent and visible ... a perpetuation of differing terminology cannot serve the best interests of professional practice.
>
> (Wallace and Gough 1995, p.944)

Within the UK, the debate about specialist and advanced practitioners may be described as having had a long and tortuous history (Wallace and Gough 1995). Over the past 20 years, numerous definitions have appeared within the nursing literature produced by the professional body which attempted to define the concepts of specialist, advanced and consultant nursing practice and associated nursing roles beyond initial registration (UKCC, 1986, 1994, 1999, 2002).

In 1994, the UKCC presented its framework for nursing following registration, identifying three levels of practice, namely primary, specialist and advanced. Primary practice focused on the period of practice following the support stage for newly registered 'novice' practitioners (UKCC 1994). Although pre-registration education was considered to provide practitioners with the knowledge, skills and competence to deliver safe and effective care, the UKCC indicated that some practitioners required further preparation to meet the specialist needs of certain individuals and groups in society. The terms 'specialist' and 'advanced' nursing practice were used to distinguish such practitioners. Specialist practice was based on the need to:

1   utilise the expertise of experienced nurses
2   value clinical practice – providing career opportunities that maintained contact with patients to deepen knowledge and skill in direct patient care
3   recognise that initial professional education was not enough for the complexity of modern nursing
4   differentiate between working in a specialty and being a specialist (Castledine and McGee 1998).

The specialist practitioner was defined as someone who will be able to demonstrate:

higher levels of clinical decision making and will be able to monitor and improve standards of care through supervision of practice, clinical nursing audit, developing and leading practice, contributing to research, teaching and supporting professional colleagues.

(UKCC 1994)

This definition revealed two components to the concept. The first was the level of practice at which a specialist practitioner was expected to work, termed 'a higher level'. Secondly, the definition highlighted the sub-roles that the specialist practitioner was expected to undertake. The UKCC emphasised that there was 'a clear difference between practising within a specialty and being a nursing specialist' (UKCC 1994), and did not associate specialist practice or the specialist practitioner role with work within a clinical specialty or with patients with particular diseases. Instead, by focusing on the level of practice of the practitioner, the UKCC definition enabled nurses working in any clinical setting to become specialist practitioners. In order to be recognised as a specialist practitioner, a framework of degree-level education and the recording of the achievement of specialist practitioner status was set out by the UKCC. Statutory standards for post-registration education, which could lead to the recordable qualification of specialist practitioner, were identified.

The UKCC also defined the advanced practitioner as being engaged in:

adjusting the boundaries for the development of future practice, pioneering and developing new roles responsive to changing needs and with advancing clinical practice, research and education to enrich professional practice as a whole.

(UKCC 1994)

This role therefore focused on leading innovations in practice and service delivery, advancing nursing practice, research and education, and the development of professionals (Wallace and Gough 1995). The level of education of the advanced practitioner was described as likely to be Masters or doctoral level. However, no formal process for recording this role was put in place.

It is interesting to note that these attempts to define specialist and advanced nursing practice in 1994 focused on the level of practice, the roles of the practitioner and stipulating the educational qualifications required for these roles. In particular, it appears that the higher level of practice of specialist practitioners was linked to the completion of an educational course rather than to demonstration of clinical competence. However, practitioners were not mandated to record a qualification, which made public verification of appropriate educational preparation difficult (UKCC 1999).

In 1997, a review of specialist and advanced practice was undertaken by the UKCC in recognition of the rapidly evolving environment of health and social care and the opportunities for new nursing roles. It was acknowledged that difficulties had arisen as the 'higher level of practice' identified within the definition of specialist practice had achieved a low level of consensus by organisations and individuals in terms of post-registration practice competencies. This had resulted in individual interpretation of the concept by NHS employers, focusing predominantly on role title and specialty rather than on level of practice, and the lack of a nationally co-ordinated approach to the development of specialist practitioner roles. The UKCC also acknowledged the confusion surrounding specialist practice as being associated with a particular clinical specialty or disease-specific group, and the lack of a national recordable qualification for the higher-level practice. Therefore, in order to address some of the confusion surrounding the concept of specialist practice and the specialist practitioner title, the UKCC conducted a pilot project aimed at clarifying higher-level practice, the development of a national standard and setting out the criteria and processes that a nurse must undergo in order to be assessed and recognised as a specialist practitioner.

The publication *Report of the Higher Level of Practice Pilot and Project* (UKCC 2002) detailed the findings from the pilot project and set out for the first time the level of practice expected from nurses undertaking this 'specialist practitioner role'. The terms 'specialist practice' and 'specialist practitioner' were replaced by 'higher-level practice' and 'higher-level practitioner' in an attempt to disassociate specialist practice from clinical specialties or disease-specific groups. Higher-level practitioners were described as using complex reasoning, critical thinking, reflection and analysis to inform their health assessments, clinical judgements and decision making. Such practitioners would act as leaders for change, crossing professional and agency boundaries and recognising ethical, legal and professional constraints on practice (UKCC 2002). The title 'higher-level practitioner' was recommended as a recordable title. Furthermore, the UKCC identified the criteria that a nurse must fulfil and the assessment process to be undertaken for recognition as a higher level practitioner. The proposed standard for higher-level practice included seven areas for assessment. The standard acknowledged that although those working at a higher level of practice had aspects of education, research and management included within their role, the main focus, purpose and impact of their work related to individuals and groups or communities (UKCC 2002) including:

1   providing effective healthcare
2   leading and developing practice
3   improving quality and health outcomes
4   innovation and changing practice
5   evaluation and research
6   developing self and others
7   working across professional and organisational boundaries (UKCC 2002).

It was envisaged that practitioners would supply evidence to demonstrate that they had achieved the standard. The proposed assessment process involved:

• practitioners developing a portfolio of evidence against the standard
• a visit by a member of the assessment panel to the practitioner's workplace, once the practitioner had submitted the portfolio, to verify its content and identify relevant factors
• practitioners appearing before an assessment panel to discuss the evidence they had presented, and the panel deciding whether there is sufficient evidence to judge the practitioner's competence against the standard (UKCC 2002).

On successful completion of this process, the UKCC proposed that this title would be recorded for three years, following which the nurse must be reassessed for re-registration as a 'higher-level practitioner'. The UKCC's proposals for the development of higher-level practice and higher-level practitioner status were presented to the NMC for discussion and further action as appropriate. In March 2003, the NMC announced details of a new three-part register and outlined the Council's intention to prescribe competencies for specialist and advanced practice nursing which will include protection of title for these roles (Nursing and Midwifery Council 2003). Nurses will therefore not be entitled to refer to themselves by specialist titles unless they are appropriately qualified to do so and have been assessed and recorded as such by the NMC (Scott 2003).

This announcement was timely. The publication of the proposals for *Agenda for Change* (Department of Health 2003) links pay progression to the achievement of particular competencies. It seems therefore that the current climate provides an opportunity for joined-up thinking between the Government and the NMC to take place with regard to specialist and advanced nursing roles. Such an approach could ensure consistency in interpretation and application at a national level of specialist and advanced nursing roles, and could limit the confusion surrounding specialist and advanced nursing practice. *Agenda for Change* may be linked with competencies for specialist and advanced nursing roles with opportunities for regulation and assessment of a nationally recognised, recordable award. Indeed, suggestion of such working together is indicated in the NMC press release (Nursing and Midwifery Council 2003), which states that the Council will work closely with employers and health departments to restrict the use of titles to those that the Council will regulate. It appears that the clarification called for by Wallace and Gough (1995) and Jeyasingham *et al.* (1999), and required by employers, patients and practitioners, may finally be addressed.

Issues for consideration for nurses working within cancer and palliative care

For nurses working in cancer and palliative care, the forthcoming proposals by the NMC for a new Register, alongside the potential links with a modernised pay system within the NHS, offer a number of areas for consideration, including the following:

1   the need to review any proposed competencies and criteria for assessment as specialist and advanced practitioners and to feed back comments during any consultation period to the NMC
2   for nurses, particularly those working in 'specialist' roles, to consider the extent to which their current practice meets any proposed NMC competencies for specialist and advanced practice, identifying any education and development needs
3   for cancer and palliative care educators to review the NMC's proposals for specialist and advanced practice and review against/integrate into current education provision
4   for network lead nurses currently developing national competencies in cancer and palliative care to liaise with Government and the NMC about this work and its compatibility with their proposals.

In conclusion, this chapter has provided an overview of the development of specialist and advanced nursing roles within the UK since the emergence of these terms in publications by the UKCC during the last 20 years. The anticipated publication of a consultation document by the NMC about regulation and registration for specialist and advanced nursing roles has implications both for nurses planning their careers in cancer and palliative care and for those in 'specialist' roles. It cannot be assumed that the post-holders will meet the NMC criteria for recognition as specialist or advanced practitioners, given the local variations which have emerged for such posts. This may result in education and development needs being identified for current post-holders. However, the opportunity to link together the NMC criteria and the proposed *Agenda for Change* pay scales is timely and may serve to promote a consistent interpretation of these levels of practice within nursing to protect both nurses and, importantly, patients and their families.

Implications for the reader's own practice

1 How might the proposed NMC competencies and criteria for assessment for specialist practitioner status affect you?

2 What evidence might you present which demonstrates that you practise at 'higher level'?

3 What education and professional development needs do you have to identify to help you to meet the criteria for specialist practitioner status?

References

Castledine G and McGee P (eds) (1998) *Specialist and Advanced Practice: issues for research.* Blackwell Science, Oxford.

Department of Health (1997) *The New NHS: modern, dependable.* The Stationery Office, London.

Department of Health (1999) *Making a Difference. Strengthening the nursing, midwifery and health visiting contribution to health and healthcare.* The Stationery Office, London.

Department of Health (2000a) *The Nursing Contribution to Cancer Care.* The Stationery Office, London.

Department of Health (2000b) *The NHS Plan.* The Stationery Office, London.

Department of Health (2000c) *The Cancer Plan.* The Stationery Office, London.

Department of Health (2003) *Agenda for Change. Proposed agreement.* The Stationery Office, London.

Humphris D and Masterson A (1998) Practising at a higher level. *Prof Nurse.* **14**: 10–13.

Jeyasingham M, Ransome S and Ward S (1999) Higher-level practice: the consumer's perspective. *Prof Nurse.* **14**: 311–14.

Nursing and Midwifery Council (2003) *NMC Begins Work on Higher-Level Practice Standards.* Press statement 104/03, 5 September 2003. Nursing and Midwifery Council, London.

Scott H (2003) Specialist nurses are to be assessed and regulated. *Br J Nurs.* **12**: 340.

United Kingdom Central Council for Nursing, Midwifery and Health Visiting (UKCC) (1986) *Project 2000: a new preparation for practice.* UKCC, London.

United Kingdom Central Council for Nursing, Midwifery and Health Visiting (UKCC) (1992) *The Scope of Professional Practice.* UKCC, London.

United Kingdom Central Council for Nursing, Midwifery and Health Visiting (UKCC) (1994) *The Future of Professional Practice: the Council's standards for education and practice following registration (PREP) – transitional arrangements for the specialist practitioner title/qualification.* UKCC, London.

United Kingdom Central Council for Nursing, Midwifery and Health Visiting (UKCC) (1999) *A Higher-Level Practice. Report of the Consultation on the UKCC's proposals for a Revised Regulatory Framework for Post-Registration Clinical Practice.* UKCC, London.

United Kingdom Central Council for Nursing, Midwifery and Health Visiting (UKCC) (2002) *Report of the Higher Level of Practice Pilot and Project.* UKCC, London.

Wallace M and Gough P (1995) The UKCC's criteria for specialist and advanced nursing practice. *Br J Nurs.* **4**: 939–44.

CHAPTER 5

Post Shipman: the impact on developing education in cancer and palliative care pain management

Fiona Hicks

I will use my power to help the sick to the best of my ability and judgement; I will abstain from harming or wrongdoing anyone by it. I will not give a fatal draught to anyone if I am asked, nor will I suggest any such thing.

(from the Hippocratic oath)

The aim of this chapter is to explore the effects of the Shipman case on attitudes to end-of-life prescribing, and to consider the value of education to counterbalance these effects.

Learning outcomes

By the end of this chapter the reader should be able to:

- put the events associated with Harold Shipman in context
- appreciate the continuing importance of dispelling 'morphine myths'
- consider the legal and ethical implications of the doctrine of double effect in pain management at the end of life.

Introduction

Much has changed in healthcare in the UK over the past five years. Public confidence in the medical profession in particular has been rocked by a series of scandals that have been widely reported in the press, including:

- the Bristol case (excess mortality in paediatric cardiac surgery which went undetected for some years)

- the Alder Hey case (retention of post-mortem tissue from children without express parental consent)
- the Shipman case (a general practitioner now thought to have murdered around 230 patients).

Although the first two cases can be attributed to the mistakes of largely well-meaning doctors, the Shipman case is different. Organisational change may prevent another 'Bristol' with the robust introduction of clinical governance (Department of Health 2000), and enhanced procedures with regard to consent may resolve the issues of retained organs, but what do we make of the doctor turned serial killer?

The case of Harold Shipman raises several uncomfortable questions. Do the appalling revelations about Harold Shipman have an impact on our own practice in palliative care or on the relationships between physicians and their patients and families? Has the criminal behaviour of Harold Shipman exposed the pre-existing concerns of healthcare professionals or patients about pain management in end-of-life care? Does the fact that he used overdoses of diamorphine to kill his patients resonate with difficult issues in end-of-life decision making in pain management? Has he undermined the public's trust in all doctors, and general (family) practice or single-handed practitioners in particular? Is this an issue that is confined to the UK, or have the effects of this case been felt across the western world?

Harold Shipman in context

Harold Shipman graduated from the University of Leeds, England, in 1970. After hospital posts, he went directly into general (family) practice in 1974, and in 1975 was investigated by the police for excessive prescribing of pethidine (meperidine). He admitted to using intravenous pethidine to treat his 'depression', and in 1976 he was convicted on drugs charges. He signed a written undertaking that he had no intention of returning to general practice, and he entered a clinic in order to overcome his addiction. In 1977 he did return to general practice. The General Medical Council, which is the body responsible for the regulation and registration of doctors in the UK, decided not to take action on the advice of Shipman's psychiatrist, who stated that it would be catastrophic to him if he were not allowed to return to practice. He worked as a single-handed general practitioner for over 20 years in two practices, where he was well respected by his patients and known as an attentive and caring family doctor. When he was found to have forged the will of an elderly female patient who died suddenly and unexpectedly, the police began to scrutinise his practice.

In 2001, at the age of 56 years, he was convicted of murdering 15 middle-aged and elderly female patients with fatal injections of diamorphine, and he became Britain's most prolific serial killer. The most likely number of victims is now thought to be 236 (Baker 2002). Medicine has arguably thrown up more serial killers than all other professions put together, with nursing a close second. Shipman is the last in a long line of such killers and is by far the most prolific. Does the profession attract people with a pathological interest in power over life and death? (Kinnell 2000). Does this make the rest of the profession more sensitive to the way in which they manage terminal illness?

Fallout from the Shipman case

The publicity surrounding the conviction of Harold Shipman on several counts of murder led to a series of articles in the medical press speculating on how it might change areas of medical practice. His case was linked with the events at Bristol, which saw the advent of the concept of clinical governance. There were concerns about the public's trust in doctors, worries about hasty political decision making on professional self-regulation and the role of the General Medical Council, and speculation about the end of single-handed general practitioners. Records of the patterns of opioid prescribing of individual doctors were examined. There were calls for the publication of mortality data from individual GPs, suggestions that death registers be kept in general practice, and calls for more effective investigation into deaths.

The publication of mortality data might well have helped to catch Shipman sooner, and many articles made valid points about how healthcare is organised and delivered, but could some of the fallout from this case be damaging to the practice of palliative care? Will patients die in pain because doctors fear to prescribe adequate analgesia, or was this always an unsatisfactory area of palliative care? Will patients be afraid to accept diamorphine from their doctors or did this issue pre-date the Shipman case?

Morphine myths revisited

Over the last 20 years or so in the UK, and increasingly across the world, the hospice movement has been responsible for extensive education of doctors, nurses and the public about the safe and effective use of morphine in palliative care (Twycross and Lack 1984). In specialist palliative care it has become routine practice to prescribe morphine, diamorphine and other strong opioids for severe pain, and to counsel patients about the benefits of such treatments. The World Health Organization (WHO) analgesic ladder (World Health Organization 1990) and the European Association of Palliative Care guidelines on the use of strong opioids (Hanks *et al.* 2001) are widely used both in practice and in education, but how well are these guidelines implemented beyond specialist practice?

The role of patients

A recent American study recruited 998 terminally ill patients from 6 US sites (Weiss *et al.* 2001), of whom 50% reported moderate or severe pain, 52% had seen a primary physician and 20% had seen a pain specialist during the previous four weeks. However, of those with pain, only 29% wanted more analgesic therapy,

62% wanted pain therapy to remain the same and 9% wanted to reduce or stop their analgesics. The reasons given for not wanting to increase pain medication were fear of addiction, dislike of mental side-effects, dislike of physical side-effects and not wanting more pills or injections. A study from Chicago also found that fears of addiction and, more particularly, tolerance among patients correlated with high pain scores (Paice *et al.* 1998). Similar findings have been reported from Hong Kong, in addition to the desire of patients to be 'good' and not to complain, especially to their doctors (Wills and Wooton 1999). A qualitative analysis of pain management autobiographies and reluctance to use opioids for cancer pain management from San Francisco uncovered a host of beliefs and misconceptions that were impeding good pain management (Schumacher et al 2002). There are clearly factors relating to the patients in these studies, and these appear to be reinforced by professional attitudes.

A Gallup poll conducted in the UK in 1995 assessed perceptions of the medical use of morphine in a sample of 1055 members of the general public aged 16 years or and over (Smith *et al.* 1995a). In total 29% thought that it signified imminent death, 36% thought that it prevented normal living and 40% believed that it impaired the ability to think clearly. Furthermore, 72% thought that morphine is addictive, 50% said they would worry about becoming addicted to the drug, 74% regarded morphine as dangerous, 48% associated morphine treatment with unpleasant side-effects and 44% stated that they would be reluctant to take morphine if their doctor prescribed it. Clearly the results of this study have enormous implications for public education and are consistent with the findings of the other studies cited above.

Nursing staff

There are several studies that highlight a lack of knowledge among nursing staff about opioid treatment for pain management, including issues such as addiction and tolerance (Brunier *et al.* 1995), in addition to equianalgesia and opioid dosing (Ferrell and McCaffrey 1997). One study evaluated the information that nurses receive during their basic education in North America (Ferrell *et al.* 1992). These researchers examined 14 nursing textbooks published between 1985 and 1991 and found that only one stated correctly the definition of opioid addiction and its likelihood following the use of opioid analgesics for pain control. Other studies have demonstrated the positive effect of experience on nursing knowledge and practice (O'Brien *et al.* 1996) and the influence of empathy on pain assessment and the use of opioids (McCaffrey and Ferrell 1997a).

Medical staff

The concept of 'opiophobia' was first coined in America to describe the customary under-utilisation of opioid analgesics. Morgan (1986) asserted that American physicians markedly under-treat severe pain based on an irrational and undocumented fear that appropriate use of opioids will lead patients to become addicts. Morgan's view was that this irrational fear, which he termed opiophobia, resists educational intervention just as phobic fears resist rational explanation and exploration. Because this phobia has become fixed in the customary behaviour of physicians, it is particularly resistant to change. His conclusion was that re-education may be better directed towards the changing of mistaken attitudes about drug use and abuse that are part of the American culture and which are not amenable to alteration by medical education. Certainly it has been found that American medical students' attitudes to prescribing opioids became more negative as they progressed through medical school (Weinstein *et al.* 2000). Several personality traits were associated not only with career intentions regarding specialty choice, but also with opiophobia as described by Morgan. This work clearly has implications for medical education, with a strong emphasis in America on changing attitudes to opioids.

In 1995, a panel of UK general practitioners (GPs) were asked about both their own and their patients' perceptions of controlled-release morphine (Smith *et al.* 1995). In total, 91% of GPs thought that their patients had specific worries about taking morphine, 36% thought that their patients associated a prescription of morphine with imminent death, and 18% considered their patients to be fearful about the side-effects of morphine. It was found that 59% of GPs thought their patients had fears about addiction, but only 7% reassured them about this. A considerable number of GPs themselves were convinced that the therapeutic use of morphine would always cause addiction.

Two studies in Scandinavia have highlighted related issues. A survey of Norwegian physicians revealed deficits relating to both knowledge and attitudes (Warncke *et al.* 1994). Of 306 physicians managing pain in cancer, only 25% had knowledge of the WHO analgesic ladder and only 86% were prepared to prescribe a strong opioid. Of those, 44% prescribed inadequate doses and only 13% had a correct understanding of opioid drug dependence. A similar Swedish study (Rawal *et al.* 1993) highlighted far greater knowledge of the WHO analgesic ladder but also a fatalism regarding the experience of pain in terminal care, with 30% of physicians believing that all patients experience moderate to severe pain at the time of their death and 78% believing that periodic severe pain is common in patients with terminal cancer.

These findings are not necessarily applicable to other parts of the world. A study of GPs in Australia revealed that these doctors were not concerned about tolerance to opioids when treating cancer pain, but were worried by opioid side-effects and cognitive dysfunction (Wakefield *et al.* 1993).

There are clearly cultural differences in knowledge and attitudes in relation to opioids and their use in the management of severe pain in cancer. The majority of published studies hail from America, and their results should not be extrapolated uncritically to other parts of the world. Sensitivity to the cultural background and existing knowledge of audiences must underpin education in this field.

Pharmacists

The role of pharmacists in patient management may be underestimated, but knowledge and attitudes may well impact on the willingness of patients to comply with prescribed medication, in addition to their important educative role for patients, nurses and medical staff. A study of 43 German patients who had been treated with strong opioids by a pain service (not necessarily for palliative care) uncovered negative attitudes among relatives, pharmacists and general practitioners (Donner *et al.* 1998). Similarly, an audit of doctors, nurses and pharmacists in a 591-bed teaching hospital in Scotland yielded some disappointing results (Welsh *et al.* 1997); 48% had not heard of cancer pain management guidelines, 71% thought that patients would develop psychological dependence on opioids, and 84% thought that patients would develop tolerance to opioids in the management of their cancer pain. This study did not include a subgroup analysis of the different professionals, but all stated that they would value more education in this area.

What's in a name?

There is certainly an issue about the perception of strong opioids and their use in pain management in palliative care. The extent of fears and knowledge does appear to vary between cultures, but all demonstrate concerns about the use of these drugs. Harold Shipman used diamorphine to murder his patients, and this is known to be one of the most addictive and abused morphine derivatives worldwide. Indeed, many countries (including North America) do not have access to legal supplies of diamorphine and express amazement at its use in palliative care in the UK. How many of our patients know that they are being prescribed heroin? Would it change their attitudes if they did know? Are strong opioids with names other than morphine more acceptable to patients and staff? Experience does suggest this to be the case, but it is an area that has not been widely researched and is therefore open to speculation. Certainly Oxycontin is now a drug of abuse in North America, and it may be that patients will show a similar concern when they are prescribed Oxycontin to that concern they express about being prescribed morphine. It appears that prescribing alternatives to morphine may be a short-term solution to allaying people's fears, but it is probably the nature of the drugs and their potential for abuse that is more important in the long term. Any adverse publicity with regard to abuse of these drugs either for murder or for recreation probably increases public and professional anxieties about their medicinal use. Educational strategies must bear this in mind.

The role of education

There is no published literature on the education of the general public about dispelling 'morphine myths' and the use of opioids for pain management. However, several studies have demonstrated that healthcare professionals are aware of the difficulties of managing severe pain in cancer, and are concerned that their own practice could be improved. There is a thirst for education in this area, as in many other areas of management of patients with end-stage disease. A survey of GPs across the UK revealed that 43% of those working in inner city areas wanted education in opiate prescribing (Shipman *et al.* 2001). There certainly appears to be a significant demand for education in this area, but much less is known about the methods of teaching that are likely to be successful and show a sustained improvement in practice.

The underlying trend of improvement

There is some evidence to suggest that nurses' knowledge of pain assessment and management has improved over the last two decades. A review of the literature by McCaffrey and Ferrell (1997b) demonstrated an encouraging trend, with improvement of nurses' knowledge of pain assessment, opioid dosing and likelihood of addiction. However, knowledge deficits were still evident.

Experiential education

Medical students in Kentucky in the USA have been involved in a programme of visiting hospice patients at home, completing a cancer pain history and performing a relevant physical examination (Sloan *et al.* 2001). They then received feedback and teaching on cancer pain management from a hospice nurse. Both the patients and the students considered this to be a valuable experience. A Canadian group assessed the value of a two-week programme of experiential learning for postgraduate physicians training in family medicine (Oneschuk *et al.* 1997). There were significant improvements in examination scores after the placement, but the authors noted that serious deficiencies were identified, particularly in the areas of pain assessment and opioid use, namely opioid side-effects and issues involving dependence, addiction and tolerance. A descriptive study comparing knowledge and misconceptions about cancer pain management between two groups of nurses in America, working in either a community-based hospice or an inpatient oncology setting, showed that the hospice nurses scored significantly higher with regard to overall knowledge of pain management, opioids, scheduling and liberalness (Hollen *et al.* 2000). The authors suggest that the practice setting in addition to education may influence both knowledge of and attitudes to pain, although the reasons behind the nurses' choices of work setting were not discussed.

Workshops

The value of oral presentations and group discussions has been assessed in a number of small studies. A study in the Netherlands found that the prescription records of general practitioners do not change one year after a single palliative care workshop (Schuit *et al.* 2000). A lecture given to physicians and nurses in Belgium led to a small improvement in knowledge immediately after the teaching (Devulder 1999), and a series of lectures and group discussions of cases was found to be effective relative to a low baseline of knowledge and attitudes in Flanders (Bauwens *et al.* 2001).

The most effective methods of teaching have yet to be elucidated for healthcare professionals, but even less is known about effective methods of education for members of the general public or palliative care patients.

The doctrine of double effect

Evidence and experience demonstrate that the use of strong opioids to relieve severe cancer pain is both safe and effective over prolonged periods of time, when doses are properly titrated (World Health Organization 1990). For specialists in palliative care, the prescription of opioids for their patients is largely routine and does not cause the physician undue concern. However, for some patients at the end of life such a prescription has the potential to cause dangerous side-effects and thus shorten the terminal phase. Such patients may include those with respiratory failure and severe pain, in whom the administration of a strong opioid may cause a degree of respiratory depression. In 1994, the House of Lords Select Committee on Medical Ethics considered this question and reported as follows:

> In the small and diminishing number of cases in which pain and distress cannot be satisfactorily controlled, we are satisfied that the professional judgement of the health care team can be exercised to enable increasing doses of medication (whether analgesics or sedatives) to be given in order to provide relief, even if this shortens life. The adequate relief of pain and suffering in terminally ill patients depends on doctors being able to do all that is necessary and possible. In many cases, this will mean the use of opiates or sedative drugs in increasing doses. In some cases patients may as a consequence die sooner than they would otherwise have done, but this is not in our view a reason for withholding treatment that would give relief, as long as the doctor acts in accordance with responsible medical practice with the objective of relieving pain and distress, and with no intention to kill.

It is this kind of situation that requires the healthcare team to carefully discuss the benefits and burdens of treatment and reach a consensus if at all possible. Such cases often cause concern among prescribing doctors, and some may under-treat patient pain or anguish for fear of the consequences. Many physicians are unclear about the law in this area and worry unduly about prosecution. The value of team discussion and decision making, with recourse to specialist advice, cannot be over-emphasised. The reporting of incidents in the press that resonate with their own experience may increase the vulnerability felt by doctors in such circumstances.

Thus it may well be that the publicity surrounding Harold Shipman and his use of diamorphine to murder his patients has increased the discomfort of doctors with regard to prescribing for symptom relief in terminal care where life may be shortened. An increased number of patients could be dying with uncontrolled symptoms. Education of staff about the ethical and legal principles underpinning treatment decisions and the doctrine of double effect, and reminders that Shipman was a murderer, not a bad doctor, could be included in education about care of the dying.

Evidence that Shipman had any effect

There is no published research about the effect that the Shipman case has had on medical practice in palliative or terminal care in the UK or elsewhere. Clearly, the myths about morphine and the strongly held beliefs of a significant number of healthcare professionals, in addition to society itself, about the medical use of opioids, pre-date the Shipman case. The palliative care movement has worked hard over the last 20 years or so to dispel these myths, with limited success outside the specialty itself. Anecdotal evidence does suggest that pre-existing concerns have been heightened for some doctors, especially in terminal care situations.

Conclusion

The prevalence of opiophobia among healthcare professionals and society in general continues to act as a barrier to effective pain relief in palliative care across most cultures. A variety of educational strategies have been adopted, with some limited success. A serial killer such as Harold Shipman who used diamorphine to murder his patients unfortunately acts to validate these fears for some people. Shipman must be put in context in palliative care education and seen for what he is. His crimes bear no relation to the practice of palliative and terminal care. An honest exposure of opiophobia should form a key part of educational programmes for both patients and professionals – there is still a long way to go.

Key points to consider
- Harold Shipman was a murderer, not a bad doctor.
- Myths about morphine (opiophobia) are still prevalent in most cultures, impeding effective pain relief in palliative care.
- Education strategies should include not only the pharmacological basis for opioid prescribing, but also the legal and ethical contexts in which healthcare professionals practise.

Implications for the reader's own practice

1 How has the Harold Shipman case affected your management of pain?
2 In the light of the Shipman case, what creative and imaginative approaches to teaching could you use to ensure high-quality pain management?
3 How prevalent is opiophobia in your clinical setting?
4 What methods of education could you introduce for patients, staff and the general public in order to combat opiophobia?
5 In what ways is a team approach taken to pain management in your clinical setting?

References

Baker R (2002) *Harold Shipman's Clinical Practice 1974–1998. A clinical audit commissioned by the Chief Medical Officer*. Department of Health, London.

Bauwens S, Distelmans W, Storme G *et al.* (2001) Attitudes and knowledge about cancer pain in Flanders. The educational effect of workshops regarding pain and symptom control. *Palliat Med.* **15**: 181–9.

Brunier G, Carson M and Harrison D (1995) What do nurses know and believe about patients with pain? Results of a hospital survey. *J Pain Symptom Manage.* **10**: 436–45.

Department of Health (2000) *An Organisation With a Memory. Report of an Expert Group on Learning from Adverse Events in the NHS*. The Stationery Office, London.

Devulder J (1999) Persisting misconceptions of Belgian physicians and nurses about cancer pain treatment. *Acta Clin Belg.* **54**: 346–50.

Donner B, Raber M, Zenz M *et al.* (1998) Experiences with the prescription of opioids: a patient questionnaire. *J Pain Symptom Manage.* **15**: 231–34.

Ferrell B and McCaffrey M (1997) Nurses' knowledge about equianalgesia and opioid dosing. *Cancer Nurs.* **20**: 201–12.

Ferrell B, McCaffrey M and Rhiner M (1992) Pain and addiction: an urgent need for change in nursing education. *J Pain Symptom Manage.* **7**: 117–24.

Hanks G, de Conno F, Cherny N *et al.* (2001) Morphine and alternative opioids in cancer pain: the EAPC recommendations. *Br J Cancer.* **84**: 587–93.

Hollen CJ, Hollen CW and Stolte K (2000) Hospital and oncology unit nurses: a comparative survey of knowledge and attitudes about cancer pain. *Oncol Nurs Forum.* **27**: 1593–9.

House of Lords Select Committee on Medical Ethics (1994). **HL Paper 21–1**: 49.

Kinnell HG (2000) Serial homicide by doctors: Shipman in perspective. *BMJ.* **321**: 1594–7.

McCaffrey M and Ferrell B (1997a) Influence of professional vs. personal role on pain assessment and use of opioids. *J Contin Educ Nurs.* **28**: 69–77.

McCaffrey M and Ferrell B (1997b) Nurses' knowledge of pain assessment and management: how much progress have we made? *J Pain Symptom Manage.* **14**; 175–88.

Morgan J (1986) American opiophobia: customary under-utilisation of opioid analgesics. *Adv Alcohol Subst Abuse.* **5**: 163–73.

O'Brien S, Dalton J, Konsler G *et al.* (1996) The knowledge and attitudes of experienced oncology nurses regarding the management of cancer-related pain. *Oncol Nurs Forum.* **23**: 515–21.

Oneschuk D, Fainsinger R, Hanson J *et al.* (1997) Assessment and knowledge in palliative care in second-year family medicine residents. *J Pain Symptom Manage.* **14**: 265–73.

Paice JA, Toy C and Shott S (1998) Barriers to cancer pain relief: fear of tolerance and addiction. *J Pain Symptom Manage.* **16**: 1–9.

Rawal N, Hylander J and Arner S (1993) Management of terminal cancer pain in Sweden: a nationwide survey. *Pain.* **54**: 169–79.

Schuit K, Otter R, Stewart R *et al.* (2000) The effects of a postgraduate course on opioid-prescribing patterns of general practitioners. *J Cancer Educ.* **15**: 214–17.

Schumacher K, West C, Dodd M *et al.* (2002) Pain management autobiographies and reluctance to use opioids in cancer pain management. *Cancer Nurse.* **25**: 125–33.

Shipman C, Addington-Hall J, Barclay S *et al.* (2001) Educational opportunities in palliative care: what do general practitioners want? *Palliat Med.* **15**: 191–6.

Sloan P, LaFountain P, Plymale M *et al.* (2001) Implementing cancer pain education for medical students. *Cancer Pract.* **9**: 225–9.

Smith R, Wade J and Gordon D (1995a) *Morphine therapy: an assessment of the public's perceptions.* Napp Laboratories, Cambridge.

Smith R, Wade J and Gordon D (1995b) *Morphine Therapy: an assessment of GP perceptions.* Napp Laboratories, Cambridge.

Twycross R and Lack S (1984) *Oral Morphine in Advanced Cancer.* Beaconsfield Publishers Ltd, Buckinghamshire.

Wakefield M, Beilby J and Ashby M (1993) General practitioners and palliative care. *Palliat Med.* **7**: 117–26.

Warncke T, Breivik H and Vainio A (1994) Treatment of cancer pain in Norway. A Questionnaire study. *Pain.* **57**: 109–16.

Weinstein S, Laux L, Thornby J *et al.* (2000) Medical students' attitudes towards pain and the use of opioid analgesics: implications for changing medical school curriculum. *South Med J.* **93**: 472–78.

Weiss S, Emanuel L, Faiclough D *et al.* (2001) Understanding the experience of pain in terminally ill patients. *Lancet.* **357**: 1311–15.

Welsh J, Fallon M and Urie J (1997) *Doctors', nurses' and pharmacists' beliefs about dependence on and tolerance to opioid analgesics in cancer patients.* Proceedings of the Fifth Congress of the European Association for Palliative Care, 10–13 September 1997, London.

Wills B and Wootton Y (1999) Concerns and misconceptions about pain among Hong Kong Chinese patients with cancer. *Cancer Nurse.* **22**: 408–13.

World Health Organization (1990) *Cancer Pain Relief and Palliative Care. Report of a WHO Expert Committee.* World Health Organization, Geneva.

CHAPTER 6

Death anxiety and death education: a brief analysis of the key issues

Graham Farley

If you are distressed by anything external, the pain is not due to the thing itself, but to your estimate of it, and this you have the power to revoke at any moment.

(Marcus Aurelius, Roman emperor and philosopher, AD 121–180)

Introduction

The aim of this chapter is to enable healthcare professionals to gain a greater insight into death anxiety as a contributory factor with regard to occupational stress (Llewellyn and Payne 1995), that is particularly associated with cancer and palliative care. The intention is to chart the evolution of death anxiety and to highlight the unique nature in relation to healthcare professionals of this particular specialty. Papadatou (2000, p.61) postulates that:

> professionals' grief has some unique features that cannot be understood within the framework of existing traditional theories ... these models refer to grief when a loved one dies ... such models are hardly applicable to health professionals who are faced with the daily events such as pain, suffering, and death as a result of the job they selected.

It is the exclusive context of this particular type of stress which develops that needs to be clearly understood by healthcare professionals so that they can have a greater opportunity to resolve issues and acquire a better understanding of the complexities that underlie this phenomenon.

One of the ways in which professionals can be enabled and empowered to deal more effectively with issues of death and death anxiety is through death education.

The approaches to death education have varied enormously over the years, and this chapter will chart and analyse them in order to shed light on the path(s) ahead.

Learning outcomes
By the end of this chapter the reader should be able to:
- show an increased understanding of death anxiety
- understand the impact of death anxiety on health professionals in cancer and palliative care
- highlight sources of support that can contribute to the working lives of the individual and the team
- develop educational approaches that engage in alleviating death anxiety.

Death anxiety

Death anxiety (thanatophobia) is defined as a feeling of dread, apprehension or solicitude when one thinks of the process of dying, or ceasing to be or what happens after death. Death is defined as a state of non-being, the termination of biological life.

(Bond 1994, p.4)

The unique perception that each individual has of death is shaped by their continued world experience (the micro- and macro-cultural infrastructure in which they reside and work). This perception is not 'etched in stone', but changes through the constant interplay between the individual and the world. These changes some-times occur month by month and at other times by the minute. Each individual therefore holds a unique perception of death, but this is shared with others, and so the 'generalised' perception is shaped and used as a frame of reference that in turn may, along with future experiences, alter the individual perception, and so the cycle continues.

So far the discussion has implied that death anxiety is a state or an attitude of mind but this oversimplifies the issue. Wong *et al.* (1994) have suggested that the terms 'death anxiety' and 'fear of death' are used interchangeably in the literature, but imply that it might be helpful to attempt to differentiate between the two. They suggest that it may be more useful to regard fear of death as specific and conscious, whereas death anxiety is viewed as more generalised and inaccessible to the aware-ness. This indeed highlights the complexity of the singular and multiple perceptions of death. It might even be illuminating to suggest that, rather than moving from different perceptions over a period of time, different perceptions are held at the same juncture. There is death's overwhelming inevitability vying with a sense of opti-mistic survival for the present and immediate future.

Vachon (1999) suggests that the hospice and palliative care movement arose out of a requirement to address the unmet needs of dying persons during the 1960s and 1970s. This, Vachon reminds us, needs to be viewed within the prevailing social context at that time, which included the sexual revolution, the questioning of social values and an increased awareness of death (in America, resulting from the murder of the Kennedy brothers, Martin Luther King and the daily exposure to deaths in the Vietnam War). As the hospice movement began to grow, the emotional intensity and its cost became more apparent, which highlighted issues such as occupational stress and burnout. Degner and Gow (1988) suggest that major shifts in the patterns of disease and treatment have affected the way in which nurses are now exposed to the dying process. Prior to this period the predominant reason for exposure to death was infection, whereas medical advances have now resulted in more patients dying as a result of chronic diseases, such as cancer.

A combination of factors has led to the way in which healthcare professionals and indeed nurses react to dying and death. These include the fact that Western society is regarded as a death-denying society (Gorer 1965). Many patients are treated aggressively, sometimes right up to the moment of death. The latter statement may give the false impression that death is an admission of failure (of medicine or the institution), rather than being viewed as something natural. The former statement also implies that death is unnatural, and that for those who have yet to succumb there is a need to sanitise it or minimise its public impact. The individual nurse's attitude to death can result in a fear of death which may be manifested in a variety of behaviours, including avoidance, denial and failure to meet the needs of the patient, carers or relatives. Boyle and Carter (1998, p.39) state that 'The delivery of effective and efficient palliative care requires the nurse to have close personal contact with the dying patient and his family, thus encouraging open awareness of the patient's impending death.' This suggests that a possible paradox may arise between the need for the nurse to develop a close relationship and the increased risk of emotional damage by becoming so closely involved. The nurse wrestles with the need to engage in a strong, meaningful relationship while conscious of the simultaneous need for self-preservation. Such cognitive dissonance coupled with the complexity of emotions poses severe threats to the working lives of these professionals, and it presents serious challenges as well as opportunities for education. However, in a phenomenological study of nurses caring for dying patients, Rittman et al. (1997), concluded that experienced nurses are able to establish different levels of intensity in their involvement with their patients. This variation in intensity is said to help the nurses to meet the emotional demands of their practice. It is not clear from this study whether this is because the nurses have a sense of control or whether it is due to a sophisticated form of avoidance.

Death acceptance

In contrast to death anxiety there is the concept of death acceptance. In their conceptual analysis of attitudes to death, Wong et al. (1994) identified three different kinds of death acceptance, namely neutral, approach and escape.

Neutral acceptance is neither fearing nor welcoming the event, but acceptance of the inevitability of death – that it is one of the immutable factors in life's trajectory.

Approach acceptance is based on belief in life after death, and may also be associated with some reward. This particular perspective, according to its proponents, is found in those who have strong religious beliefs. Powell and Thorson (1991) suggest that religiosity (the quality of being religious or devout) is related to lower levels of death anxiety. Furthermore, Leming (1977) views religion as a means of giving people a sense of harmony and cohesion. However, those who have a strong faith but consider themselves to have committed major sins may feel that they have even more to fear in the afterlife.

Escape acceptance is seen as a welcome alternative to a life that is full of misery and pain. The state of death acceptance may therefore exist for a variety of reasons, and it is possible to surmise that individuals may hold any or all of these beliefs at one or the same time. In this respect, imagine for a moment that a terminally ill patient is being cared for by a range of nurses who have varying beliefs about death acceptance. Apart from the patient's own state of death acceptance, a variety of transactions might occur between the patient and these nurses depending on the nurses' particular beliefs. This may result in some nurses who hold an 'approach acceptance' interacting in a more optimistic fashion than nurses who view death as nihilistic.

Payne *et al.* (1998) in a study that compares death anxiety in hospice and Accident and Emergency nurses, suggest that there may be an element of self-selection for those who undertake hospice work, because they are more comfortable with the open acknowledgement of death. This assumption opens up an argument of causality in the prevalence, nature of death occurrence and the clinical setting in which these professionals find themselves. An equally plausible argument is that self-selection may be facilitated by the prevailing attitudes and culture of the team rather than by the individual's personal feelings about death. Further research is recommended to delineate these factors. To illustrate this point, a student who finds herself in a caring and supportive environment which nurtures the staff as well as the patients may find that this helps to significantly balance or nullify any pre-existing fears about death. What this also suggests is that, rather than attempting to view all hospices as a magnet for nurses with open acceptance of death, there is a need to acknowledge that each hospice may have its own individual culture, and that there can be significant variations (in relation to death attitude) between them. The particular culture that develops in any hospice, community or ward may therefore owe its dynamic influence to the prevailing collective beliefs and attitudes of the healthcare professionals with regard to death, rather than the clinical setting in which they find themselves.

Personal meaning of death: the philosophical perspective

From a philosophical perspective, Erikson (1963) states that in order for individuals in the final stages to reconcile themselves with death, they need to resolve the crisis of integrity vs. despair. Integrity is referred to as a state of mind, and relates to the firm belief that life has been worthwhile and meaningful. It also means that there is an acknowledged acceptance of the differences between the reality of that lived life and what would have been the ideal. The differences between the two are reconciled. In contrast, individuals who feel that they have frittered away the years without true investment in their life are likely to feel a sense of despair, and in this case will fear death. Frankl (1965) suggests that finding a meaning in life helps to negate a person's fear of death.

The personal meaning of death: the clinical perspective

From a clinical perspective, Papadatou (2000) stresses the importance of making sense of a person's death, as this will increase the opportunity for integration that allows for investment in new relationships. In the absence of meaning, difficulties may arise in integrating the loss. Vachon (2003) suggests that a sense of spirituality can be perceived as supportive by professionals who may otherwise struggle to find meaning in the work that they are doing. Vachon also claims that nurses who are attracted to hospice work are more religious than others. Again this is an argument of causality, as it may be that those who are attracted to hospice and palliative care have a need to search within themselves as a result of the increased exposure to death. This in turn may create an environment in which a propensity to spirituality can develop. Papadatou (2000) claims that professionals ascribe meaning to death by relying on spiritual or religious beliefs, but that when this explanation does not bring comfort, the professional focuses on the seriousness of the illness that medicine has not yet been able to cure. This meaning relates to a sense of relief for the long-suffering patient and relates closely to the escape acceptance theory of Wong *et al.* (1994). When professionals cannot reconcile the deaths with these types of belief frameworks, then new frameworks are developed that usually focus on some aspect of the practice which involves a sense of satisfaction in 'doing'. This is seen as being both an individual and a team activity, as they construct shared meanings of death (Papadatou 2000).

Death education

The development of death education

Carr and Merriman (1996) claim that healthcare professionals who work in hospices have lower levels of death anxiety than colleagues who work in other settings. Factors that correlated strongly with scores on the Death Attitude Index (i.e. greater comfort working with the terminally ill) were education and a sacred value system. Although it would be difficult (if not questionable) to influence the sacred value system, it is feasible to influence healthcare professionals' attitudes, beliefs and behaviours through education. Durlak (1994) states that death education programmes started in the USA in the 1950s and were influenced by the work of Kubler-Ross among other noted thanatologists of this period. Downe-Wamboldt and Tamlyn (1997) suggest that death education began to appear as a topic for discussion, research and education in the late 1960s, and remains an educational challenge four decades later. These authors also state that although a range of programmes originated in the USA, there is significantly less information about similar programmes that were developed in the UK and Canada. Doyle (1987) intimates that not only were there reports from students of inadequate preparation for providing terminal care, but also there was inadequate professional training for those working in the hospice. Downe-Wamboldt and Tamlyn (1997) clearly highlight the need for a greater focus on theory-based educational approaches, as well as the need to identify which educational approaches would be most effective.

Didactic and experiential approaches to death education

There have been two principal educational approaches to death education, namely the didactic and the experiential approach. Durlak (1994) suggests that the didactic programmes highlight knowledge and information about the study of death, whereas the experiential programmes might share some of the techniques, but emphasise and encourage the examination of feelings and issues related to death. However, the point Durlak is making is that there is considerable overlap between the content and strategies for delivery between the two approaches. In this case it may also be helpful to view this as a didactic–experiential continuum, rather than viewing these approaches as completely dichotomous and discrete entities. Maglio and Robinson (1994) performed a meta-analysis which looked at the effects of death education on death anxiety. Whereas individual studies report reduced levels of death anxiety, this comprehensive review suggests that both didactic and experiential methods are likely to increase death anxiety, although didactic interventions caused higher levels of death anxiety than experiential methods. However, these authors do not specifically differentiate between the two approaches in terms of the strategies used, and they admit that there is a degree of heterogeneity of the approaches within each of these spheres. There may be some 'grey area' or 'cross-over' in the interpretation of what constitutes a didactic and an experiential approach – hence a continuum perspective may prove more helpful here. As discussed previously, each term can equally relate both to the overall educational approach and to the specific interventions and strategies involved. What the study also reveals is that other independent variables (in addition to the educational approaches) need to be taken into consideration. These variables include gender, occupation, education level, number of participants, age of the participants, duration of the programme, previous exposure to death and religiosity. Spall and

Johnson (1997) note that experiential methods can produce both positive and negative outcomes. The positive outcomes related to the attitudes towards death, but this was at the expense of possible emotional distress and anxiety felt by participants. As a corollary to this, these authors offer a range of safety recommendations which include ensuring that there is adequate peer support, care in selection of attendees, acknowledgement of the motivation to undertake such training, the addition of a second trainer to diffuse any negative feelings, and allowing for informal follow-up.

Hurtig and Stewin (1990) conducted an experimental study to examine these different approaches to death education and the effects on nursing students in Canada. Students were allocated to one of three programmes, namely didactic, experiential and placebo (in this case the placebo programme was the control group). The didactic group included a format of lectures, films and group discussion on topics such as death in our society, a developmental view of death, the dying process, the tasks of the dying and the value of death. The experiential group had a more personal focus, using death awareness exercises, music, drawing and dyadic encounters between students. The placebo group consisted of a simulation which dealt with independence in the ageing adult (and did not deal with death education). The findings of the study suggest that inexperienced students who were in an experiential programme benefited from a positive effect on death confrontation more than those who had been randomised to the didactic or placebo programme. However, this study also acknowledged that experienced students were negatively affected by the experiential approach. The authors do not suggest or assume that experienced students may benefit more from didactic approaches. However, it may be that students who have had recent experience of death may find the experiential approaches rather 'raw' and discomforting. Interestingly, prior to undertaking this study the authors reflected that there had been an inability to distinguish between those who harbour yet deny a fear of death, and those who maintain a sense of acceptance yet exhibit some fear. However, a tool developed by Klug (1976) called the Confrontation–Integration of Death Scale (CIDS) attempts to measure two components of the reconciliation of death construct, namely death confrontation (the conscious contemplation of one's death) and death integration (the positive emotional assimilation of one's own death). Hurtig and Stewin (1990) used the CIDS, but concluded that the scores indicated that neither death education nor the personal experience of death independently produced a significant variation in death confrontation or death integration scores.

The requirement to meet the needs of the student

In contrast to the previous methodological approach, Beck (1997) conducted a phenomenological study of students' experiences of caring for dying patients. Beck claims that before educational strategies are planned, perhaps a backward step would be prudent in order to capture the students' experiences of caring for dying patients. Beck states that:

If educational strategies are targeted for specific issues identified by nursing students, perhaps more consistent findings will be reported, and nursing students will be better prepared for death and dying.

(Beck, 1997, p.409)

A total of 26 sophomore and junior-level undergraduate nursing students were included in the study. Collaizi's method of content analysis (Collaizi 1978) was used to examine the written transcripts of the students' experience of caring for dying patients. Six themes emerged.

- *Theme 1*. Nursing students experienced a gamut of emotions while caring for the dying patients. This included experiences of fear, emotional distancing, anger and frustration.
- *Theme 2*. Contemplation of the patient's life and death occurred as the nursing students cared for the patients. As the students developed relationships with the dying patients, their realisation and perspective of them changed from a dying body in a bed to a person with whom they identified and who had lived a life.
- *Theme 3*. Supporting the dying patient's family became an integral part of the care. Students realised that the dying patient was not their only responsibility, and that the grieving family needed their support as well.
- *Theme 4*. Helplessness was experienced by the nursing students with regard to their role as patient advocates. This refers to a variety of issues about which the students felt powerless, including feeling trapped when the dying patient was unaware of the diagnosis. Other concerns included not having enough authority to increase the patient's medication so that they could die a more peaceful death.
- *Theme 5*. Nursing care for dying patients involved giving comfort physically, mentally and spiritually. Nursing students discovered that just sitting quietly and holding the patient's hand was in itself an effective nursing measure.
- *Theme 6*. While caring for dying patients nursing students learning flourished. Nursing students learned a variety of things. They learned to become less judgemental and to care unconditionally. These students also learned that not only did they help people to get well, but also they helped people to die.

This proactive approach advocated by Beck (1997) should be applauded from a critical social theory perspective, as it attempts to meet the direct needs of the student rather than, as has perhaps been the case in the past, merely surmising and assuming what the student wants. Nursing curricula sometimes have a tendency to follow fickle fashions during the evolution of educational and nursing philosophy rather than necessarily meeting the needs of the practitioner, which in turn are influenced and driven by the needs of the patient. As Beck (1997) concludes, these themes have implications for nurse educators in helping to prepare these practitioners to care for the terminally ill. This study highlights the fact that assumptions from previous death education programmes were designed to meet the (assumed) death anxiety that might emanate from facing one's own demise, the assumption being that students face their own mortality every time they care for dying patients. This phenomenological study challenges such an assumption in that the nursing students' death anxiety emerged from feelings of personal inadequacy and limited clinical experience. Beck (1997) suggests that educational programmes which meet the needs of clinical inadequacy may then help nursing students to move on to face their own fears of death.

Problem-based learning and emotion-focused approaches

A more recent educational strategy that attempts to meet the needs of the student has been initiated by Wong *et al.* (2001), who advocate a problem-based learning approach. From a series of three segmented scenarios based on cancer, nursing students were encouraged to work through identified problems and to keep a reflective journal. Three themes emerged from the findings – the nurses acknowledging their emotions when facing death and dying, a need for the nurses to be better equipped with regard to communication and counselling, and a holistic and family-centred approach to care. What is particularly interesting about this study is that these students, through increased self-awareness, were able to identify their own coping strategies (e.g. avoidance) and gradually to change their attitude to one of confrontation of the difficult issues normally associated with care of the dying. This appears to have been achieved through a variety of prevalent factors. The first was support from their peers and as students are 'care agents', the very fact that they felt 'cared for' may in itself be a salient feature. This educational initiative afforded opportunities to discuss and reflect on difficulties that may in fact have helped the students in two other important ways. First, individual students may have benefited from the knowledge that they were not suffering in isolation (and otherwise labouring under the false impression that only they were finding it difficult to cope). The shared difficulty in this respect may have proved to be a comfort. Second, the educational strategy was actively seeking healthy alternative coping strategies (in this case problem solving) rather than a total reliance on emotion-focused strategies that could result in avoidance or a blunting of the emotions. It would be fallacious to suggest that problem-focused coping had any superiority over emotion-focused coping. In fact, Lazarus and Folkman (1984) suggest that rather than being employed in isolation, the two approaches may often be engaged together and can be mutually facilitative or can impede each other. In addition to the possible emotional benefits that may arise from such strategies, Wong *et al.* (2001) attest that the salient features of such a teaching methodology allow the facilitation and encouragement of a range of key skills, including critical thinking, creativity in learning, personal growth, teamwork, research skills and community focus. The authors of this study suggest that such a methodology calls for a process known as 'elaboration' (Coles 1997, cited in Wong *et al.* 2001), which affords the students opportunities to develop more complex networks of knowledge. Apart from the obvious academic development that this offers, it also provides a platform for students to learn how to overcome and work through difficult issues. In other words, it teaches self-mastery and reduces the risk of hopelessness and helplessness as a learned behaviour. The strategy of Wong *et al.* (2001) highlights the need for collaboration within the clinical area as well as the classroom. This further endorses the role of clinical supervisors and mentors in the support of students. Boyle and Carter (1998) offer a word of caution, that regardless of the educational approach the effectiveness of its impact can be marred by inappropriate attitudes and behaviour of mentors and supervisors, who themselves may experience high levels of death anxiety and who at the same time are acting as role models and teachers for those under their supervision.

It should also be noted that those practitioners who experience high levels of death anxiety may be using coping strategies that are both inappropriate and ineffective (e.g. alcohol, drugs and, in extreme cases, possibly self-harm). A difficulty arises in that researching this particular aspect further may result in an irreversible alteration of the public perception of these healthcare professionals. This in turn may affect public confidence in both healthcare practitioners and the health institution as a whole. The media are more concerned with sensationalism than a sensitive analysis of the facts in context. Public perception of healthcare professionals is usually based on an ideal stereotype which tends to neglect the human frailties that are common to all. Many healthcare professionals may attempt to aspire to the stereotypical ideal (rather than acknowledging their own human limitations), and this may have dire consequences.

Direct and indirect patient involvement

Apart from well-established teaching strategies, in a recent survey of medical training in the UK, Field and Wee (2002) refer to the use of terminally ill patients in teaching programmes, and at least seven schools admitted that this included the patient addressing the class directly. Controversially, this raises ethical issues as to whether the patient feels some degree of obligation that is weighted against his or her need or desire to participate in such events because of the meaning and utilitarian benefit that this may provide. It also raises issues in relation to the professionals' emotional discomfort which such a strategy may provoke. A less controversial strategy that appears to be gaining in popularity is simulation involving the use of actors, recently advocated by Kruijver *et al.* (2001) in communication skills training.

Conclusion and recommendations

Death anxiety is a complex phenomenon which, although pervasive in wider society, takes on a significantly different character within the arena of cancer and palliative care. In order to appreciate the unique character of death anxiety within this specialty, it is necessary to acknowledge the intrinsic factors (knowledge, beliefs, attitudes and rituals) as well as the extrinsic factors (the prevailing culture, and organisational and management philosophy). It is recommended that, in order to allow professionals to face and work through their negative feelings and attitudes towards death, educational approaches need to be developed that foster a climate of acceptance and support (Durlak 1994), which in turn facilitates and motivates participants to share, work and learn together. The ethos of care requires a foundation-stone that needs to be laid by educational strategists and clinical institutions alike.

Implications for the reader's own practice

1   What do you consider to be the key influences that help to shape your perception of death?
2   Should death anxiety feature as an appropriate topic of discussion between you and your colleagues, your patients and carers?
3   How would you consider initiating the topic of death anxiety with colleagues, patients and carers?
4   How would you develop your own understanding of death anxiety?
5   How would you develop students' understanding of death anxiety?
6   How would you consider enhancing effective educational strategies concerned with death and death anxiety?
7   How would you consider evaluating the outcomes of education about death anxiety?

References

Beck CT (1997) Nursing students' experiences of caring for the dying patient. *J Nurs Educ.* 36: 408–15.

Bond CW (1994) Religiosity, age, gender and death anxiety: http://dunamai.com/survey/fddyq.htm

Boyle M and Carter DE (1998) Death anxiety amongst nurses. *Int J Palliat Nurs.* 4: 37–43.

Carr M and Merriman MP (1996) Comparison of death attitudes among hospice workers and health care professionals in other settings. *Omega.* 32: 287–301.

Collaizi P (1978) Psychological research as the phenomenologist views it. In: R Valle and M King (eds) *Existential Phenomenological Alternatives for Psychology.* Oxford University Press, New York.

Degner LF and Gow CM (1988) Evaluations of death education in nursing: a critical review. *Cancer Nurs.* 11: 151–59.

Downe-Wamboldt B and Tamlyn D (1997) An international survey of death education trends in faculties of nursing and medicine. *Death Stud.* 21: 177–88.

Doyle D (1987) Education and training in palliative care. *J Palliat Care.* 2: 5–7.

Durlak JA (1994) Changing death attitudes through death education. In: RA Neimeyer (ed.) *Death Anxiety Handbook: Research Instrumentation and Appreciation.* Taylor & Francis, Washington DC.

Erikson E (1963) *Childhood and society* (2e). Norton, New York.

Field D and Wee B (2002) Preparation for palliative care: teaching about death, dying and bereavement in UK medical schools 2000–2001. *Med Educ.* **36**: 561–7

Frankl VE (1965) *The Doctor and the Soul.* Knopf, New York.

Gorer G (1965) *Death, Grief and Mourning in Contemporary Britain.* Cresset Press, London.

Hurtig WA and Stewin L (1990) The effect of death education and experience on nursing students' attitude towards death. *J Adv Nurs.* **15**: 29–34.

Klug L (1976) *An empirical investigation of the relationship between self-actualization and reconciliation with death.* Unpublished doctorial dissertation. Univerity of Ottawa, Ottawa.

Kruijver IPM, Kerkstra A, Bensing JM and van de Wiel HBM (2001) Communication skills of nurses during interactions with simulated cancer patients. *J Adv Nurs.* **36**: 772–9.

Lazarus RS and Folkman S (1984) *Stress, Appraisal and Coping.* Springer Publishing Co., New York.

Leming M (1977) Religion and death: a test of 'thesis'. *Omega.* **10**: 347–63.

Llewellyn S and Payne S (1995) Caring: the costs to nurses and families. In: A Broome and S Llewellyn (eds) *Health Psychology: processes and application* (2e). Chapman & Hall, London.

Maglio CJ and Robinson SE (1994) The effects of death education on death anxiety: a meta-analysis. *Omega.* **29**: 319–35.

Papadatou D (2000) A proposed model of health professionals' grieving process. *Omega.* **41**: 59–77.

Payne SA, Dean SJ and Kalus C (1998) A comparative study of death anxiety in hospice and emergency nurses. *J Adv Nurs.* **28**: 700–6.

Powell F and Thorson J (1991) Construction of death among those high in intrinsic religious motivation: a factor-analytic study. *Death Stud.* **5**: 131–8.

Rittman M, Paige P, Rivera J, Sutphin L and Godown I (1997) Phenomenological study of nurses caring for dying patients. *Cancer Nurs.* **20**: 115–19.

Spall R and Johnson M (1997) Education. Experiential exercises in palliative care training. *Int J Palliat Nurs.* **3**: 222–6.

Vachon MLS (1999) Reflections on the history of occupational stress in hospice/palliative care. *Hospice J.* **14**: 229–46.

Vachon MLS (2003) Occupational stress in palliative care. In: M O'Conner and S Aranda (eds) *Palliative Care Nursing: a guide to practice.* Ausmed Publications, Victoria, Australia.

Wong TP, Reker GT and Gesser G (1994) Death Attitude Profile – revised: a multidimensional measure of attitudes toward death. In: RA Neimeyer (ed.) *Death Anxiety Handbook: research, instrumentation and application.* Taylor & Francis, London.

Wong FMY, Lee WM and Mok E (2001) Educating nurses to care for the dying in Hong Kong: a problem–based approach. *Cancer Nurs.* **24**: 112–21.

CHAPTER 7

Exploring the territory: nurses' perceptions of spirituality and the implications for nursing care and education

Elizabeth Foster

'Pooh', he whispered. 'Yes Piglet?'. 'Nothing,' said Piglet, taking Pooh's paw, 'I just wanted to be sure of you.'

AA Milne, *The House at Pooh Corner*

The aim of this chapter is to explore how concepts of spirituality and spiritual care are influenced by the nurse's own self-awareness and life experience. The educational implications of this are then considered.

Learning outcomes
By the end of this chapter the reader should be able to consider:
- the importance of the spiritual dimension
- the role of the nurse in spiritual care
- life factors which may inform the concept of spirituality
- the educational implications of the above.

Introduction

Significant social and psychological distress is commonly associated with the diagnosis and treatment of cancer, and this may be further exacerbated in those patients who require active palliative care. The key factors involved are uncertainty about the future, loss of control, the search for meaning and the need for support (Faulkner and Maguire 1994). Addressing such issues while at the same time achieving symptom control and physical comfort requires a holistic approach to care. Holistic care is that which encompasses the dimensions of body, mind and spirit. Care of the spirit is related to 'low death fear, low discomfort, decreased loneliness, emotional adjustment and positive death perspectives' (Narayanasamy 1991, p.53). These factors are at the heart of the most defining and distinctive principles of palliative care. However, the evidence suggests that nurses vary widely both in how well they understand the concept of spirituality and in their expertise in translating the principles into clinical practice. Various reasons are cited for this, but of significance is the nurse's own awareness of spirituality (Ross 1997; Newshan 1998).

In this chapter we shall look at the concept and perception of spirituality and spiritual care. The findings of a recent research study undertaken by this author and related literature will be discussed, in particular the far-reaching implications for addressing spirituality within nurse education.

Definition of spirituality

Spirituality as a term is beset by definitional ambiguities. However, as a concept that includes living our life according to certain values and precepts it is a universal phenomenon. Everyone – atheists and agnostics alike – seeks to make sense of and understand their world, especially at times of personal difficulty and crisis. A seminal definition of spirituality is that proposed by Murray and Zentnor:

> A quality that goes beyond religious affiliation, that strives for inspirations, reverence, awe, meaning and purpose ... The spiritual dimension tries to be in harmony with the universe, and strives for answers about the infinite, and comes into focus when the person faces emotional stress, physical illness or death.
>
> (Murray and Zentnor, 1989, p.259)

McSherry and Draper (1998) integrate the above elements into the visual representation of a football which makes the definition accessible to our notions of daily life (*see* Figure 7.1). Each of the components (patches) is of equal importance, tightly bound to the others and unable to function in isolation. The football (spirituality) is kicked (life events) many times throughout the game (life). Such knocks come from unexpected events over which we often have little control. This is analogous to the diagnosis of a life-threatening illness (McSherry 2000). If we approach the definition of spirituality in this way, it becomes clear that spirituality is not synonymous with religion, although expression of the spiritual dimension may indeed include rituals such as prayer and religious observance. Instead, these core elements are at the heart of our every relationship and action.

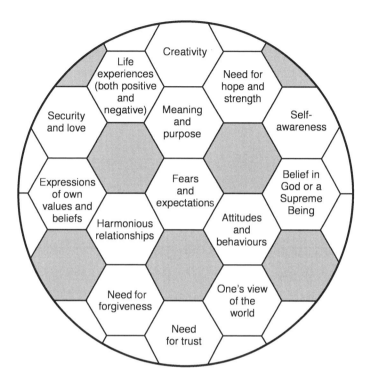

Figure 7.1   Diagrammatic model of spirituality

Each of the major religious traditions addresses spirituality in a different way, and this diversity of understanding requires acknowledgement. However, one thing on which they are all agreed is that simply considering the body as a group of mechanistic systems fails to recognise a vital quality of being human (Bush 1997).

Holism and palliative care

The term 'holism' is derived from the Greek word '*holos*' meaning 'whole'. A holistic approach to care is one that integrates and balances the physical, social, psychological and spiritual aspects of care, not as a summary of discrete parts but rather so that all of the dimensions are inextricably woven together. It aims to go beyond the presenting symptoms, to explore the history and circumstances of the patient's life. By contrast, the reductionist or biomedical model views the individual as a group of body systems, with little consideration of the relationship between each dimension. Currently there is growing acknowledgement that the biomedical model fails to respond fully to the nature of human suffering, because suffering is recognised as involving more than biological malfunction, and can arise from any facet of our being (Nettleton 1995; Clark and Seymour 1999). Thus our spirituality is not isolated in a vacuum, but is housed in a human and physical body.

Spirituality and palliative care

The principles of palliative care that are applicable to all healthcare professionals include:

- a focus on the patient's quality of life
- a whole-person approach that involves present and past experiences
- care of both the patient and those who matter to the patient
- respect for patient autonomy and choice
- sensitive and competent communication skills
    (National Council for Hospice and Specialist Palliative Care Services 1995).

Patients who are dying have been described as people on a journey '... uprooted ... dispossessed, marginalised, travelling fearfully into the unknown' (Cassidy 1988, p.4). This is a discomforting image of patients who, when facing a life-threatening illness and death, are confronted with the possible disintegration of their values, meaning and purpose in life. Doyle (1983) estimates that around 75% of palliative care patients will voice spiritual concerns related to this sense of isolation and disorientation. Reviewing the palliative care principles alongside the definition of spirituality, it is difficult to envisage how we might meet these aims without addressing spiritual care. This suggests that to care for patients competently, nurses need to be aware of spirituality and the components of spiritual care.

The nurse's role and spiritual care

There is debate about how nurses should both assess and provide spiritual care. However, there is consensus that they should acknowledge spiritual care as a legitimate area of concern. Indeed, various professional guidelines and standards refer to the spiritual dimension of patient care, stating that nurses should be able to promote and protect patients' interests and value the concept of individualised care (National Association of Health Authorities and Trusts 1996; Nursing and Midwifery Council 2002).

   Nurses in particular have a unique opportunity to integrate spirituality into healthcare. Their access to personal details, the potential intimacy of their relationship with the patient and their 24-hour responsibility are all potent factors (Lancaster 1997; Smith 1999). At this clinical level, spiritual care is about forming a nurturing, interpersonal relationship. It is not a separate entity self-consciously performed, but rather it is about the receptivity between patient and professional, allowing the expression of feelings and emotions alongside nursing procedures and clinical aspects of care (Bradshaw 1994). Its aim is to recognise the value and uniqueness of each patient, paying attention to personal accounts of illness that challenge and disrupt the structure of everyday life. The relationship can be described as *skilled companionship* – it is a ministry of presence that has its emphasis on 'being with' rather than 'doing' (Cassidy 1988, Stoter 1995). Spirituality concerns life's meaning and purpose, and spiritual care is about exploration of these dimensions of our lives, not about rigid frameworks of information giving. Consequently, the required underpinning expertise involves a knowledge of counselling skills, and skills such as empathy, unconditional positive regard, congruence, reflection and honesty. Importantly, these skills, which themselves encapsulate spiritual values, necessitate a level of self-awareness (Rogers 1961; Egan 1994).

The research study

Methodology

A recent study undertaken by the author of this chapter used focus groups to explore nurses' understanding of spirituality and the training they received to provide spiritual care. The aim was not to reach a consensus, but to facilitate the free flowing of ideas and explore the diverse opinions generated (Sim 1998; Robinson 1999). Attention was given to how viewpoints are developed, the information being conveyed in the respondent's own language.

At these focus groups the relevant questions pertaining to this chapter were as follows.

1   What do you understand by the term 'spirituality'?
2   What training have you undertaken that included spirituality and spiritual care in the programme?
3   To what or to whom do you attribute your own meaning of spirituality?

The sample population was taken from the qualified nursing population in two care settings (a nursing home and a hospice). Purposive sampling was used to identify the respondents and the settings. A number of categories emerged from the research data.

The following data show how the nurses defined spirituality and what they felt informed their knowledge.

A significant number of the participants described an awareness of spirituality that was woven into their own personal life events and experiences. The nurses who had thought about their own spirituality spoke articulately about the need to incorporate this dimension into care. None of the respondents had attended an educational session or programme that explicitly incorporated spirituality as a topic area.

Defining concepts of spirituality

Each focus group began by exploring what was meant by the term 'spirituality'. The discussion ranged over a variety of ideas and concepts (*see* Table 7.1).

Table 7.1   Respondents' views of components of the concept of spirituality

Uniqueness of the individual
Universal need
Finding meaning/purpose
Need for forgiveness
Search for inner peace
Incorporates physical care
Integral to holistic care
Importance of relationships

One participant identified spirituality as being aligned to having a faith. However, the majority of the respondents saw spirituality as being separate from religion, although it may include religious belief.

Participant 3:   'I think people tend to focus on the religious aspect, but I don't think it is that at all ...'

Participant 1:   '... spirituality has a wider meaning I think than just religion ...'

Participant 2:   '... I don't think always that spirituality has anything much to do with the church ...'

Participant 9:   '... it's to do with the whole inner self ...'

Participant 7:   'I think religion is a very big part of it ... but it's not the whole of it ... it's about the whole person'.

Spirituality is often equated with religious belief, but the majority of nurses in the study recognised that it has a wider dimension than this, and that it should not be confined to a particular ethnicity, culture or religious observance. One nurse commented on looking after someone with clear religious convictions. As death approached, the patient continued to be distressed as he raised questions about life's purpose.

Participant 8:   'I looked after a patient ... he was actually a minister of religion ... he did not seem to be spiritually calm, and you would expect purely on a religious basis that he would have been ...'.

For the nurse this reinforced the belief that spirituality was more than religious observance.

The nurses commented that spirituality encompassed every other dimension and was an integral part of holistic care. They considered spirituality as an overarching concept that had an impact upon physical, psychological and social domains. They believed that the goal was to achieve a harmonious balance.

Participant 5:	'It includes the physical ... emotional ... and everything else ... it all comes under the same spiritual umbrella ... you can't just deal with one thing and not with the other ... they all sort of slot in like a jigsaw puzzle ...'.

The imagery of the jigsaw puzzle fits with the football model of spirituality and how the elements incorporated exert an important effect on each other. If one aspect was out of balance, it affected everything else – hence the importance of paying attention to spirituality. For this nurse, the visual image of everything fitting under a spiritual umbrella reinforced the view that other aspects of our personhood are affected by the meaning, values and beliefs that we hold in life.

The nurses recognised the concept of holism and also appeared to invest time and energy in their relationships with patients. To explain their understanding of spirituality they related what they understood to be spiritual issues as raised by patients.

Participant 2:	'Have I been a good person? Have I been a bad person? ... getting the demons off your chest ...'
Participant 5:	'Have I had a useful life? ... Am I worthy?'
Participant 7:	'... if there is anything that you want to put right ... to say your goodbyes ... tell people how you feel about them'.

These comments show an understanding that a search for meaning and purpose is part of the concept of spirituality. The explanations are also outside a religious framework, fitting with their earlier discussions around definitions. This is encouraging, as the view is sometimes taken that nurses are only aware of spirituality and spiritual need when there is concrete religious expression of these.

One participant explored the idea that not only does spirituality encompass what is happening for the patient, but also that the relationship between the nurse and the patient informs the concept. This suggests a participative model of care rather than simply an informative one, supporting the ideals of both palliative and spiritual care.

Participant 1:	'I can't really describe how I interpret spirituality, but it can't just be whether they believe in God or not ... it's how we help them as well, isn't it ... it's not just their spirituality'

Desire to nurture

Linking back to the historical roots of nursing, an idea was expressed by one participant that the role of the nurse was fundamentally spiritual in itself.

Participant 1:	'... as a nurse I feel it's a kind of spiritual job in as much as a vicar can do their bit ... we can do our bit ...'.

Some literature suggests that nurses always refer to the chaplain. However, this nurse defines nursing as having a spiritual dimension. They considered that the chaplain, who while maintaining the confidentiality of their unique role empowered the nurses to contribute, helped to facilitate an open environment for spiritual care. They were also appreciative of the chaplains who recognised that this was demanding work for the nurses, touching on ideals of staff support.

Importantly, if spirituality is a universal dimension, it is unrealistic to consider that the chaplain alone could meet all needs. It would therefore seem important to explore this partnership of care further.

A number of nurses spoke explicitly about the nurse's desire to nurture as a motivation for working in palliative care and for wanting to understand and address spiritual needs. When the situation allowed them to discuss intimate and private subjects, they found this hard and demanding. Nevertheless they also described it as a privilege.

Participant 1:	'I believe that it's right in there ... your total desire to nurture ... cherish ... ease pain ...'.

They felt that a willingness to engage with patients was undervalued both by nurses and by other professionals. This drive focused them upon the patient's needs and facilitated their recognition of spiritual care. This was the investment in the therapeutic relationship.

Participant 2:	'You've got to have machines ... research and science ... but ... nursing to me is actually to do with the patient ... people [dying patients] are so vulnerable that it's so important to feel valued ... in a fast world people are seen as disposable items ... nursing seems to be seen as rocket science these days ...'.

This innate desire to be with people and demonstrate empathy was described by one participant as something so integral to the nurse that she was almost unaware of it. This perhaps describes the intentional and unconscious use of self in the encounter.

> Participant 3:   'I think it's probably an unconscious way of [being] as you are ...'.

Their comments could be interpreted as those made by nurses not involved in critical care, consequently emphatically supporting fundamental nursing skills. However, this sense of valuing the patient and providing a supportive presence is clearly a way of demonstrating the patient's self-worth and esteem, and is perhaps the nub of spiritual care. Describing their desire to nurture, the nurses spoke of the heart and pointed to their own hearts as a way of explaining their feelings. Such ideals of care move the patient–professional interaction to a medium where the human relationship is paramount. This personal way of caring can be described as sacred work (Prior 2001, p.341).

Life experience

All of the participants considered that the experience of the nurse, in both her personal and professional life, had an impact on how spirituality was understood and how spiritual care was delivered. All of the nurses spoke movingly and articulately about the situations that they had encountered. The discussion ranged over incidents such as difficult bereavements and seminal moments in life that were transforming.

> Participant 3:   'things that happen in your life that change you forever ...'.
> Participant 1:   ' things that happen to you have a bearing on how ... you care for others ...'.
> Participant 2:   'I don't think you realise how final it all is until maybe you have an episode in your life where things happen ...'.

Expanding on these views, the nurses described how situations had caused them to reflect on their values and beliefs, and how new ways of thinking were opened to them. With hindsight, they understood how such experiences had altered their perceptions of spirituality and that this had also changed the way in which they now considered patient care.

Self-awareness

The majority of nurses explored the idea that this engagement with experience was an active and conscious step. It was a lifelong process to develop one's values and to make personal sense of life meaning. They described it as being self-aware about needing to work on self-awareness.

> Participant 7: 'I think it's about developing your own self-awareness ... you're aware of what makes you feel angry or what makes you feel glad, and that is something you are developing the whole of the time and how to deal with that ... that helps you with other people'.

These respondents felt that further reading or training could enhance skills, but this was still dependent on the nurse's character and life experience.

> Participant 5: 'I think you must have feelings to start with ... with your training ... all they do is bring out these skills ...'.
>
> Participant 2: 'I think it's everything ... your experiences of life ... what you've learnt in the classroom ... and being able to implement that ...'.
>
> Participant 4: 'It's both reading and life experiences ...'.

Participants were wary of training if it had a purely formulaic format, which they considered would lead to a stilted approach.

Links to practice

The sample size of the research study and the directive nature of the sampling, among other limitations, mean that these findings may not be generalised to other populations. However, although it was a small study, it provides rich phenomenological data with a valuable clinical and educational link.

There is a tension between the identified benefits of addressing spirituality in palliative care and the fact that no guidelines exist on how to prepare nurses. It is thought that those who have not considered their own attitudes to suffering or spirituality may be less well able to provide that care for others, yet there has generally been little focus on this aspect (Wright and Sayre-Adams 2000; Cobb 2001). The majority of nurses in this study had considered their attitudes to suffering and sadness, and one could speculate that this was because of their particular work area, but most of the respondents also referred to specific personal events outside their work that had challenged their thinking. If, as this study and the literature suggest, nurses' understanding of spirituality is informed by personal experience and self-awareness, how can nurse education effectively prepare nurses to engage with spiritual care?

Spirituality and nurse education

Palliative care makes considerable mention of attitudes to death and dying, but there is little evidence that nurses, or any other group of staff, are encouraged to think through and explore their own attitudes, values, beliefs and motives. It may be the patient's search for meaning which acts as the catalyst for the nurse to personally reflect on spirituality. This was defined by one respondent as a 'wake-up' call for her.

Participant 2:	'It sort of wakes you up ... and you think ... this woman is looking for a bed for her husband who she knows is going to pass away in possibly eight weeks ... I just thought it was mind blowing'.

Clearly it would be preferable for nurses to have some understanding and aware-ness of their own inner dimension before being faced with such situations and the distress and anguish encountered in aspects of palliative care (Bush 1997; White 2000). This may both enhance their potential as caregivers and also reduce their vulnerability to burnout and exhaustion as they become self-aware about what sustains them. Developing self-care prevents them becoming 'dispirited'. There is little emphasis on the art of caregiving – the concept of skilled presence – yet one of the prominent claims of palliative care is attention to humanistic caring values.

Participant 7:	'... it's what we do all day ... and perhaps don't even acknowledge just how much we do listen to patients'.

To prepare for caregiving, enhanced by self-awareness, perhaps the role of educa-tion is to promote reflection and self-appraisal, a thoughtful process that addresses the jumbled issues and inconsistencies of being human, allowing us to access our (sometimes unconscious) thoughts and feelings. In the study, the nurses described their own developing spiritual awareness in the context of ongoing personal experi-ence at home and at work. They had discovered, like their patients, that spirituality was a dynamic entity related to their values, personality and coping strategies. Perhaps from both a clinical and a formal educational setting we could enquire into our own spirituality, articulating questions by asking what relevance the core aspects (the patches on the football) have for us in our own lives. If the evidence that a spiritual dimension supports people at times of change and life crisis is robust, perhaps we need to really espouse the concept of holism, rejecting the dualism that sees patients as 'them' and nurses as 'us'. As human beings sharing the lived experience of the world, we all need to stand in right relationship with ourselves and with each other.

Conclusion

Spirituality is rooted and nurtured in the smallest of our daily activities, and in recognising this the nurse's role becomes vitally important. The research data substantiate the literature which suggests that self-awareness as a way of knowing is a significant factor in recognising the spiritual dimension and in considering the legitimacy of spiritual care. Consequently, there needs to be discussion of spirituality within what we consider to be formal education, although isolated workshops based solely on information giving may not be helpful. It is worth noting just how much a focus group was enlivened to debate and discuss ideas, exploring spirituality and its meaning. Perhaps such an open forum allowing creative interaction has potential for the future. There is also learning in the clinical situation, exploring and developing personal qualities of empathy and compassion. Building trusting and open relationships with patients can raise awareness of the inherent spirituality in each nursing encounter.

Importantly, we must allow our patients to feel sure of us, and to have confidence that we are fully present, open and attentive to them. This certainty is not built on our demonstration of knowledge and busy professionalism – instead it involves using our greatest gift, 'which is our ability to be there, to listen, to enter into solidarity with those who are suffering' (Nouwen 1981).

Key points to consider
- Spirituality is a universal dimension.
- Spiritual concerns have the potential to cause significant distress to patients.
- Nurses have a valuable role to play in providing spiritual care. This needs to be acknowledged by educators, managers and nurses themselves in order that they might work together to provide the most appropriate ways of incorporating it into practice.
- Nurse's ability to understand and engage with spiritual care is informed by personal life events and self-awareness. The challenge here is to facilitate nurses gaining insight into their own spiritual beliefs or lack of them. Recognising our own limitations should not deter us from staying alongside the patient or providing a supportive presence in times of need.
- Education could play a role in preparing nurses, by allowing them to reflect and consider their own spirituality. This needs to be incorporated more fully into pre- and post-registration courses for the future.
- This application of education necessitates taking the long view, including support and supervision by clinical as well as educational staff.

> **Implications for the reader's own practice**
> 1 How do you currently integrate the spiritual dimension of nursing into your practice?
> 2 In what ways do you provide a supportive presence?
> 3 How can your involvement in nurse education effectively prepare nurses to engage with spiritual care?
> 4 What innovative ways can you think of to explore the nature of spirituality in your educational programme and teaching sessions?
> 5 How can you develop a dynamic approach to challenge and change colleagues' perceptions of spirituality?

References

Bradshaw A (1994) *Lighting the Lamp. The spiritual dimension of nursing care.* Scutari Press, London.

Bush T (1997) Spirituality in care. In: S Ronaldson (ed.) *Spirituality. The heart of nursing.* Ausmed Publications, Victoria, Australia.

Cassidy S (1988) *Sharing the Darkness.* Darton, Longman and Todd Ltd, London.

Clark D and Seymour J (1999) *Reflections on Palliative Care.* Open University Press, Buckingham.

Cobb M (2001) *The Dying Soul. Spiritual care at the end of life.* Open University Press, Buckingham.

Doyle D (1983) *Coping With a Dying Relative.* MacDonald Printers Ltd, Edinburgh.

Egan G (1994) *The Skilled Helper: a problem management approach to helping* (5e). Brooks Cole Publishing Co., Pacific Grove, CA.

Faulkner A and Maguire P (1994) *Talking to Cancer Patients and their Relatives.* Oxford University Press, Oxford.

Lancaster R (1997) The meaning of spirituality and the nurse's role in providing spiritual care to the dying patient. In: S Ronaldson (ed.) *Spirituality. The heart of nursing.* Ausmed Publications, Victoria, Australia.

McSherry W (2000) *Making Sense of Spirituality in Nursing Practice. An interactive approach.* Churchill Livingstone, Edinburgh.

McSherry W and Draper P (1998) The debates emerging from the literature surrounding the concept of spirituality as applied to nursing. *J Adv Nurs.* **27**: 683–91.

Murray RB and Zentnor JB (1989) *Nursing Concepts for Health Promotion.* Prentice Hall, London.

Narayanasamy A (1991) *Spiritual Care. A resource guide.* Quay Publishing, Lancaster.

National Association of Health Authorities and Trusts (NAHAT) (1996) *Spiritual Care in the NHS. A guide for purchasers and providers.* NAHAT, Birmingham.

National Council for Hospice and Specialist Palliative Care Services (1995) *Specialist Palliative Care: a statement of definitions.* Occasional Paper no. 8. National Council for Hospice and Specialist Palliative Care Services, London.

Nettleton S (1995) *The Sociology of Health and Illness.* Polity Press, Cambridge.

Newshan G (1998) Transcending the physical: spiritual aspects of pain in patients with HIV and/or cancer. *J Adv Nurs.* **28**: 1236–41.

Nouwen HJM (1981) *The Way of the Heart.* Harper, London.

Nursing and Midwifery Council (2002) *Code of Professional Conduct.* Nursing and Midwifery Council, London.

Prior D (2001) Caring in palliative nursing: competency or complacency? *Int J Palliat Nurs.* **7**: 339–44.

Robinson N (1999) The use of focus group methodology – with selected examples from sexual health research. *J Adv Nurs.* **29**: 905–13.

Rogers C (1961) *On Becoming a Person.* Houghton Mifflin Co., Boston.

Ross L (1997) The nurse's role in assessing and responding to patients' spiritual needs. *Int J Palliat Nurs.* **3**: 37–42.

Sim J (1998) 'Collecting and analysing qualitative data: issues raised by the focus group. *J Adv Nurs.* **28**: 345–52.

Smith M (1999) Spiritual Issues. In: J Lugton and M Kindlen (eds) *Palliative Care. The nursing role.* Churchill Livingstone, Edinburgh.

Stoter D (1995) *Spiritual Aspects of Health Care.* Mosby, London.

White G (2000) An inquiry into the concepts of spirituality and spiritual care. *Int J Palliat Nurs.* **6**: 479–84.

Wright S and Sayre-Adams J (2000) *Sacred Space. Right relationship and spirituality in health-care.* Churchill Livingstone, Edinburgh.

CHAPTER 8

Art and artistry in practice: a reflective account

Angela Brown and Gill Scott

it is something to be able to paint a picture, or carve a statue, and to make a few objects beautiful. But it is far more glorious to paint the atmosphere in which we work, to effect the quality of the day. This is the highest of arts.

Henry David Thoreau

In this chapter, the reader will be jolted a little out of the familiarity of traditional ways of looking at palliative and cancer care education. This will be achieved by examining the value of art as a medium for learning about practice, as well as the recognition of artistry in the process of learning. The approach that the authors have taken is justified by the fact that art's very nature demands a unique interpretation and response from every observer. This chapter is offered in this spirit, and it is hoped that the reader will make a unique interpretation and response. As a consequence, the learning outcomes are not predetermined in the behaviourist tradition but in the humanist tradition, in that the chapter is offered as a learning opportunity, for the reader to reflect upon and identify the meaning of art and artistry for him or herself.

The chapter itself claims to be an art form, created by the distinction, contrast and interweaving of reflective portfolio extracts written in the first person and presented in handwritten font type. These are contrasted with the contextual theoretical underpinning, which is presented in the third person. At a qualitative health research conference in North America, one of the authors (AB) had previously encountered the presentation of numerous theories expressed three-dimensionally and culturally true to the American genre of quilting. In this sense the context of this discussion written in the third person is the 'base cloth' of the chapter, and the portfolio and teaching exemplars written in the first person are the quilt patches that create the form, imitation and expression of the chapter's concepts (Rose 1997). Thus the chapter itself becomes an art form, a quilting together of styles, and becomes a metaphor of both its interpretative and interpretable style and stance. It is a reflective educational account illustrated with examples from palliative and cancer care and their respective educational contexts. Reading this chapter should provide an opportunity for the reader to review their own collection of patchwork scraps and potential components of an art form that becomes an expression of the very values that they hold and espouse, a self-actualisation of the experience that they aim to comprehend in their practice through their reflection on practice.

Although this discussion is framed within the context of specialist palliative and cancer care, the authors are anxious that the reader comprehends that art and artistry as a learning vehicle have the potential to enrich the learning experiences for a broader range of specialists and practitioners. Indeed, these are already in existence – for example, the use of carer narratives in inter-professional palliative care education workshops (Sheldon 2001). Nevertheless, the authors purport that the locating of this non-traditional strategy within cancer and palliative care education is a valuable catalyst for a special type of emancipatory learning (Rogers 1994). In the palliative and cancer care field, the nature of contact with human frailty and vulnerability may already engender in its practitioners an acceptance of imperfection and life's inevitable ending (Nyatanga 2001). This may foster in its students a greater acceptance of an ontology that respects and does not strive against the course of life-threatening illness and its associated impact. Thus the vehicle of art as one of freedom of thought and interpretation is a potentially undervalued component of our professional development, experience and delivery, but perhaps particularly within end-of-life care and education.

Art for art's sake

Art is all around us in many forms. Generally we think of paintings, sculpture, music and literature, which to many may constitute the aesthetic component of art – that which is concerned with its beauty or with the appreciation of beauty. How art and artistry are seen may conjure up an entirely different vision for each onlooker. Art is not only descriptive – it is also expressive and individual.

Representations may be in oil-paint or watercolour, charcoal or pencil, photographs or engravings. Sculptures may be real or abstract, functional as architecture or ornamental. Music may be classical or modern, listened to, played or read. And literature may be stories (real or fiction), poetry or plays. If one pauses for a moment to think what constitutes art in our lives, it is surprising what can be conjured up. More unusually other creations may be included such as needlecraft, quilting, cookery, storytelling and keeping a diary/journal. This begins to widen the definitions of art, art forms and artist, and as most of us will be able to appreciate and maybe achieve at least one of those listed, art is accessible to all. These thoughts are supported by Gablik (1991), who identified two traditions in the modern art world:

1   'artlike art', which is separate from life and everything else
2   'lifelike art', which is connected to life and to everything else.

So what do these traditions have to do with nursing, we may wonder? *A* short meander into the purpose of art may assist us in our thoughts. From the dialogue of Rose (1997), this can be distilled as *form, expression* and *imitation*. Form is the arrangement of its constituent parts – for example, colours and shapes in painting, drawing or needlecraft, notes, rhythms and instruments in music, and words, grammar and intonation in literature (Rose 1997). Expression is a communication of and the arousal of emotion (Sheppard 1987). Sheppard (1987) also described imitation or representation as 'providing a bridge between eternal ideas, such as love and beauty, and the way in which they are sensed by individuals, by expressing them in a perceivable form such as poetry or music' (Rose 1997). Rose (1997) illustrates her discussion with the way in which nursing may be considered as an art form utilising these attributes, and concludes that it is possible to consider nursing as an art form. At this juncture it is necessary to make it clear that we are not suggesting nursing is an art and not a science, but asking the reader to consider nursing as art, as a form, expression and imitation (representation). This may assist us in how we critically analyse nursing practice by providing an alternative approach.

Art and artistry in nursing – educational rationale

We are all familiar with the visual representations of reality (models – conceptual and real, diagrams, pictures, exposition) as a mechanism for conveying meaning, purpose, beliefs and values. The use of art and artistry to discover knowledge, skills, attitudes and emotions in relation to nursing is offered as an alternative approach to presenting meaning, purpose, beliefs and values in relation to practice through artistic representations of reality. This provides opportunities to further develop critical thinking and dialogue, and it gives us permission to be expressive in alternative ways and provide evidence of innovative and creative intellectual thought.

The educational rationale and framework for this approach can be identified as humanistic, reflecting the work of Maslow (1970) and Rogers (1994). The philosophy is student-centred, based on active discovery and leading to self-actualisation. The learning experience is cognitive and experiential, the educative role is one of facilitation, and the role of the learner is participative. The examples offered here are reflections on this educative process in action.

Using lifelike art to understand nursing

Lifelike art can be used in a variety of ways to help nurses to understand their nursing as it is 'connected to life and everything else' (Gablick 1991).

The following two examples – art and professional practice and narrative or storytelling – are illustrations of how lifelike art may be used in the learning experience to facilitate critical thinking through reflection on practice, and expression through creativity and innovation.

Art and professional practice

Marks-Maran and Rose (1997), in *Reconstructing Nursing: Beyond Art and Science*, 'attempted to go beyond some traditional ways of understanding nursing' and inspired the approach to this learning opportunity. The student was invited to identify something that they considered to be an art form. They were asked to bring along to the next session a vision of their art form and be prepared to describe their art form and engage in discussion with the group on why this constituted art for them. The three groups of students who engaged in this learning opportunity participated in the activity whole-heartedly. Their art forms ranged from classical pictures (of which they brought photographs) to pieces of music played for the group, examples from nature (a leaf), a photograph of a polar bear swimming in Arctic waters and photographs of their children and other significant people or objects. The descriptions and discussions were always enlightening, often emotional and highlighted the characteristics of lifelike art. They also contributed to the process of self-awareness of what constitutes beauty and the appreciation of beauty. The second part of the seminar involved analysing the literature on what constitutes art in nursing or the practice of aesthetic knowledge (Chinn and Kramer 1991). The students were invited to consider what aspects of their practice could be considered lifelike art and therefore begin to engage with the notions of Carper's (1978) *Aesthetics: The Art of Nursing*.

Another example of art conveying meaning was at a conference in 2002, when one of the authors (GS) projected the picture shown in Figure 8.1 as an introduction to the reality of hospice nursing practice. The audience laughed spontaneously prior to any explanation of its meaning from her. It was a simple parallel of a Jackson Pollock painting that successfully attempted to portray the complexity and messiness of everyday palliative care nursing. However, there is more to her analogy in the following portfolio extract than meets the eye.

The deliberacy of a Jackson Pollock

There is a deliberacy as well as randomness in the quality of nurse–patient interactions that I have understood in this life-changing experience of deep reflection. It can be best understood by thinking about the work of Jackson Pollock, whose large-scale paint-drip compositions aroused much interest in the 1940s (Gombrich 1995). They may seem thrown together, but upon close examination and an understanding of the process of the composition, one appreciates that there is far more construct and form woven together to produce a pleasing colour and movement arrangement. Interestingly, it was a return to childlike simplicity and spontaneity, a railing against convention, that underpinned Pollock's radical painting methods of paint drips. Take a typically busy clinical setting and you have nursing's answer to the

Figure 8.1   The reality of hospice nursing practice

Jackson Pollock. To the untrained eye, there may not seem to be much difference between an infant's nursery painting and this masterly painting, but the knowledge and wisdom that produced them are poles apart. The value of the finished products is also incomparable, although the expert's and the preschooler's work have their own value dependent on the eye of the beholder.

For some practitioners it may seem unfamiliar to introduce within their therapeutic exchanges a metaphorical reference to a parallel concept or representation. However, an image such as Jackson Pollock's may well illustrate to the patient the reality of experiencing clinical diagnosis or treatment. For example, the technique of visualisation has long enjoyed acceptance within healthcare, and the Bristol Cancer Help Centre continues to offer this self-help treatment within their residential courses as a component of their 'gold standard for complementary care in cancer' (Sikora 2003). Kearney (1996) has similarly argued the place of mythological storytelling as a powerfully therapeutic tool for patients facing the finality of their life, and Petrone (2003) has documented the emotional journey of the cancer experience with the aim of promoting 'an opportunity to create a dialogue with those we serve and care for, with his powerful, hopeful and beautiful images' (Felton 2003). We can learn from these examples to promote therapeutic and even cathartic exchanges with our patients by creating shared moments through the media of such accessible imagery.

Narrative or storytelling

> We dream in narrative, daydream in narrative, remember, anticipate, hope, despair, believe, doubt, plan, revise, criticise, construct, gossip, learn, hate and love by narrative.
>
> (Widdershoven 1993).

To facilitate the discovery of the knowledge used in practice, in our second example of how lifelike art may be used in the learning experience, each student was invited to tell a story and thus begin to critically analyse what it is that they do and what it is that they know. The narratives were introduced as encounters in practice. They did not need to be rare or racy but could be ordinary, and they had to be patient focused. The process was modelled for the students with a narrative from practice, and then they were invited to prepare their narratives and present them to their peers.

The following seminar information was given to students.

- Choose an aspect of practice – it may be ordinary.
- Tell a story – try to include as much detail as possible.
- Attempt to identify the knowledge you are using in practice.

These events were always stimulating and emotionally charged, 'nurses talking nursing' promoting that tingling sensation of hair raised on the back of the arms. The nurses were able to identify the biological, psychosocial and cultural perspectives of their practice and their caring. The subsequent critical thinking highlighted nursing not only as doing, but also as knowing and therapeutic. In addition, it also provided the opportunity to begin the process of clarifying one's own philosophical underpinnings while exploring the practice–theory interface. The study of narrative 'offers a possibility of developing an understanding that cannot be arrived at by any other means' (Greenhalgh and Hurwitz 1999), as it is often difficult in our experience to identify and separate the sources of knowledge within the complexity of practice.

These two approaches are illustrated by Gill Scott as part of her experience as a participant researcher on the Royal College of Nursing (RCN) Expert Practice Project (Hardy *et al.* 2002). Gill illustrates how those artistic characteristics from which she had reluctantly separated in making a nursing career choice were rediscovered and integrated into her world view of nursing and nurse expertise, and how through this process her personal epistemology of practice could be articulated. The following excerpts suggests how life, like art, may be considered as evidence to demonstrate expertise in practice and used in portfolio development. The resultant portfolio was in itself a work of art. Presented in a pleasing blue script font style, it contained narratives, feedback from colleagues, paintings, quotations and poetry, while also demonstrating expertise in practice. The following are excerpts from the portfolio.

Artistry as expertise in palliative care nursing

Art or science?

I confessed to my critical companion, Angela, the mentor I chose to challenge and support me through the Expertise in Practice Project pilot upon our first meeting when we explored our values with regard to nursing. I said that I had a love–hate relationship with nursing. The fantasy that I always return to if I feel overwhelmed by the constraints and challenges of my work is of becoming an art student. I would take a year on a foundation course to experiment with various media and find the expression that suited me. Art was the alternative career option for me when I chose to become a nurse, and I have always had a secret regret that it was superseded by what seemed to be the more sensible option at the time. Art is the antithesis of everything I see as prescriptive and restrictive about nursing ... or it was, for now I really do see that what I can do for or with a patient is indeed as much a creative act as the application of brush to paper. There will always remain a tension in that bureaucratic restraints upon true nursing will cause frustration and even despair of ever making a difference to the world of the patient. But this is the mark of an artist, one who is sensitive enough to recognise the anomalies and idiosyncrasies of life.

Recognising reality through art

When I first encountered the Titchen (2001)* model and its description of 'antennae' of the sensitive engagement of the nurse with the patient, the environment and self, I struggled to interpret the practical or operational equivalent of Titchen's 'antennae' through which skilled companions sense what is happening within themselves, the relationship, and outside within the clinical context. But during one of those defining moments with my critical companion, we recognised something in my daughter's old homemade painting pinned over my desk.

It was an abstract wheel that threw out paint streaks as the paper had revolved around a turntable. It suddenly epitomised the nature of the patient–expert nurse interaction. Without movement of the turntable there would still be a painting, but of random dots and splashes although the very same actions had taken place. Movement had created cohesion, patterning and beauty that reflected Titchen's antennae. This spoke to me of either connected or disconnected nursing, relationship or task orientation, proactive or custodial care, and self-giving or self-preservation (because revolving the turntable is far more messy!). Making explicit what is different between the paintings with and without rotation was difficult, even though the finished products look completely different. The difference was in the heart of the action, the underpinning movement itself and at the

---

*'Companionship' is a metaphor for a helping relationship. The complete model is too detailed to describe here, and the reader is referred to the referenced text for further information.

Figure 8.2 The sensitive engagement of the nurse with the patient, the environment and self

moment of its creation. The portfolio recreated some of the moments that were demonstrative of my own expertise in nursing.

Expressing reality through art

The portfolio I produced as a reflective participant researcher has become a metaphor for the artistry of nursing. The evidence itself, including a collection of reflections, narratives and peer responses, was a metaphor for the individual acts of everyday nursing. Title pages graphically and descriptively suggested their contents, in the spirit of an unfolding nursing interaction that had to be interpreted and reinterpreted with all of one's wisdom, intuition and hindsight. This is a comment upon the covertness of many of my nursing interactions. Naive pictures represented the spontaneity with which I understood both my practice and myself through the process of reflection. They spoke of the vulnerability I recognise I need to approach the patients with whom I work, and of the childlike ease with which something of beauty can be formed and pass away almost without value or comment. The rewards of delving below the surface of one's ordinary nursing narratives, analysing a wealth of expertise in my reflective portfolio, proved to be a rich and awe-inspiring experience.

I would argue that it is time we examine our own practice and profession until we understand it deeply and can produce a convincing case for the attainment of genuine and authentic nursing care. As Watson so carefully identifies:

> The art of caring evokes the most human and humane processes of sustaining and expanding our being. It creates opportunities for full expression of self as ultimate caring art/act. Caring is relational, and a caring moment transcends and transforms both the one caring and the one cared for (not unlike a work of art both transcending and transforming the viewer). Any nurse who has stood in that sacred place where they have truly, artistically touched the life spirit, the life force of another, understands the power and beauty, the aesthetic arrest of the connection – soul to soul.
>
> (Watson 1999)

Round peg in a square hole

During the project, I became engaged in a conversation with a colleague about the nature of nurse training and some of the traits of our own very different nurse educations. I think conceptually and holistically – strengths and weaknesses that I am sure are a combination of thinking style and training. My colleague thinks logistically and has a phenomenal memory for sequential data. She was trained in the 1970s, given hard facts without rationale, and gained a thorough grasp of anatomy, physiology and disease processes. Although she has a questioning mind, it was seen as a nuisance by her then tutors! The combination of her knowledge and enquiry resulted in a thorough if pedantic attention to detail, protocols and procedures that I felt was consistently thorough, but sometimes stifling.

My own undergraduate training tackled nursing from a health–wellness perspective and although, for example, I was well versed in the physiology of oxygen exchange, I would not have had a clue about how to take a bag of blood from the hospital blood bank! This kind of local and logistical information was not always easy to find out, and the reasons for some of the procedures that existed were even less clear! This has created in me a tendency to oversimplify, generalise and contextualise, as well as an ability to spot inconsistencies or anomalous practices and to feel justified in challenging them.

However, I do consider that a combination of detail and holism is the ideal, although I am never satisfied that I have obtained enough information to merit the title 'expert'! I actually have an un-researched hunch that most nurses are serialists according to Pask (1975), and that there are proportionally far fewer in nursing that are holists. Those who are holists tend to be square pegs in a round hole, or as I prefer to put it, a round peg in a square hole, dogged by a sense of inadequacy yet having been some of the most perceptive characters I have worked with.

Reflections

We hope you have enjoyed our quilt! In the spirit of this chapter, the authors do not wish to draw conclusions for the reader, but invite them to reflect upon how they may incorporate these notions into in palliative and cancer care practice and education. The value of art as a medium for palliative and cancer care education is surely made evident by these examples. As we have explored art forms, so it is possible to enquire from others what they perceive as art forms, and to use these as vehicles to explore aspects of palliative and cancer care. The challenge is to find metaphors that engage others and to utilise them to make that which is obscure more explicit. For example, for those who perceive cooking to be an art form, a recipe approach to academic writing or to a treatment plan might help them to 'see' the end result.

Educationalists and learners who are continually seeking to address and challenge the existential consequences both of facing and of denying death oneself, either as the patient or as the professional alongside them, could do worse than embrace this approach. If these types of approach are adopted, it is also time for us to review the systems of reward and recognition of those who have achieved or benefited. Demonstration of learning should be meaningful, inspirational and enjoyable for the student, and demonstrative of the highest level of internalisation. This requires a different approach to valuing the learning demonstrated. The challenge is for us to become accomplished connoisseurs or 'art' critics with a more holistic philosophy than the singular academic processes of assessment and accreditation that predominate.

Personal reflections

The authors would like to share their individual personal reflections on the experience of incorporating art and artistry into the educative process.

An artist has the courage of their convictions to portray a representation of the world as they see it. In doing so, they bring a facet of interpretation that was previously embedded within them. Whether this impression is understood or rejected, applauded or ignored, it has meaning and value. Such authenticity is a trait of the artist and must be the goal of every practitioner.

It was Gill's experience that disclosure of reflection and critical thought led to a freedom to practise authentic palliative care. For a palliative or cancer care nurse, coming into contact with human loss, fear, exposure, disappointment and separation is a regular challenge or opportunity to translate the face of patient suffering and felt professional incapacity into deeper learning about one's resources and weaknesses that can create a common understanding between the professional carer and the patient being cared for. Lifelike art is a common and universally comprehended medium for learners, be they nurses or patients. 'Presencing' oneself, or 'being with' a patient rather than 'doing to' them, has been recognised as an important attribute of palliative care nursing (Davies and Oberle 1990).

In Angela's experience the introduction of art and artistry into learning episodes was both risky and time consuming. However, the results more than justified the energy and anxiety. Creating opportunities to learn in this way is a liberating experience, providing opportunities to clarify one's own values with regard to education and live them as an educator within the traditional academic/accreditation frameworks that exist in healthcare education. These humanistic approaches to learning and assessment reflect the personal philosophy of nursing and nurse education, and provide the opportunity to incorporate more holistic approaches to the recognition and assessment of learning.

Both Gill and Angela found the experience emancipating and self-actualising. They both further developed their critical thinking and a form of expression that was reflective of their creativity.

They are inspired by the words of Marianne Williamson (1992), and feel that these reflect the challenge to educationalists to embrace art and artistry in the learning experience.

> Our deepest fear is not that we are inadequate; our deepest fear is that we are powerful beyond measure. It is our light, not our darkness, that most frightens us. We ask ourselves 'Who am I to be so brilliant, gorgeous, talented, fabulous?'. Actually, who are we not to be? You are a child of God. Your playing small does not serve the world. There is nothing enlightened about shrinking so that other people won't feel insecure around you. We are meant to shine, as children do. It is not just in some of us, it is in everyone. As we let our light shine, we unconsciously give other people permission to do the same. As we are liberated from our own fears, our presence automatically liberates others.'
>
> (Williamson 1992, often cited as from Nelson Mandela's Inauguration Speech, 1994)

Implications for the reader's own practice

1 How can you discover your own innate artistry?
2 How could you use artistry in your teaching?
3 Can you recall any examples of situations when you have used artistry?
4 How will you apply artistry in nursing to palliative and cancer care in the future?
5 Are there some examples from life that are useful for illustrating your practice?

References

Carper BA (1978) Fundamental patterns in knowing in nursing. *Adv Nurs Sci.* 1: 13–23.

Chinn P and Kramer, M K (1991) *Theory and Nursing: a systematic approach.* Mosby Year Book, St Louis, MO.

Davies B and Oberle K (1990) Dimensions of the supportive role of the nurse in palliative care. *Oncol Nurse Forum*. **17**: 87–94.

Felton M (2003) The Emotional Cancer Journey and Health Promotion; www.mapfoundation .org/exhib.suff/exhib1.html

Gablik S (1991) *Re-enchantment of Art*. Thames & Hudson, New York.

Gombrich E (1995) *The Story of Art* (16e). Phaidon, London.

Greenhalgh T and Hurwitz B (1999) Narrative-based medicine: why study narrative? *BMJ*. **318**: 48–50.

Hardy S, Garbett R, Titchen A and Manley K (2002) Exploring nursing expertise: nurses talk nursing. *Nurs Inquiry*. **9**: 196–202.

Kearney M (1996) *Mortally Wounded*. Marino, Dublin.

Marks-Maran D and Rose P (eds) (1997) *Reconstructing Nursing: beyond art and science*. Bailliere Tindall, London.

Maslow A (1970) *Motivation and Personality* (2e). Harper and Row, New York.

Nyatanga B (2001) *Why is it so difficult to die?* Mark Allen Publishing, Dinton.

Pask G (1975) *The cybernetics of human learning and performance: a guide to theory and research*. Hutchinson, London.

Petrone MA (2003) www.mapfoundation.org

Rogers C (1994) *Freedom to Learn* (3e). Macmillan, Oxford.

Rose P (1997) Science and technology: tools in the creation of nursing. In: D Marks-Maran and P Rose (eds) *Reconstructing Nursing: beyond art and science*. Bailliere Tindall, London.

Sheldon F and Turner P (2001) The contribution of carers to professional education. In: S Payne and L Ellis Hill (eds) *Chronic and Terminal Illness – new perspectives on caring and carers*. Open University Press, Buckingham.

Sheppard A (1987) *Aesthetics: an introduction to the philosophy of art*. Oxford University Press, Oxford.

Sikora K (2003) The Bristol Cancer Help Centre; www.bristolcancerhelp.org

Titchen A (2001) Skilled companionship in professional practice. In: J Higgs and A Titchen (eds). *Practice Knowledge and Expertise in Health Professions*. Butterworth Heinnemann, Oxford.

Watson J (1999) *Post-modern Nursing and Beyond*. Churchill Livingstone, Edinburgh.

Widdershoven G (1993) The story of life: hermeneutic perspectives on the relationship between narrative and life history. In: R Josselson and A Lieblich (eds) *The Narratives of Life*. Sage Publications, London.

Williamson M (1992) *A Return to Love: reflections on the principles of a course in miracles*. Harper Collins, London.

Further reading

Brykcznska G (1997) Art and literature: nursing's distant mirror? In: G Brykcznska (ed.) *Caring: the companion and wisdom of nursing*. Arnold, London

Byham WC and Cox J (1988) *Zapp! The lightning of empowerment*. Century Business, Random House, London.

Derbyshire P (1999) Nursing art and science: revisiting the two cultures. *Int J Nurs Pract.* **5**: 121–31

Keoning JM and Zorn CR (2002) Using storytelling as an approach to teaching and learning with diverse students. *J Nurs Educ.* **41**: 393–402.

CHAPTER 9

The role of psychoneuroimmunology in oncology and palliative care education

Sally-Ann Spencer-Grey

He made her melancholy, sad, and heavy, and so she died; had she being light like you of such a merry, nimble, stirring spirit, she might ha' been a grandma ere she died; and so may you, for a light heart lives long.

(William Shakespeare, *Love's Labour's Lost*)

In this chapter I shall endeavour to introduce the notion, research base, evidence and practical applications of psychoneuroimmunology in relation to oncology and palliative care education.

Learning outcomes

This chapter will:

- introduce the reader to the concept of psychoneuroimmunology
- outline the current oncology and palliative care perspectives of psycho-neuroimmunology
- enable the reader to appreciate how psychoneuroimmunology supports the underlying philosophy of integrative whole-person care
- provide an example of psychoneuroimmunology in practice in education.

Introduction

Reductionism and materialism as related to science, technology and medicine have informed and underpinned modern healthcare practice and provided powerful resources that have successfully tackled and banished many dreaded diseases. The acute infections that threatened human life up until the 1950s, such as tuberculosis (TB), syphilis, rheumatic fever, polio, pneumonia, meningitis and septicaemia (Porter 1997), have been usurped by chronic conditions and diseases related to life-style, environment and increased longevity (Department of Health 2000).

The continued search for detailed and specialised knowledge has achieved enormous insights in reductionistic modern science (the biomedical approach), but investigation and understanding of single elements do not guarantee an explanation or prediction of the reactions of an individual organism as a whole. From this an awareness of the interconnections and interdependency between element, human systems and scientific and medical disciplines (e.g. dualism) has developed. This appreciation of holism has in turn led to a growing interest in systems, systems theories and the use and role of systemic, mind–body/integrative therapies and practices (Jonas 1997).

It is in this holistic paradigm that integrative therapies, also known as complementary and alternative medicine (CAM), have become increasingly popular both with the general public and with those living with chronic and life-threatening illness/disease. These 'unconventional' or 'unorthodox' therapies are defined as any practices which are not standard within medicine. In oncology this usually means those therapies that fall outside the domains of surgery, chemotherapy, radiotherapy, and hormone therapy (Gray *et al.*, 1998).

These therapies are employed by what are often disparagingly termed the 'worried well' to maintain or improve health and prevent disease, while those living with disease/illness most often use these therapies to improve their quality of life and treat illnesses or symptoms of their illness for which conventional therapies have proved ineffective.

Complementary therapies have had a mixed reception from healthcare professionals, and their acceptance and support in mainstream healthcare have been sporadic. Healthcare professionals may be sceptical or cynical, but are overall more tolerant of complementary rather than alternative therapies, considering them to be harmless on the whole and maybe of some benefit. The most readily accepted therapies are those considered to be the most established or common place (e.g. chiropractic, osteopathy, aromatherapy, reflexology, acupuncture and massage). The more 'exotic' and 'imprecise' therapies (e.g. homeopathy, herbal therapy, Reiki, diet) are often considered 'risky' or 'quackery', as are the majority of alternative therapies.

The problems with CAM and its acceptance, particularly in the current climate of evidence-based medicine, are the perceived lack of 'legitimate' research (randomised controlled clinical studies to measure outcomes in a scientific way) and a lack of scientific theoretical underpinning. The lack of research is being addressed, as are the quality of the studies and the methodologies employed. The limitations of the research 'gold standard' randomised controlled trial (RCT) in investigating CAM have been well described, and necessitated a creative and innovative approach to research in order to provide meaningful information (e.g. 'dual-blind' studies and multifaceted intervention trials over single interventions). Psychoneuroimmunology and associated disciplines will provide the scientific underpinning.

The increasing interest in and use of CAMs, especially within oncology and palliative care, must be reflected in healthcare education in order to equip healthcare professionals with an understanding and working knowledge that will enable them to best support and inform individuals' healthcare choices.

Psychoneuroimmunology

Be wary of simple answers to complex questions.
(George F. Solomon, Professor Emeritus, University of California at Los Angeles)

As already stated, inherent in many integrative therapies is the notion of holism and the connection between mind, body and spirit.

The scientific field of psychoneuroimmunology moves away from the traditional view that the immune system is autonomous – that is, self-regulatory and functioning separately and independently from the rest of the body. It provides an explanation of why mind–body therapies can improve psychological and physical functioning, quality of life and perhaps even disease-related outcomes (Bauer-Wu 2002).

Psychoneuroimmunology is the result of converging data from different disciplines. It helps to define the interrelatedness of psychology, neurobiology, endocrinology, immunology, neurology and psychiatry while recognising the biological, psychological, sociological and spiritual essence of being human. The compelling evidence provided by psychoneuroimmunology emphasises the need for multi-disciplinary studies and education aimed at integrating these disciplines in terms of research and clinical implications.

Psychoneuroimmunology has its modern roots in the 'psychosomatic medicine' studies of the 1930s (Kiecolt-Glaser *et al.* 2002b) and then through George Engel's work during the 1950s, resulting in the publication of *Psychological Development in Health and Disease* (Engel 1962), which outlined his psychoanalytically grounded psychobiological system. This is referred to as Engel's *biopsychosocial model*.

However, the term 'psychoneuroimmunology' was first coined in 1964 by Solomon in his landmark discussion entitled *Emotions, Immunity and Disease: a Speculative Theoretical Integration* (Solomon and Moos 1964). From then until the 1980s very little was written about this phenomenon and science, until in 1981 Robert Ader started the exponential expansion of this field of enquiry with the publication of his book *Psychoneuroimmunology* (Ader *et al.* 1991). Today the topic of psychoneuroimmunology can be found in numerous journals and papers published from all over the world.

Psychoneuroimmunology has been defined by a number of authors, including the following:

- Lovejoy and Sisson (1989):
  the study of the interactions among the mind, the immune system and the neurological system that modulate susceptibility to disease or its progression

- Klazien Matter-Walstra (2001):
  a discipline which studies the relation, co-operation and modulation of functions of the central nervous system, immune system and the psyche.

Robert Ader says of psychoneuroimmunology research that 'we are not talking about causation of disease, but the interaction between psychosocial events, coping and pre-existing biologic conditions' (Ader *et al.* 1991).

The premise of psychoneuroimmunology is that the immune system, like any other system, is operating in the interests of homeostasis, and that to this end it is integrated with other psychophysiological processes and is therefore influenced by and capable of influencing the brain (Ader 2000). This mind and body connection is a bidirectional communication that is mediated by direct nervous tissue connections (de Kooker 2001) and a flow of hormones, neuropeptides and cytokines (Ader *et al.* 1991).

Stress research overlaps into the field of psychoneuroimmunology because stress is the environmental condition under which homeostasis is interrupted. The pathways mentioned above are activated because of the body's response to stress (physical and psychological).

Living organisms are macro-phenomena consisting of micro-elements. However, research at the molecular level has revealed that the material properties of (reacting) substances themselves are not sufficient to explain what happens in a living system (Matter-Walstra 2001).

Not only may a biochemical substance contain and transmit several 'meanings' (pleiotropy), but also a certain 'meaning' may be shared by different substances (redundancy) (Matter-Walstra 2001). In addition, research is showing that people respond to the same stressful event in different physiological ways depending on how they appraise it (personality and coping styles) (Kiecolt-Glaser *et al.* 2002a), and that the presence of psychosocial factors such as optimism and social support can moderate stress responses (De Angelis 2002).

The aim of psychoneuroimmunology is to link the isolated mechanisms that have been determined with the complexity of the human condition. Research that uses a psychoneuroimmunology framework therefore seeks to determine whether valid associations exist between stress, immune function and health, but the multi-faceted and complex nature of psychoneuroimmunology means that the research is fraught with methodological difficulties (Robinson *et al.* 2002).

There is no space here to discuss in detail the different mind–body pathways or the models of psychoneuroimmunology, but they are very eloquently described in a number of publications (e.g. Watkins 1997).

What are the limitations of psychoneuroimmunology? Does it include practices related to energy theory, spirituality and Eastern medicine? Does it explain integrative therapies such as therapeutic touch, Reiki, reflexology and homeopathy? Does it take into account the subtle but profound effects of the caring relationship? Some authors believe that psychoneuroimmunology has limited applications and that these limitations must be recognised (Bauer-Wu 2002), although perhaps it is not psychoneuroimmunology that is limiting but rather our understanding, interpretation and narrow application of it.

What we have done is to coin a phrase and name a science of which that we have very little knowledge. What we must do now is allow this science to grow unhampered by its label. Our understanding can only develop if we widen our horizons to include other fields of enquiry, such as quantum physics (Lindley 1996), chaos theory (Gleik 1987), Buddhist void, universality and relational holism (Kearney 2000). Integration of these with the fields of enquiry of biology, psychology, health and illness will result in mutually beneficial symbiotic consortia – non-competitive combinations engaging in joint ventures.

Current oncology and palliative care perspectives of psychoneuroimmunology

Introducing psychoneuroimmunology as a topic in oncology and palliative care education, relating it to the use of CAMs, and examination of psychological, immunological, endocrinological and sociological studies in psychoneuroimmunology will help healthcare practitioners to communicate more effectively with other individuals about the use of such therapies.

Although there has been surprisingly little research involving the study of specific patient groups and their use of CAM, the majority of the published studies that are available concentrate on cancer patients (Cassileth *et al.* 1984; Downer *et al.* 1994; Maher *et al.* 1994; Miller *et al.* 1995; Begbie *et al.* 1996; Jacobson *et al.* 1999; Penson *et al.* 2001).

One of the findings identified in this work is the gap between what healthcare practitioners perceive their patients to be using and what those patients are actually using. This highlighted the fact that patients were often not telling their health carers (physicians in particular) that they were using CAM (Downer *et al.* 1994; Begbie *et al.* 1996), reflecting a deficiency in the health carer/doctor–patient relationship (York University Centre for Health Studies 1999).

Many healthcare professionals create communication barriers between themselves and patients with regard to CAM. As a result, many individuals engage in the use of CAM with little information and support. Around 80% of patients seem to be using CAM, and less than half will inform their GP of this (Penson *et al.* 2001). Whereas many forms of CAM do not interact with more conventional practices, some do, and this can lead to unsafe/dangerous interactions and a greater potential for exploitation of vulnerable individuals.

Psychoneuroimmunology also supports and underpins the innovative interventions that are being introduced more frequently into oncology and palliative care, some examples of which are given below.

Hypnotherapy is used in the palliative care setting to benefit both patients and healthcare providers with stress reduction, while enabling patients to find ways that may help them to cope better with their illness and the prospect of death (Curtis 2001).

Psychological interventions such as relaxation, visualisation and guided imagery are used as 'adjunctive psychological therapy' (APT) to 'reliably improve the quality of life of most cancer patients' (Cunningham 2000, p.368). Their effects on the immune system, levels of anxiety, depression and coping (Walker *et al.* 1999) and on longevity/survival (Spiegel *et al.* 1989) are also being investigated.

The use of humour to improve mood and to effect immunological changes indicated by elevation of natural-killer-cell (NKC) levels and activity (Takahashi *et al.* 2001) is discussed further in Chapter 13.

Psychosocial support and support groups (e.g. bereavement support groups, cancer support groups) are used to ameliorate the potentially damaging effect of negative emotions and distress on immune function, which may otherwise impair health and hasten disease progression (Goodkin *et al.* 2000; Kiecolt-Glaser *et al.* 2002a).

In oncology, but especially in palliative care, two of the main healthcare outcomes are adaptation and coping. With the dynamics of chronic illness, homeostasis (whereby the internal environment remains constant) is virtually impossible to achieve, but allostasis (the ability to achieve stability through adaptation) (Pendleton 2002) is a possibility. Margaret Dimond, an American Professor of Nursing, in 1983 quoted by Helmut Milz (1992) commented that:

> The ultimate measure of achievement of successful adaptation to a chronic illness is found in a way of life that sustains hope, diminishes fear and preserves a quality of living that takes account of, perhaps transcends but is not controlled by, the limitations of an illness.

In addition to the benefits to communication between healthcare professionals and patients, psychoneuroimmunology will also bring awareness of CAM and insight into the complexity and interrelatedness of disease and treatment. It will promote holistic, evidence-based medicine whereby practitioners will objectively evaluate all therapeutic interventions with a view to translating this knowledge into routine practice and thus enhancing patient care (Sackett *et al.* 1996).

Psychoneuroimmunology underpins oncology and palliative care

The facts of psychoneuroimmunology have far-reaching implications for basic biological sciences, academic and clinical medicine and the effectiveness of healthcare (Kiecolt-Glaser *et al.* 2002b). Holistic, patient-centred care advocated by modern healthcare providers and receivers – shared decision making and 'relationship-centred care' (Tresolini 1994) – is supported by psychoneuroimmunology. It is then a natural extrapolation to envisage psychoneuroimmunology as an underpinning philosophy of healthcare from health promotion through to terminal care and bereavement support.

Oncology and palliative care are complex specialties, but are importantly broadly representative of the gamut of complete healthcare and of psychoneuroimmunology theory. These specialities, like psychoneuroimmunology, acknowledge the multifactorial nature of wellness and illness (Birney 1991), and are inherently multidisciplinary in scope, involving many of the healthcare professions across different healthcare settings. Oncology and palliative care specialties emphasise searching beyond the traditional therapies and concepts of allopathic medicine (although not excluding them) to meet healthcare needs (de Kooker 2001).

They encompass groups of diseases with multiple aetiologies (Anderson *et al.* 1994) which provide for a disparate group of patients unrelated by age, gender or pathology.

Oncology and palliative care can in fact provide unique opportunities to examine the complexity of the human condition in relation to the whole person. Psychoneuroimmunology theory is the link between the clinical, scientific and epidemiological elements of oncology and palliative care and the humanistic dimension – 'whole-person care' (WPC) (Thompson and Zollman 2001). Psychoneuroimmunology theory can therefore be maximised in oncology and palliative care education to enrich understanding and enable practice development.

Psychoneuroimmunology has been demonstrated to underpin holistic (therapeutic) nursing (Bennett 1994) and to support research themes and approaches, and is used to support the vertical theme of 'whole-person care' (WPC) in medical training (Thompson and Zollman 2001). It is eminently suitable as an underpinning model of oncology and palliative care.

Measures must be taken to ensure the application of this new knowledge in the wider healthcare setting. This is achieved by facilitating meaningful connections between theory and practice, promoting an integrative approach, maintaining the humanistic dimension and operating under a WPC premise that sustains the art and science of good medicine (Thompson and Zollman 2001). This is achieved through education.

Human complexity needs to be reflected in healthcare approaches and interventions to encompass not just the complexity of health and illness but also the complexity of individual variation – culture, beliefs, values (Li *et al.* 1998), personality and emotions.

The type and variety of care interactions available to healthcare professionals are most frequently (at least initially) based on their professional educational preparation.

Review of doctors and oncology nurses who received CAM and psychoneuroimmunology education as part of their training showed that they communicated more effectively with patients in this area than did their colleagues (Perry and Dowrick 2000).

Developing and advancing practice requires expansion of knowledge, skills and understanding achieved through a combination of education from formal and informal learning opportunities, and from experience (Glen and Leiba 2002).

The driving force for advancing practice therefore comes from promoting a learning culture by creating learning environments and implementing lifelong learning strategies.

> Fundamental to the basis upon which students are prepared for their profes-
> sional career is the provision of programmes of academic study and practice-
> based learning which lay the foundation for career-long professional develop-
> ment and lifelong learning to support best professional practice and the
> maintenance of professional standards (Quality Assurance Agency for Higher
> Education 2001).

A psychoneuroimmunology-based philosophical approach to oncology and palliative care introduced through oncology and palliative care education will ensure
that the art and humanity of medicine always accompany and are balanced with
the science, thus ensuring 'good medicine' (Thompson and Zollman 2001).

Psychoneuroimmunology in practice in education

The next challenge is to translate into practice the theory and philosophy of psychoneuroimmunology that have been discussed in the chapter so far. How do you put
psychoneuroimmunology into action in education?

The following information comes from the authors' experience in developing,
writing and delivering a two-module course at academic levels 2 and 3. This course
sought to enlighten, examine and educate health and complementary therapy
professionals in CAM approaches to healthcare and their integration with conventional healthcare.

The aim of the course was to provide education and awareness of holism and
holistic approaches to healthcare, and it was designed to provide a holistic learning
experience – the integration of intellectual, social and emotional aspects of learning
(Cove and Goodsell Love 1996). Student learning was focused on the whole
learning experience, with meaningful connections made between theory and
practice, and with personal experience and insight encouraged and as valued as
theory, while bidirectional communication was established and maintained. Focus
on a part of the whole and students' education becomes no more than the sum of
its parts (Cove and Goodsell Love 1996).

Students were not being trained as CAM practitioners – the course enabled better
understanding and use of holistic principles. It was intended that this increased
awareness and knowledge would enable better facilitation and support of patients'
healthcare choices. A narrow awareness and knowledge base with regard to CAM
may inevitably lead to narrow application, recommendation and use. This is
supported by evidence reported in Chapter 10.

To achieve this holistic end and to ensure overall coherence, the course embraced
psychoneuroimmunology as an integrative tool to enable meaningful connection

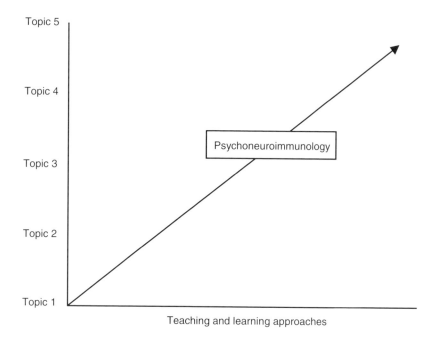

Figure 9.1   Progression of the course with psychoneuroimmunology

between topics, skills and experience more usually addressed in different subject areas and disciplines (Drake 1998). The philosophy of psychoneuroimmunology was used as a vertical and horizontal theme. As a vertical theme it was integrated into all subjects/teaching throughout the two modules to encourage the development of skills and attitudes that would provide a basis for lifelong learning. As a horizontal theme it was used to underpin course development and all teaching and learning approaches, providing flexibility and the capacity to introduce new material in response to change (*see* Figure 9.1).

This was a directed holistic approach that endeavoured to serve the needs of the individual (professionally and personally), the 'profession' (the students' professional discipline) and the 'service' (be it within the public or private sector) while reflecting current policy, guidelines and professional driving forces.

The holistic approach was reflected in topic selection, teaching methods, assessment strategy and evaluation and course administration, each of which will be discussed in more detail below.

Student mix

Course access enabled healthcare professionals and complementary therapists from different disciplines to undertake this module either as part of a diploma or BSc in health professional studies (oncology) or as a stand-alone module. The course attracted a wide mix of students, including the following:

- healthcare professionals (e.g. nurses, physiotherapists and radiographers from acute, community, hospice, oncology and palliative care settings)
- healthcare professionals with CAM qualifications, some of whom were enabled by their job description to use their CAM skills within their professional role
- complementary therapists originally from a healthcare background (e.g. nursing)
- complementary therapists with a purely CAM background.

Course structure

The course consisted of two 12-week modules, for one full day a week, which included clinical placements/visits. The intention was for students to commence with module 1 and progress to module 2. However, each module could be studied independently.

Although both modules addressed the central themes, they each had a specific focus.

- Module 1 was directed mainly at providing the philosophical, theoretical, scientific and research underpinning, and encouraging self-awareness and development.
- Module 2 was directed at providing an introduction to a range of CAM and therapeutic interventions, and providing examples of integrative healthcare.

Administration

In any social relationship (family, study group or institution) there are vertical and horizontal relationships. These relationships include a top-down vertical perspective where 'responsible behaviour at the top level creates responsible behaviours down to the level of the individual' (Colceag 2003). There is also a 'bottom-up' vertical perspective which accommodates the adjustments made by and the influence of the lower hierarchical levels and individuals on the higher levels, enabling 'mobility and adaptation to new demands'. The third perspective is horizontal, recognising peer interactions (Colceag 2003).

These relationships can inhibit or enhance the learning experience, and although they are often recognised in the immediate learning environment, their influence is not limited to in-class experience, but equally relates to out-of-class activity and to course administration.

The learning experience can be adversely affected as much by poor administration and organisation and unpleasant surroundings/poor facilities as by poor content and teaching. Effective administration and organisation are a co-responsibility that is based on open and good communication, and are as much a result of vertical and horizontal social relationships as learning is.

Therefore when adopting a holistic perspective there is no dominance of or reliance on those 'at the top' to determine behaviour, there is co-responsibility (both vertically and horizontally), and there is potential for bidirectional adaptation and evolution. The result is 'social capital', in that the relationships between people enhance those individuals' abilities (World Bank 2003).

Pleasant surroundings with adequate parking, heating, lighting, toilets and refreshments available may seem an obvious requirement, but sometimes it does require creativity and co-operation to achieve them.

Teaching and learning methods

Adult learners are by definition adults. Their process of growth is continuing rather than starting, and they come to the learning situation with a set of experiences and values, intentions and expectations. They also have competing interests and established patterns of learning (Rogers 1996). A positive learning environment will embrace all of this.

The course adopted a radical constructivist approach (von Glasersfeld 1970), building on what the students already know and can do, and creating an atmosphere that inspires individuals 'to explore, to experiment, to make mistakes and have wonderful ideas' (Piaget, quoted by von Glasersfeld 1970). According to this constructivist perspective, knowledge is constructed by the individual through their interactions with their environment. To this end, and to further ensure a holistic learning approach, the curriculum and academic goals were closely linked with the student's life (both personal and professional) outside the classroom. Students were regularly asked to illustrate how they were using course material in other areas of their lives. Therefore, through the use of reflection, clinical placements/visits and the nature of the assessments linking programmes and activities across the academic and out-of-class dimensions of students' lives, student learning was able to transcend the artificial boundaries set between in-class and out-of-class learning (Kuh *et al.* 2000). As well as learning specific knowledge and skills and the attitudes that underpin them, the value of self-evaluation was highlighted, and its importance as a core professional skill that will form part of continuing professional development.

It is recognised that learning is facilitated or hampered by emotions (Boekaerts 1993; Goleman 1995), and that emotions drive learning and memory (Sylvester 1994). Current learning can be affected positively or negatively by previous experiences of learning. In addition, learning can be a source of stress (physiological and psychological, social and spiritual) and, as with any other stressful situation, support can help to effect a more positive experience and outcome.

> Students in learning communities provide social, emotional and intellectual support for each other's learning.
>
> (Kuh *et al.* 1991)

According to this premise, tutor and peer support was established to contribute to the positive learning experience and, it was hoped, to help to provide some recompense for previous negative experiences.

The teaching and learning strategies employed were chosen to provide variety to accommodate individual experience and learning styles, to optimise presentation of the subject matter, to enable experiential learning and to develop a positive learning environment/community, creating an environment and situation in which all students have the opportunity to participate and contribute, and that would enhance learning by capitalising on students' strengths and addressing their learning needs. The methods employed included lectures, group work, experiential learning opportunities (e.g. creative arts days and clinical visits), peer presentations, peer feedback and tutorials.

The course recognised, encouraged and provided for the following (Jacobsen 1997).

- Learning is considered partly as a social process between students and students/ teachers, and partly as an individual process.
- Students are given a real co-responsibility for their own progress and that of their group.
- The course leader will provide for both group and individual learning.
- Student activation is stimulated.
- Co-operative skills are practised.
- Individual reasoning is subject to collective reflection.
- The theoretical learning objectives are placed in a 'real' patient setting.
- A basis for lifelong learning is provided.

Topics

The topics included here do not represent an exhaustive list, and can be added to or replaced, but it is important to endeavour to maintain the range of aims described by these topics.

Module 1

Each topic is a broad heading that incorporates a variety of approaches, theories and ways of thinking to describe it. For example, the lecture on *concept of holism* with underpinning psychoneuroimmunology looked at what holism could be, giving no definitive answers but opening the mind to enquiry. It included the following:

- traditional Chinese medicine – beliefs about dynamic balance
- holographic principle – perspective on energy patterns in which every piece contains information about the whole (the whole is in every part)

- holistic paradigm – living systems function as irreducible 'wholes' rather than as clockwork biomachines, and subjectivity can directly influence the observable physical world (dualism, reductionism, etc.)
- development of new physics from classical physics – quantum physics, wave-particle duality
- relational holism – a single atom acts unpredictably, but a group of atoms works collectively in relation to each other and to an extent predictably
- Buddhist void and potentiality
- measurement – objective and subjective measurement
- chaos theory and practice – sensitive dependence on initial conditions
- universality and sensitive chaos
- complexity theory
- chaotic systems and diseases
- self-regulation, regulation and mode locking
- potential problems of a holistic approach.

Other topics included the following:

- concepts of health and illness
- health and social policy – oncology, supportive and palliative care, CAM (development, implications, interpretation and future)
- person-centred care – self-awareness, quality of life
- therapeutic relationships – professionalism, health and safety, etc.
- allopathic vs holistic – patient assessment and practice
- presentation skills, including PowerPoint
- reflection and reflective practice
- introduction to research and critical analysis – research issues with regard to CAM.

Module 2

This included the following topics:

- aromatherapy
- reflexology
- reiki
- homeopathy
- herbal therapy
- iridology
- hypnotherapy
- relaxation and visualisation
- communication and counselling – counselling skills and counselling theories
- nutrition and diets
- creative arts day – enneagrams, mandalas, drama and drama therapy, creative writing/journals, art and art therapy, dreams and sleep
- holistic centres (CAM centres, integrative approaches and projects, etc.).

The CAM topics were delivered by CAM practitioners from a variety of settings, including the NHS, the voluntary sector and private practice. Each speaker was asked to:

- discuss philosophy, history and holistic principles
- address training, qualifications, registration, continuing professional development, etc.
- address client assessment and review
- discuss recommendations for use (particularly with regard to oncology and palliative care)
- discuss health and safety, cautions and contraindications
- outline the research base and any current research issues and give a perspective on attitudes of and integration with conventional healthcare (potential problems/issues)
- provide a practical demonstration or experience for students whenever possible.

Assessment

Once again the assessment strategy had been determined by the holistic approach, and consisted of a combination of formative and summative assessment. It included reflection on an experience (e.g. clinical visit) or an aspect of care (e.g. case study), as well as reflection through the learning journal/portfolio. Assessment also involved:

- research critique and analysis via a presentation and through academic writing
- peer review of a presentation.

Evaluation

Evaluation of success is based on evaluation of increased knowledge, skills and changes in attitude, together with benefits to the individual and impact on practice.
The following evaluation modalities were employed.

- *Self-evaluation* by the students and lecturers, who were asked to address perceived individual benefits and impact on practice, and to comment on their participation.
- *Portfolio/learning journal.* This was reviewed at tutorials and at the end of the course. Although it was mainly considered to be a personal portfolio and an individual record of the development of the practitioner's skills, knowledge, attitudes, understanding and achievements, rather than a professional profile, it was structured with the possibility of sharing the document with a specific audience (i.e. the tutor).
- *End-of-course evaluation.* This provided an opportunity to comment on all aspects of the course (administration, structure, organisation, content, lecturer quality)

and to remark upon what worked well and what worked less well. Observations on the topics covered were encouraged, as were suggestions for future topics.

- *Review day at three months.* The review day is an opportunity for the learning group to meet again and catch up with each other. On a more formal note, each student is asked to provide information/comment on how they have incorporated their learning from the course into their practice and their own life. In addition, students are asked to comment on how they intend to develop this learning in the future. It is also an opportunity to provide additional teaching on a new topic that has been requested by students, or one that was missed during the course due to cancellation/unforeseen circumstances.

Conclusion

This chapter has introduced the reader to the concept of psychoneuroimmunology, translated within the context of cancer and palliative care education. It further demonstrates that this appreciation of holism, systems and systems theories underpins mind–body/integrative therapies and practices which have increasing significance in cancer and palliative care provision.

Finally, this chapter has demonstrated that an oncology and palliative care education experience, when provided within a holistic, psychoneuroimmunology-based framework and philosophy, will ensure that the art, humanity and science of healthcare are balanced to provide whole-person care. In addition, whole-person care in this context encompasses the student and their education experience whereby a holistic learning experience – that is, the integration of intellectual, social and emotional aspects of learning (Cove and Goodsell Love 1996) – enables personal and professional growth, while the relationships established provide 'social capital' and the education experience becomes more than the sum of its parts.

Key points to consider
- Course content should be developed to incorporate student suggestions, to keep abreast of policy, political and professional driving forces, and to accommodate new insights.
- The popularity of this course as well as the need for education in this field would support the development of additional similar courses that would 'stand alone' as discrete learning opportunities, encompassing a wider student population.
- It is necessary to raise awareness of psychoneuroimmunology as a topic, and although it may be used already, its profile is in need of more overt attention and publicity.
- Psychoneuroimmunology needs to be integrated into other subject areas.
- Evaluation techniques need to be developed not only to be robust but also to ensure holistic evaluation that fits with the model.

Implications for the reader's own practice

1 Is psychoneuroimmunology an integrated element in your educational practice?
2 If the answer is yes, in what way is it integrated?
3 If the answer is no, how might this be achieved?
4 What knowledge and understanding of psychoneuroimmunology do you need to initiate a programme that utilises psychoneuroimmunology in the clinical setting?
5 In what innovative ways might you use psychoneuroimmunology?

References

Ader R, Felten DL and Cohen N (eds) (1991). *Psychoneuroimmunology* (2e). Academic Press, San Diego, CA.

Ader R (2000) On the development of psychoneuroimmunology. *Eur J Pharmacol.* **405**: 167–76.

Anderson BL, Kiecolt-Glaser JK and Glaser R (1994) A behavioural model of cancer stress and disease course. *Am Psychol.* **49**: 389–404.

Bauer-Wu SM (2002) Psychoneuroimmunology. Part II. Mind–body interventions. *Clin J Oncol Nurs.* **6**: 167–70.

Begbie SD, Kerestes ZL and Bell DR (1996) Patterns of alternative medicine use by cancer patients. *Med J Aust.* **165**: 545–8.

Bennett M (1994) Multidimensional factors affecting well being: a PNI-based model for therapeutic nursing intervention. Unpublished paper. Rush-Presbyterian St Luke's Medical Center, College of Nursing, Chicago.

Birney M (1991) Psychoneuroimmunology: a holistic framework for the study of stress and illness. *Holistic Nurs Pract.* **5**: 32–8.

Boekaerts M (1993) Being concerned with well-being and with learning. *Educ Psychol.* **28**: 149–67.

Cassileth B, Lush EJ, Strouse TB and Bodenheimer BJ (1984) Contemporary unorthodox treatment in cancer medicine: a study of patients, treatments and practitioners. *Ann Intern Med.* **101**: 105–12.

Colceag F (2003) *Horizontal and Vertical Social Relationships*; www.austega.com.

Cove PG and Goodsell Love A (1996) *Enhancing Student Learning: intellectual, social, and emotional integration*. ERIC Digest. ERIC Clearing House on Higher Education, Washington, DC.

Cunningham AJ (2000) Adjuvant psychological therapy for cancer patients: putting it on the same footing as adjunctive medical therapies. *Psycho-Oncology.* **9**: 367–71.

Curtis C (2001) Hypnotherapy in a specialist palliative care unit: evaluation of a pilot service. *Int J Palliat Nurs.* **7**: 604–9.

De Angelis T (2002) A bright future for PNI. *Monitor Psychol.* **33**: 6.

de Kooker M (2001) *Psychoneuroimmunology: an overview*. The Wellness Support Programme: www.wellness.org.za/html/pni.html

Department of Health (2000) *The NHS Cancer Plan*. Department of Health, London.

Downer SM, Cody MM, McCluskey P *et al.* (1994) Pursuit and practice of complementary therapies by cancer patients receiving conventional treatment. *BMJ.* **309**: 86–9.

Drake SM (1998) *Creating Integrated Curriculum: proven ways to increase student learning.* Corwin Press, Thousand Oaks, CA.

Engel G (1962) *Psychological Development in Health and Disease.* Saunders, Philadelphia, PA.

Gleik J (1987) *Chaos: the amazing science of the unpredictable.* Vintage, London.

Glen S and Leiba T (2002) Interprofessional education: the way forward. In: S Glen and T Leiba (eds) *Multiprofessional Learning for Nurses.* Palsgrave, London.

Goleman ID (1995) *Emotional Intelligence. Why it can matter more than IQ.* Bloomsbury Publishing Ltd, London.

Goodkin K, Tuttle RS, Blaney NT *et al.* (2000) Bereavement, immunity, and the impact of bereavement support groups in HIV-1 infection. In: K Goodkin and AP Visser (eds) *Psychoneuroimmunology: stress, mental disorders and health.* American Psychiatric Press, Washington, DC.

Gray RE, Fitch M and Greenberg MA (1998) Comparison of physician and patient perspectives on unconventional cancer therapies. *Psycho-Oncology.* **7**: 445–52.

Jacobsen N (1999) *Curriculum Overview.* Faculty of Dentistry, University of Oslo; www.odont.uio.no

Jonas WB (1997) Foreword. In: A Watkins (ed.) *Mind–Body Medicine.* Churchill Livingstone, Edinburgh.

Kearney M (2000) *A Place of Healing,* Oxford University Press, Oxford.

Kiecolt-Glaser JK, McGuire L, Robles TF and Glaser R (2002a) Emotions, morbidity and mortality: new perspectives from psychoneuroimmunology. *Ann Rev Psychol.* **53**: 83–107.

Kiecolt-Glaser JK, McGuire L, Robles TF and Glaser R (2002b) Psychoneuroimmunology and psychosomatic medicine: back to the future. *Psychosom Med.* **64**: 15–28.

Kuh, G, Schuh J, Whitt E *et al.* (1991) Involving Colleges: successful approaches to fostering student learning and development outside the classroom. Jossey-Bass, San Francisco, CA.

Kuh GD, Branch Douglas K, Lund JP and Ramin-Gyurnek J (2000) *Student Learning Outside the Classroom: transcending artificial boundaries.* Jossey-Bass, San Francisco, CA.

Li BUK, Caniano DA and Comer RC (1998) A Cultural Diversity Curriculum: combining dialactic, problem-solving and simulated experiences. *Jamwa.* **53**: 127–9.

Lindley D (1996) *Where Does the Weirdness Go?* Vintage, London.

Lovejoy NC and Sisson R (1989) Psychoneuroimmunology and AIDS. *Holistic Nurse Pract.* **3**: 4: 1–15.

Maher EJ, Young T and Feigel I (1004) Letters: complementary therapies used by patients with cancer. *BMJ.* **309**: 671–2.

Miller MJ, Boyer MJ, Dunn SM *et al.* (1995) Why do Australian cancer patients use unproven therapies? *Procedures of the Clinical Oncology Society of Australia.* **22**: 78.

Matter-Walstra K (2001) www.datacomm.ch/kmatter/content.htm

Milz H (1992) Healthy ill people: social cynicism or new perspectives? In: A Kaplan (ed.) *Health Promotion and Chronic Illness: discovering a new quality of health.* WHO Regional Publications, No. 44.

Pendleton V (2002) *Health Psychology Seminar 1. Psychophysiological basis of health and illness*; www.hms.uq.edu.au

Penson R, Castro M, Seiden M, Chabner B and Lynch T (2001) Complementary, alternative, integrative or unconventional medicine? *Oncologist*. **6**: 463–73.

Perry R and Dowrick C (2000) Complementary medicine and general practice: an urban perspective. *Compl Ther Med*. **8**: 71–5.

Porter R (1997) *The Greater Benefit to Mankind*. Harper Collins, London.

Porter R (2001) *Bodies Politic. Disease, Death and Doctors in Britain, 1650–1900*. Cornell University Press, London.

Quality Assurance Agency for Higher Education (2001) *Benchmark Statement: health care programmes. Phase 1: radiography*. Quality Assurance Agency for Higher Education, London.

Robinson FP, Mathews HL and Witek-Janusek L (2002) Issues in the design and implementation of psychoneuroimmunology research. *Biol Res Nurs*. **3**: 165–75.

Rogers J (1989) *Adults Learning*. Penguin Books, Harmondsworth.

Rogers A (1996) *Teaching Adults* (2e). Open University Press, Buckingham.

Sackett DL, Rosenberg W, Muir Gray JA, Haynes RB and Richardson WS (1996) Evidence-based medicine: what it is and what it isn't. *BMJ*. **312**: 71–2.

Solomon GH and Moos RH (1964) Emotions, immunity and disease: a speculative theoretical integration. *Arch Gen Psychiatry*. **11**: 657–74.

Spiegel D, Bloom JR, Kraemer HC and Gottheil E (1989) Effect of psychosocial treatment on survival of patients with metastatic breast cancer. *Lancet*. **2**: 888–91.

Sylvester R (1994) How emotions affect learning. *Educ Leadership*. **52**: 60–65.

Takahashi K, Iwase M, Yamashita K *et al*. (2001) The elevation of natural killer cell activity induced by laughter in a crossover-designed study. *Int J Mol Med*. **8**: 645–50.

Thompson TDB and Zollman C (2001) Whole Person Care: a vertical theme; www.epi.bris. ac.uk/phc/teaching/y1wpcare.doc.

Tresolini CP (1994) *Health Education and Relationship-Centered Care*. Pew Health Professions Committee, San Francisco.

von Glasersfeld E (1970) *Cybernetics, Experience and the Concept of Self*; www.oikos.org/constructivism.htm.

World Bank (2003) *The Scope of Social Analysis: the five entry points. Institutions, rules and behaviour. The Social Analysis Sourcebook*; www.worldbank.org/socialanalysissourcebook/5elements2.htm.

Walker L, Walker M, Ogston K *et al*. (1999) Psychological, clinical and pathological effects of relaxation training and guided imagery during primary chemotherapy. *Br J Cancer*. **80**: 262–68.

Watkins A (ed.) (1997) *Mind–Body medicine. A clinician's guide to psychoneuroimmunology*. Churchill Livingstone, Edinburgh.

York University Centre for Health Studies (1999) *Complementary and Alternative Health Practices and Therapies: a Canadian overview*. York University Centre for Health Studies, York.

Further reading

Brandon D (1976) *Zen in the Art of Helping*. Penguin Books, Harmondsworth.

Cardinal M (1983) *The Words to Say it*. The Women's Press, London.

Downie RS (ed.) (1994) *The Healing Arts*. Oxford University Press, Oxford.

Gerber R (2000) *Vibrational Medicine for the Twenty-First Century*. Judy Piatkus, London.

Gladwell M (2000) *The Tipping Point: how little things can make a big difference*. Little, Brown and Company, London.

Goosman-Legger AI (1986) *Zone Therapy Using Foot Massage*. CW Daniel Company Ltd, Saffron Waldon.

Gordon JS and Curtin S (2000) *Comprehensive Cancer Care*. Perseus Publishing, Boston, MA.

Gould SJ (1996) *Life's Grandeur*. Jonathan Cape, London.

Le Fanu J (1999) *The Rise And Fall of Modern Medicine*. Little, Brown and Company, London.

Lessell CB (1994) *The Infinitesimal Dose*. CW Daniel Company Ltd, Saffron Walden.

Lewin R (1993) *Complexity: Life on the edge of chaos*. Phoenix, London.

Pirsig RM (1974) *Zen and the Art of Motorcycle Maintenance: an inquiry into values*. Vinatage, London.

Reid D (1996) *The Shambhala guide to Traditional Chinese Medicine*. Shambhala Publications Ltd, Boston, MA.

Root-Bernstein RM (1997) *Honey Mud Maggots and Other Medical Marvels*. Macmillan, London.

Sachs O (1985) *The Man who Mistook his Wife for a Hat*. Picador, London.

Sachs O (1990) *Awakenings*. Picador, London.

Snellgrove B (1996) *The Unseen Self*. CW Daniel Company Ltd, Saffron Walden.

Tisserand R (1988) *Aromatherapy for Everyone*. Penguin Books, Harmondsworth.

Wolpert L (1993) *The Unnatural Nature of Science*. Faber and Faber, London.

Wright R (2000) *Non-zero: the logic of human destiny*. Little, Brown and Company, London.

CHAPTER 10

Aromatherapy and community nursing: implications for educational planning

Marie Nicoll

The holistic approach of aromatherapy emphasising the interrelatedness of the mind, body and spirit ... plus the idea of giving people control over their own health ... would seem to complement many nursing theories.

(Johnson 1995, p.129)

The aim of this chapter is to evaluate the understanding and use of aromatherapy for palliative care patients by nurses in the primary care setting, and to discuss the implications that this may have in planning future education initiatives for nurses.

Learning outcomes

By the end of this chapter the reader should be able to:

- identify what evidence exists for the effectiveness of aromatherapy
- identify whether aromatherapy is a patient or nurse preference in palliative care
- identify whether patients or nurses consider aromatherapy is an appropriate therapy for nurses to practise
- identify whether nurses are sufficiently educated to practise or advise aromatherapy
- identify the education implications and training needs of nurses with regard to aromatherapy.

People are holistic beings composed of many interactive systems. The role of the nurse is to plan health interventions in partnership with the patient, by seeking to understand his or her unique characteristics and view of the world. The focus of nursing care is on helping patients to develop models of self-care in order to achieve optimal levels of holistic health via internal and external sources (Rider 2001).

The opening quote also intimates that nursing and aromatherapy share a common holistic philosophy, which may be the reason for its current popularity among nurses.

Aromatherapy is said to have been used by the ancient Egyptians. Its present-day use is attributed to Gatefosse, who found that a burn on his hand healed quickly after the application of lavender oil (Stevensen 1994). The surgeon De Valnet reputedly found essential oils to be effective alternatives to conventional medication during the Second World War (Westwood 1992). There are contrasts between the use of aromatherapy in the UK and in Europe, where it is practised by doctors who use the oils as internal medicines. In the UK, the oils are highly diluted and used externally in massage, baths or inhalations, by aromatherapists who are not generally medically qualified (Price 1998).

Definitions and claimed properties

Aromatherapy is one of the fastest growing complementary therapies, and has been defined as 'the treatment of disorders and disease using a distinctive ... smell' (Lis-Balchin 1997, p.324), 'the use of organic essences of aromatic plants for healing' (Westwood 1992, p.7) and 'the systemic use of essential oils in holistic treatments to improve physical and emotional well-being (Aromatherapy Organisations Council 1994, p.4). Aroma is not mentioned in the last definition, which indicates that the council perceives it is the absorption of the oils via the skin which is beneficial.

None of these definitions mentions clients with an impaired sense of smell, begging the question of whether aromatherapy is appropriate for those who are unable to detect aroma. This may be pertinent to cancer patients, whose sense of smell may be altered by disease or treatments.

Essential oil is 'an aromatic, volatile substance extracted from a single botanical source by distillation or expression' (Aromatherapy Organisastions Council 1994, p.4).

Authors indicate that different conditions may be addressed by aromatherapy. Stress, anxiety and pain are the most consistently mentioned. Specific properties are attributed to essential oils, some examples of which follow. All of the camomiles are said to be anti-inflammatory, calming and soothing. Many oils are claimed to have anti-depressant properties, including rose, patchouli, lavender, jasmine, basil and sandalwood. Marjoram, lavender and rosemary are said to reduce pain, and camomile, lavender, peppermint and lemon are claimed to relieve vomiting (Davis 2000). Lavender oil is said to reduce stress (Buckle 1993).

It is difficult to find irrefutable scientific evidence for claims regarding the properties of specific oils. It is not possible to check the validity of original research. Many authors make different claims for properties of the same oil, and suggest different oils for specific conditions. They do not state whether the properties depend on the differing needs of individuals, or whether several different oils may have similar effects. They make general claims, with no advice about the blending of oils tailored to individual requirements (Vickers 1997). Properties of essential oils may have been mistakenly taken from *Culpeper's Herbal*, which describes the properties of tinctures and teas – different preparations with different compositions (Lis-Balchin 1997).

Similar confusion occurs with regard to claimed adverse effects (Vickers 1997). There is disagreement about the potential toxicity of essential oils. Aromatherapy teachers tend to fall into one of two groups – those who advise that the majority of essential oils carry little risk, and those who advise extreme caution (Burfield 2000). This calls into question the credibility of claims made for properties of specific oils. In the absence of a sound scientific evidence base, how are students of aromatherapy to judge what is appropriate? This is a crucial point, as some oils may harm the fetus during pregnancy (Burfield 2000), and some may cause seizures or skin burns (Buckle 2000).

Some authors claim that the effects of essential oils may be due to associating aromas with past life events (Shenton 1996; Lis-Balchin 1997). If this is so, it is necessary to avoid scents linked with previous sad or bad issues. This may cause a 'catch-22' situation for the aromatherapist if the client is perceived to need an essential oil which has bad associations for the practitioner. Not using the oil may deprive the client of potential gain, but using it and causing the aromatherapist distress may transmit negative feelings to the client. Either of these scenarios may deprive the client of benefit.

There is a paucity of scientific evidence for the effectiveness of aromatherapy, despite much anecdotal evidence. (Stevensen 1994; Freshwater 1996; Mantle 1997; Hehir 1999), and 'the implementation of complementary medicine has occurred in response to public and professional need rather than on a basis of research evidence of effectiveness' (Stone 1999, p.47).

'Clients and practitioners of aromatherapy perceive it to be effective, but physicians are often sceptical' (Cooke and Ernst 2000, p.493). This appears to be due to the lack of scientific data pertaining to properties of essential oils. Doyle (1996, p.86) recognises that there are benefits for patients in having previously unmet needs addressed, but he:

> looks forward to seeing the results of controlled studies which clearly demonstrate that benefit is related to the specific aroma and not the understandable comfort of a caring, gentle person devoting so much time to the patient as an aromatherapist always does.

More research is needed, especially with regard to the effects of specific oils, possibly by inhalation, or by using impregnated adhesive patches to eliminate massage as a variable (Mackereth 1995). However, there are inherent difficulties when conducting double-blind trials when different odours are used, and individual clients need a unique blend of oils, which may differ each time they are treated because of changes in their health status (Lis-Balchin 1997, p.324).

In order for research to be valid, studies must be undertaken on a large sample of recipients. This appears to be a stumbling block for many of those who undertake research into aromatherapy, because of resource implications. Research into pharmacological products is generally sponsored or undertaken by large drug companies, but it is debatable whether they will support or undertake research into aromatherapy, which may provide an effective and cheaper alternative to their own product. 'Clearly there is a need for good-quality studies exercising imagination and commitment, but these require a higher level of funding and expertise than seems to be available' (Kohn 1999, p.10). Studies to date appear to be too small to be conclusive, although patients have indicated that the use of aromatherapy helps to reduce anxiety and tension (Tavares 2003).

Cooke and Ernst (2000) undertook a literature search of randomised controlled trials involving massage. All of them were small and appeared to have methodological flaws. For example, in those studies which used unscented oil for the control group it would have been virtually impossible to mask the fact that essential oil was not being used, because of the absence of aroma. Although all of the studies found aromatherapy to be more effective in treating anxiety than the controls, the effects were transient. However, this does not necessarily indicate that the effect of aromatherapy is any different from conventional treatments. Most prescribed drugs have to be taken at regular intervals in order to maintain their effectiveness, because they are continually excreted from the body.

Small studies undertaken by Dunwoody et al. (2002) and Wilkinson (1995) suggested that massage performed by nurses qualified in aromatherapy enhanced quality of life in palliative care patients. Touch or massage may be components of aromatherapy, and contribute to reduced anxiety and the promotion of well-being (Turton 1989; MacGuire 1991, Sayre-Adams and Wright 1995; Wilkinson 1995; Dunwoody et al. 2002).

Essential oils have been used instead of conventional medication. Gravett (2000) describes a clinical trial of conventional mouthwash compared with chamomile in 164 patients with oral mucositis caused by chemotherapy. No difference in effectiveness was demonstrated, but because the chamomile was preferred by patients, and was also cheaper, it has now been adopted as standard treatment.

Many authors question whether conventional methods of research can be relevant to this topic (Osborne 1994; Bay 1995; Bell and Sikora 1996). However, in the absence of alternative methods, the author questions how this therapy will ever gain credibility.

Aromatherapy and nursing practice

Nurses are increasingly interested in incorporating some form of complementary therapy into their practice. 'Aromatherapy has done an excellent marketing job.... Is it the therapeutic claims or alluring smells ... that draw them in droves?' (Mackereth 1995, p.4)

Among nurses surveyed who had not yet used any complementary therapies,

92% would be prepared to do so in the future (Trevelyan 1996, p.42). This raises concerns about the appropriateness of their use. Nurses have a duty of care to patients: '... nurses must be able to support their actions with reference to relevant research findings ...' (Norton 1995, p.346).

Stone (1999) asks how nurses can be sure that the complementary therapies they are offering are providing benefit without evidence. This highlights the need for education and training in these aspects prior to integrating the therapies into nursing practice.

Mackereth urges caution, suggesting that 'Nurses need to think about how flexible a therapy is and not be immediately drawn to a fashionable well-packaged product which ... is complex, may have emotional and physical effects and could interact with conventional drug therapy regimes' (Mackereth 1995, p.6).

The literature indicates that nurses may be interested in complementary therapies because of increased job satisfaction because they perceive patients to benefit from them, in addition to a personal preference for hands-on nursing. However, it is necessary for nurses to provide evidence for using aromatherapy in the client's best interest. Stone (1999) comments on the need to discuss the appropriateness of its use with other members of the healthcare team, and Norton confirms the need for discourse with medical practitioners, commenting that 'the British Complementary Medicine Association (1992) states unequivocally in its Code of Conduct that "Practitioners must not countermand instructions or prescriptions given by a doctor"' (Norton 1995, p.345).

In May 2003, national guidelines for the use of complementary therapies in supportive and palliative care were published by the National Council for Hospice and Specialist Palliative Care Services. These are included as part of the National Institute for Clinical Excellence (NICE) guidance on improving supportive and palliative care for adults with cancer. The guidelines incorporate education and training, quality and accountability via the clinical governance framework. It is essential that nurses follow these guidelines in order to ensure accountability for high standards of appropriate care (Tavares 2003).

Avis (1999) suggests that the public perceives aromatherapy oils as a harmless luxury. Aromatherapy seems to be increasingly popular with patients, and is used in many palliative care settings, with nurses and patients alike attesting to its effectiveness in reducing symptoms and enhancing quality of life (Norton 1995; Stevensen 1997). Aromatherapy is therefore a therapy favoured by patients and nurses, with both groups appearing to believe that it is appropriate for nurses to practise. However, some authors question whether this is appropriate in the absence of scientific proof (Mackereth 1995; Stone 1999; Johnson 2000). This raises a number of salient points:

- If a nurse suggests aromatherapy, the fact that she is a trained professional may validate the treatment to the patient.
- Nurses may or may not have the knowledge necessary to discuss the appropriateness of aromatherapy.
- Perhaps, for palliative care patients, the issues regarding how aromatherapy

works are less important than whether it is effective in improving quality of life. As Tattam (1992, p.17), quoting Denton, states: 'If we have accepted that pain is what the patient says it is, then why can't we accept that well-being is what the patient says it is?'.

- Community nurses with limited knowledge of this topic may be unaware of their own limitations regarding the appropriateness of its use, potential side-effects, or interactions with conventional cancer and palliative care treatments.

A two-phase study undertaken by this author aimed to identify community nurse knowledge and understanding of palliative care and aromatherapy, while at the same time identifying nursing opinions on aromatherapy. The second phase aimed to elicit from patients whether they had any knowledge or experience of aromatherapy, whether it had been recommended, and if so, by whom.

Research method

Survey methodology was used to elicit quantitative and qualitative data from community nurses and patients in the author's locality.

In this study, the majority of nurses who returned the questionnaire reported that they would consider suggesting aromatherapy to palliative care patients, thus confirming views indicated in the literature that this form of therapy is popular among nurses.

The majority of nurses were unable to give a complete definition of palliative care or aromatherapy. This observation indicates the need for education and training, and supports the recent Government initiative with regard to training in palliative care for district and community nurses (NHS Executive 2001).

Patients were unable to fully define aromatherapy, but the majority indicated that it may be of benefit.

The most popular reasons for nurses suggesting aromatherapy massage were touch and symptom control, confirming indications in the literature. It would have been valuable to follow up the nurses' questionnaire with interviews in order to establish specifically why nurses perceived touch to be important. However, informal discussion appeared to confirm that they felt touch was beneficial in communicating with patients, because it conveyed empathy and support.

Some patients indicated that touch was important in aromatherapy, although it appeared that they appreciated the physical effect of touch on tired muscles more than well-being engendered by the sense of being touched. This may be comparatively new data, which contradicts nursing assumptions that it is the concerned touch of another which is beneficial. It would be interesting to conduct further studies of patients' views on therapies that incorporate touch, in order to ascertain their opinions and needs.

The results of the study indicated that the majority of community nurses would suggest an oil burner to a palliative care patient. The reasons given pertained mainly to masking of unpleasant odours. Half of the patients suggested that oil burners were beneficial, but the main reason cited was to aid relaxation, although a significant minority mentioned pleasant odour as a benefit. The opinions of nurses and patients clearly differed here.

Patients were asked to indicate where they had first heard about aromatherapy. The majority stated that it was from a nurse. This observation appears to show that some nurses in this area may be promoting aromatherapy to palliative care patients, even though the majority of them are not trained in its use, few can fully define it, and only one could fully define palliative care. It appears that nurses' attitudes may be influencing patients to use aromatherapy, because if the suggestion comes from a health professional, it may be perceived as being validated by someone who has appropriate knowledge, skills and training. The evidence in this study clearly indicates that the nurses who responded do not have such abilities. It is therefore necessary to consider in what ways nurses' knowledge may be enhanced by the development of appropriate education.

Education and training implications

Nursing training and practice have changed dramatically over the past two decades. Previously, nurses were indoctrinated into being obedient to traditional practices, whereas now they are encouraged to be proactive agents for change. There is a recognised need for qualified nurses to ensure that they pursue a path of lifelong learning, as exemplified by Post Registration Education Preparation (PREPP) (United Kingdom Central Council for Nursing and Midwifery 1992) and clinical governance (Department of Health 1999). Among qualified nurses there is now a complex mixture of attitudes, knowledge, skills and training requirements, with some nurses clinging to the security of traditional roles, others rushing to embrace new opportunities for development, and the majority fitting somewhere along the trajectory between these two extremes.

It is vital that the patient remains central within this maelstrom of differences, wherever he or she is nursed. Palliative care is concerned with quality of life, and many patients seek strategies for coping and therapies that claim to increase feelings of well-being. Kenny (2003) states that 'The ultimate goal of palliative care education must be to influence, improve or change practice so that it benefits patients and their families'. For many patients, most of their palliative care takes place in the community setting, and their key worker is a member of the district nursing team. Community nurses should therefore have a basic knowledge of aromatherapy because it is growing in popularity and patients are likely to request information in order to help them to make informed choices about treatment and coping strategies, as making a positive choice about health can be a self-empowering process' (Ewles and Simnet 1992, p.159). Self-empowerment is an important concept in healthcare, as health is a matter of conjecture – individuals' opinions about the nature of health differ, and they may wish to make their own decisions regarding health and life (Coutts and Hardy 1985). It could be argued that self-empowerment is even more vital in palliative care, as these patients often experience a series of losses and decreasing empowerment due to disease progression.

Having thus established that community nurses should have at least a basic knowledge of aromatherapy, it is necessary to assess what should be taken into consideration when creating a framework for education.

The student should have an awareness of national guidelines, which have been explored in more detail in Chapter 1. Those relevant to this chapter include clinical governance, National Institute for Clinical Excellence guidelines and evidence-based practice.

Clinical governance (Department of Health 1999)

This is the framework by which quality of services and outcomes is improved, in order to address patient safety.

National Institute for Clinical Excellence (NICE)

This is the body that makes recommendations regarding service provision by identifying quality models of care. In palliative care, this includes guidelines on training and qualifications.

Evidence-based practice

It is recognised that the absence of evidence with regard to complementary therapies does not necessarily indicate that they are ineffective. Practitioners should 'integrate the best external evidence with individual clinical expertise and the patient's choice' (Tavares 2003, p.12).

Professional and ethical issues

These include professional accountability, consent and confidentiality, all of which pertain to protecting the client by promoting the best possible standards of confidential care, which the client understands and agrees to (Tavares 2003).

Education should also incorporate local policies, procedures and standards. In their absence, students should be aware of those of other organisations, in order to become catalysts for the development of policies in their own localities.

Aromatherapy is popular among palliative care patients, who may request information from nurses. It is therefore necessary to find appropriate ways of educating nurses about the ways in which aromatherapy may be pertinent to patients – this applies to all nurses, whatever their previous training, education and experience. It has been indicated that traditional research methods may not be appropriate to aromatherapy, and it could be argued that traditional methods of teaching may not be appropriate either. We routinely apply the term 'holistic' to nursing and aromatherapy. Perhaps we should now consider applying it to methods of teaching nurses about aromatherapy – in allowing that the patient is a unique being, with individual characteristics and needs, it would appear only fair to acknowledge that the student is equally distinctive.

Each nurse is individual, with unique personality traits, life experience and professional knowledge, skills and attitudes. In order to optimise their learning, it is necessary to acknowledge their uniqueness, and to begin by an assessment of their needs, in order to tailor education to their individual requirements with regard to aromatherapy. This could be undertaken individually by the nurse. However, the potential problem of the nurse assessing their own needs is that they may not be aware of what they do not know. Education-profiling sessions specific to aromatherapy and its relevance in palliative care, undertaken in a supportive and non-threatening arena and facilitated by an appropriate person, may allow the nurse to explore more fully gaps in their knowledge and ways of addressing them. It is necessary to involve students in planning their own education (Kenny 2003). It may be that conventional methods of learning are appropriate for the individual (e.g. lectures, seminars, etc. in a traditional area of learning such as a university), or it may be more appropriate to explore more innovative approaches.

It has been suggested that palliative care education should be provided and mentored in those areas where the care is given, by appropriately experienced and qualified professionals (Kenny 2003). This appears to intimate that it is appropriate for clinical nurse specialists to include such provision within their role. If so, it is necessary for such professionals to ensure that they are both educated to an appropriate standard in the area of aromatherapy and skilled in the provision of education, in order to identify and address the needs of specific individuals. This would allow them to begin a process of cascading information down to other nurses.

The field of aromatherapy abounds with claims about the properties of oils which cannot be substantiated scientifically, and if the nurse accepts them all at face value, they will not be in a position to give patients factual information. Nurses are responsible for their own actions, and must ensure that their knowledge base is sound and up to date. It is thus necessary for them to develop a critical attitude to research, and in order to give objective information, nurses need to be taught how to critique aromatherapy literature. Articles must be critically analysed in order to differentiate between 'good' and 'bad' aromatherapy research. Journal clubs are unthreatening ways in which a group may learn to critique aromatherapy articles. The group agrees on a topic, one or two individuals collect pertinent data, and the group discusses whether it is sound, guided by a facilitator who is familiar with the analysis of research.

Aromatherapy courses may encourage continuing education via aromatherapy interest groups. These can be run at dates and times that are suitable for specific communities of nurses – the group identifies its own needs and learning objectives. The chairperson can provide outside speakers or education as appropriate.

It is vital that nurses are honest with patients with regard to the lack of scientific evidence for aromatherapy. However, it may be necessary to educate nurses that aromatherapy can be a valuable therapy for certain patients. As far as quality of life and well-being are concerned, anecdotal evidence and audit of practices appear to show that many palliative care patients derive much benefit from this therapy. Therefore, it is necessary for nurses to be given opportunities to explore possible outcomes of aromatherapy, and to identify its relevance in palliative care. To this end, teaching should link aromatherapy with ethics, particularly the ethical principles of autonomy and beneficence. For this purpose, group discussion would appear to be an appropriate medium, with each individual being encouraged to contribute valuable personal and professional experience, perspectives and insight.

Debate is another valuable learning medium, with volunteers arguing for and against the therapy, a group discussion, and a final vote as to its value. However, it is necessary for an experienced facilitator to lead the debate in order to ensure equity and order.

Lectures by aromatherapy practitioners may be of value, although this may be tempered by the fact that they are prejudiced in favour of their own subject! Nevertheless, for those unfamiliar with the topic, this may be a useful introduction and an opportunity to try for themselves some products and techniques.

It has become clear that the challenge for educators is to demonstrate to nurses the need to strike a balance between how the patient says he or she feels and the professional security of a scientific evidence base. It is necessary for nurses to adhere to both local and national policies, but it is also essential that we hear what patients are saying. We must teach nurses to reflect on which is most important – why a therapy works or whether it is effective in addressing the patient's problems. It appears that the core of this issue is the essence of good-quality nursing, namely communication. If we are truly hearing what the patient is saying, and empowering them to make their own decisions, we must respond to their request for information about aromatherapy with honesty. It may be necessary to state that scientific evidence for this therapy is unsubstantiated, but we have been told by other patients that it helps. In the author's experience, patients do not expect us to have all the answers, but they do expect and deserve honesty.

Key points to consider
- *Finances.* The provision of education that is specifically tailored to aromatherapy, or to complementary therapies in general, may not be a priority either nationally or locally. Funding for specific education initiatives may not therefore be available, and it may be necessary to discover economical and innovative ways of teaching aromatherapy, such as nursing special interest or 'link' groups, cascading information, or exploring the use of endowment funds to provide teaching packs specific to this topic. Provision would have to be made for the reviewing of such packs annually, because of the need for a continually updated evidence base.
- *Ethical issues.* Apart from those discussed earlier in this chapter, it is also

necessary to take into account potential financial considerations for patients. Informal enquiry by the author has revealed that a one-hour aromatherapy session may cost around £30. If a nurse suggests that a patient may benefit from aromatherapy, and it is not provided locally free of charge or for a nominal fee, the patient may spend a considerable amount of money for a course of treatment which they may eventually perceive to have been of little benefit.

- *Who should teach aromatherapy to nurses?* Several organisations offer training in complementary therapy for potential therapists (Tavares 2003), but there do not appear to be specific guidelines regarding who should provide training about aromatherapy for those who wish to learn about the topic but do not intend to practise it. As mentioned earlier in this chapter, the problem with aromatherapists teaching nurses is that they may be prejudiced in favour of the effectiveness of their own therapy. The challenge is to find someone who is a skilled educator, is able to address the training needs of individual nurses, has a contemporary evidence base and has an unprejudiced viewpoint.

- *Public education and aromatherapy.* The public is bombarded with advertisements for aromatherapy products. The author has observed that there is a plethora of toiletries and household products bearing the discription 'aromatherapy', and the media appears to abound with stories of its effectiveness. It is therefore necessary to consider who should undertake public education with regard to aromatherapy. It may be seen as an appropriate task for those nurses who work in a health promotional role, such as health visitors. In this case, the same challenges would apply as for teaching nurses.

Conclusion

A high proportion of the literature questions the advisability of including aromatherapy in nursing practice. However, the majority of the nurses who responded to the survey viewed aromatherapy as an appropriate adjunct. Most would consider training in the future, and would use aromatherapy professionally as nurses. Further research is necessary to determine whether the local gaps in knowledge regarding aromatherapy are typical of the wider nursing community. Nursing journals abound with articles hailing its effectiveness, and it is used in many nursing and palliative care settings. In this rapidly changing nursing climate, when many traditional nursing tasks which may have provided hands-on, patient-centred job satisfaction are being delegated to other care providers, aromatherapy may provide a perceived 'safe haven' for qualified nurses to return to hands-on care. If they do so, it will be necessary to provide evidence for advising the use of or providing aromatherapy, to obtain recognised qualifications and registration and to adhere to national and local guidelines, in order to protect both patients and themselves.

As far as evidence is concerned, it is debatable whether the abundance of anecdotes about the effectiveness of aromatherapy can be cited as justification for its use, in the absence of scientific proof. Palliative care patients may clutch at straws with regard to any claims which may be made by the ignorant or unscrupulous, in an attempt to heal the spirit even if the body is beyond help. Nurses have a responsibility to offer all patients the highest standards of care via evidence-based practice. The difficulty in addressing aromatherapy is that the evidence does not appear to be irrefutable. If a patient requests treatment or asks for information, the nurse must be honest about this evidence and its limitations, and must ensure that their information is updated appropriately. Thus the nurse will be acting in a professionally responsible manner and retaining the holistic nature of his or her role by allowing the patient to be in control, and the patient will be in a position to make their own informed choices, in order to develop their own unique model of care which is responsive to individual needs.

Education for nurses regarding aromatherapy should therefore incorporate the same degree of honesty, in order to allow nurses to make appropriately informed choices about their practice.

Implications for the reader's own practice
1 How would you ensure that your knowledge of aromatherapy is relevant and up to date?
2 What are the implications for public education in empowering patients to ask the right questions?
3 How and when would you deem yourself or another professional competent to teach this topic?
4 What aspects of this topic would you consider essential when putting together a teaching pack?
5 How would you motivate colleagues to value the need for increased education in aromatherapy?

References

Aromatherapy Organisations Council (1994) *General Information Booklet*. Aromatherapy Organisations Council, London.

Avis A (1999) When is an aromatherapist not an aromatherapist? *Compl Ther Med*. 7: 116–18.

Bay F (1995) Complementary therapies – just another task? *Compl Ther Nurs Midwifery*. 1: 34–6.

Bell L and Sikora K (1996) Complementary therapies in cancer care. *Compl Ther Nurs Midwifery*. 2: 57–8.

Buckle J (1993) Aromatherapy. Does it matter which lavender essential oil is used? *Nurs Times*. 89: 32–5.

Buckle J (2000) Risk management. *Int J Aromather*. 10: 30–36.

Burfield T (2000) Safety of essential oils. *Int J Aromather*. **10**: 16–29.

Cooke B and Ernst E (2000) Aromatherapy: a systematic review. *Br J Gen Pract*. **50**: 493–96.

Coutts LC and Hardy LK (1985) *Teaching for Health*. Churchill Livingstone, London.

Davis P (2000) *Aromatherapy: an A–Z*. The CW Daniel Company, Saffron Walden.

Department of Health (1999) *Clinical Governance: quality in the new NHS*. NHS Executive, Leeds.

Doyle D (1996) *Domiciliary Palliative Care*. Oxford University Press, Oxford.

Dunwoody L, Smyth A and Davidson R (2002) Cancer patients' experiences and evaluations of aromatherapy massage in palliative care. *Int J Palliat Nurs*. **10**: 497–504.

Ewles L and Simnet I (1992) *Promoting Health: a practical guide*. Scutari, London.

Freshwater D (1996) Complementary therapies and research in nursing practice. *Nurs Standard*. **10**: 43–5.

Gravett P (2000) Aromatherapy treatment of severe oral mucositis. *Int J Aromather*. **10**: 52–3.

Hehir B (1999) Opiate of the people. *Nurs Times*. **95**: 32.

Johnson G (1995) *Complementary therapies in nursing*. Implications for practice using aromatherapy as an example. *Compl Ther Nurs Midwifery*. **1**: 128–32.

Johnson G (2000) Should nurses practice complementary therapies? *Compl Ther Nurs Midwifery*. **6**: 120–23.

Kenny LJ (2003) An evaluation-based model for palliative care education: making a difference to practice. *Int J Palliat Nurs*. **5**: 189–94.

Kohn M (1999) *Complementary therapies in cancer care*. MacMillan, London.

Lis-Balchin M (1997) Essential oils and 'aromatherapy': their modern role in healing. *J R Soc Health*. **117**: 324–9.

MacGuire J (1991) Tailoring research for advanced nursing practice. In: R McMahon and R Pearson (eds) *Nursing as Therapy*. Chapman & Hall, London.

Mackereth P (1995) Aromatherapy – nice but not essential. *Compl Ther Nurs Midwifery*. **1**: 4–7.

Mantle F (1997) Implementing evidence in practice. *Br J Commun Health Nurs*. **2**: 36–39.

NHS Executive (2001) www.doh.gov.uk/cancer/edsup.htm.

Norton L (1995) Complementary therapies in practice: the ethical issues. *J Clin Nurs*. **4**: 343–8.

Osborne S (1994) *The future of homeopathy and other complementary therapies as part of the British NHS*. Guest editorial. *J Adv Nurs*. **20**: 583–4.

Price S (1998) Using essential oils in professional practice. *Compl Ther Nurs Midwifery*. **4**: 144–7.

Rider P (2001) www.nur.utexas.edu/Rider/nursing/sld080.htm

Sayre-Adams J and Wright S (1995) Change in consciousness. *Nurs Times*. **91**: 44–5.

Shenton D (1996) Does aromatherapy provide an holistic approach to palliative care? *Int J Palliat Nurs*. **2**: 187–91.

Stevensen C (1994) Aromatherapy: the essentials. RCN Nursing Update Learning Unit 050. *Nurs Standard*. **9**: 1–15.

Stevensen C (1997) Complementary therapies and their role in nursing care. *Nurs Standard*. **11**: 49–53.

Stone J (1999) Using complementary therapies within nursing: some ethical and legal considerations. *Compl Ther Nurs Midwifery*. **5**: 46–50.

Tattam A (1992) The gentle touch. *Nurs Times*. **5**: 16–17.

Tavares M (2003) *National Guidelines for the Use of Complementary Therapies in Supportive and Palliative Care*. The Prince of Wales Foundation for Integrated Health, London.

Trevelyan J (1996) A true complement? *Nurs Times*. **92**: 42–3.

Turton P (1989) Touch me, feel me, heal me. *Nurs Times*. **85**: 42–4.

United Kingdom Central Council for Nursing and Midwifery (UKCC) (1992) *Code of Professional Conduct*. UKCC, London.

Vickers A (1997) Yes, but how do we know it's true? Knowledge claims in massage and aromatherapy. *Compl Ther Nurs Midwifery*. **3**: 63–5.

Westwood C (1992) *Aromatherapy. A guide for home use*. Amberwood Publishing, Rochester.

Wilkinson S (1995) Aromatherapy and massage in palliative care. *Int J Palliat Nurs*. **1**: 21–30.

CHAPTER 11

Palliative care education: establishing the evidence base

Vanessa Taylor

... increasingly, human service programmes are requested to be more accountable for the resources they consume. Those directing educational, medical and social programmes are being asked to document what they are doing and the impact of their efforts on people. Failure to take accountability seriously can have deleterious consequences on future funding.

(Kreuger 1994, p.4)

Palliative care education is delivered by a range of providers in a variety of settings, from higher education institutions and specialist palliative care services within hospital and community settings to uni- and multi-professional audiences. Education provision may include higher education accredited undergraduate and post-graduate modules and programmes, as well as non-accredited study days and short courses. Kreuger's (1994) stark statement quoted above serves as a reminder to healthcare professionals and education providers that they are accountable for the resources they use, with a requirement to justify their actions and demonstrate an evidence base for their care and service provision. This chapter aims to identify the need for evaluation of palliative care education, and to discuss how evaluation of palliative care education has developed in meeting the demands of stakeholders for evidence-based practice. The discussion will initially explore the context of education provision delivered by higher education institutions and specialist palliative care services. Subsequently, the theory of evaluation research will be discussed. The extent to which the evaluation of palliative care education has been developed will be explored alongside issues for consideration when planning and undertaking evaluation research in this field.

Learning outcomes
By the end of this chapter the reader should be able to:
- examine the need for evaluation of palliative care education
- explore the theory of educational evaluation research
- discuss how evaluation of palliative care education has developed and identify issues for consideration when planning and undertaking evaluation research in this field.

The need for evaluation of palliative care education

The provision of palliative care is evolving. While developing outside the mainstream of healthcare provision, often in charitable organisations, palliative care is re-emerging as an integrated part of mainstream healthcare (National Council for Hospice and Specialist Palliative Care Services (NCHSPCS) 1996; Llamas *et al.* 2001) influenced by healthcare policy (Clark *et al.* 1997). Recent Government policy within the UK supports the broadening of palliative care provision to include patients with palliative care needs from a diagnosis of cancer onward and those diagnosed with life-limiting illnesses (Department of Health 2000; NCHSPCS 2002). In order to meet the needs of patients and their families, palliative care service provision has therefore been defined as either general or specialist (NCHSPCS 2002). General palliative care services are delivered by the usual professional carers of the patient and their family, with low to moderate complexity of palliative care need. In contrast, specialist palliative care services are provided by multi-professional teams specialising in the provision of palliative care to patients and their families with moderate to high complexity of palliative care need (NCHSPCS 2002). This model of service delivery requires all health professionals to have, as a minimum, access to appropriate education in the basic principles and practice of palliative care, skills in assessing the palliative care needs of patients and their families, and training in communication skills (NCHSPCS 2002). This suggests that education providers need to question and evaluate the model of education used, and the strategies for teaching and learning adopted in the development and delivery of palliative care education, in order to ensure and demonstrate the 'appropriateness' of any education provision.

Many qualified healthcare professionals have had a limited introduction to the principles of palliative care. The demand for palliative care education – be it study days or academically accredited programmes – has mushroomed from the 1990s onwards (House of Lords 1994; NCHSPCS 1996, p.6), and is likely to increase as the application of palliative care to non-cancer patients is recognised (Lloyd-Williams and Field 2002). Lifelong learning for healthcare professionals is therefore viewed as an investment in quality by a Government that spends significant sums of money each year supporting training and education for clinical staff (Department of Health 1998, 2001). For this investment in the NHS workforce, however, the Government is committed to ensuring that this leads to the delivery of the best, most effective care for patients (Department of Health 1998). The NHS is therefore accountable for the resources and monies provided, and in turn education providers face demands from purchasers to demonstrate the value and effectiveness of their education provision in supporting the delivery of evidence-based care for patients, thereby influencing the need for evaluation of education provision.

Furthermore, for palliative care education providers within specialist services, Government reforms have also meant that palliative care services have had to justify their existence in more than purely humanitarian terms (Clark *et al.* 1997). Specialist palliative services have faced demands from a range of external and internal stakeholders to demonstrate the effectiveness of the specialty through evaluation of aspects of patient care, service organisation, service delivery and policy, as well as educational provision (Robbins 1998). External stakeholders may include service users, healthcare commissioning agencies and regulatory bodies. Internal stakeholders may include lecturers, administrators, trustees and managers of the providing institution in order to justify the use of resources away from direct patient care.

Equally, within the higher education arena, a growth in demand for educational evaluation has emerged because of the requirement for institutional autonomy and public accountability as publicly funded services have been placed within a framework reminiscent of profit-making businesses (Robson 1993, p.171; Brindley *et al.* 1998, p.97). Higher education institutions are expected to demonstrate their value to a variety of stakeholders, based on a diverse set of criteria that include research achievement, service to local communities, promotion of lifelong learning and preparation of large and diverse student populations for labour markets characterised by change, uncertainty and high expectation of performance (Henkel 1998, p.291). Within healthcare education, legislative and professional policies have created a market-led approach to the development and delivery of pre- and post-registration, undergraduate and postgraduate professional courses. This market for education has emphasised the demand for evaluation studies in an attempt to demonstrate the effectiveness of such education for improving patient care as well as continuing professional development. Each stakeholder has their own specific expectations and criteria on which to judge the educational provision, and therefore the opportunity to exercise power over educational processes at a variety of levels (Ashcroft and Palacio 1996, p.93). The varying requirements of particular stakeholders appear to have fuelled an increasing need for educational evaluation.

It may be argued, therefore, that there are demands for an evidence base for the development, delivery and outcomes of palliative care education which are present for education providers within both higher Education and specialist palliative care services. These demands may be as a result of external and internal stakeholders as well as to satisfy the curiosity of individual lecturers. However, it appears that the evaluation of palliative care education for participants and the subsequent care of patients have remained either relatively unexplored or under-reported within the literature (Robbins 1998; Langton *et al.* 1999).

The theory of educational evaluation

Evaluation research is described as applied research that is designed to answer questions about the functioning or impact of services, policy or programmes (Robbins 1998, p.3; Robson 1993, p.171). It is about using the tools and techniques developed in basic research and applying them to questions of need, effectiveness, efficiency, appropriateness and acceptability (Robbins 1998, p.3). This contrasts with traditional research studies where the aim of the researcher is to understand the phenomena under investigation and draw conclusions about it (Popham 1988, p.11), and reveals the undercurrent of power as well as accountability for evaluators. The survival of institutions and individuals may be affected by evaluators who act as gatekeepers, controlling access to information and deciding which information will be gathered, how it will be processed and which parts to report (Nisbet 1987, p.50). The findings of evaluation studies may also be ignored or manipulated for political means in any decision-making process by stakeholders if studies do not support the desired direction (Ashcroft and Palacio 1996, p.105). This may adversely affect the integrity and influence of such studies. Robson (1993, p.180) therefore asserts that evaluations are to be avoided unless one has a good chance of doing them properly. The term 'properly' is defined using four criteria which should be satisfied before the researcher commits him- or herself to undertaking evaluation. The criteria include a consideration of the utility or usefulness of the study and ensuring that it is feasible to conduct within the political and practical milieux. Furthermore, Robson reinforces the point that evaluators should be satisfied that the study can be undertaken with propriety and technical adequacy (Robson 1993, p.181). It appears therefore that evaluation studies for educators may pose problems both politically and methodologically, which may limit the extent to which such research is undertaken beyond that which is deemed 'essential' to secure future funding.

The literature is replete with definitions and models of educational evaluation that vary in the level of abstraction, scope of purpose and methodological approaches. Suchman (1967, cited in Robson 1993, p.175), in a somewhat dated definition, defined evaluation as 'a method for determining the degree to which a planned programme achieves its desired objective'. More recently, Holzemer (1980, p.33) defined evaluation as a process of description and judgement conducted for the purposes of determining programme effectiveness and improving the programme itself. Furthermore, Melrose (1998, p.37) suggested that curriculum evaluation is a process by which a judgement is made about the worth or merit of a curriculum or its appropriateness for the individual, group, organisation offering it or society within which it operates.

These authors concur in defining a limited purpose for evaluation studies concerned primarily with the evaluation of curricula or programmes. In addition, the role of educational evaluation to enable decision making aimed at the development of better policies and practices in education is reinforced (Wolf 1990, p.5). These definitions also reveal subtle differences. Suchman's definition focuses on the extent to which predetermined objectives have been achieved, and this definition is considered to neglect any unanticipated or unplanned outcomes (Robson 1993, p.175). In contrast, Holzemer and Melrose seem to embrace the potential for both anticipated and unplanned consequences within their definitions. Furthermore, Suchman and Holzemer appear to suggest that such programme or curriculum evaluation studies may be undertaken primarily to serve the interests of individual lecturers or course teams in determining the outcomes of programmes. However, Melrose highlights the potential for broader interest in such studies by not only the individual and the organisation delivering it, but also the society in which such learning is applied. Finally, although each author reinforces the importance of evaluating the outcome of any education provision, Holzemer also considers the use of evaluation studies for the purposes of improvement. It appears therefore that educational evaluation may be either formative in approach (where the intention is to identify ways to improve programmes) or summative (where the aim is to assess the merits of a programme) (Scriven 1967). However, the distinction between the two approaches may not be so clear-cut, since a formative evaluation may have summative elements, and a summative evaluation can have formative effects on the future developments of a programme.

A distinction is often made between outcome and process evaluation (Robson 1993, p.179). Outcome evaluation represents the traditional view of evaluation focused on measuring to what extent a programme, practice or policy meets its stated objectives. Process evaluation, in contrast, is concerned with studying what actually occurs in the practice or programme that is being evaluated (Robson 1993, p.180), and would therefore constitute an important aspect of both summative and formative approaches (Robbins 1998, p.7). An emphasis on the impact or outcome of a programme, in terms of the extent to which it has achieved its objectives, is considered to provide an impoverished account of the overall impact of the programme in relation to both its intended and unintended consequences (Robbins 1998, p.7). Nevertheless, some stakeholders may only be interested in the evaluation of anticipated outcomes of programmes for decision-making purposes. This reveals the potential tension between evaluators and stakeholders/commissioners in education evaluation. Educational evaluation, it appears, may be a compromise that requires researchers to recognise the opportunities which will be forgone if a particular design is adopted.

The scope of educational evaluation may also extend beyond programme or curriculum evaluation. Evaluation studies may be used for the purposes of assessing the effects and effectiveness of educational policy, practice or service (Robson 1993, p.170). This highlights the wider scope for investigation and the range of perspectives that are open to evaluators. Patton (1982, cited in Robson 1993, p.175), for example, views evaluation studies more broadly and defines evaluation as involving the systematic collection of information about the activities, characteristics and outcomes of programmes, personnel and products for use by specific people to reduce uncertainties, improve effectiveness and make decisions. This definition reinforces the need for information to be collected systematically, and concurs with the view of the authors above that evaluation studies may be used to aid decision making (Robson 1993, p.175).

The field of evaluation is therefore extremely wide and varied, since evaluations are carried out for a number of purposes. There have been several attempts to categorise the different kinds of evaluations. Stecher and Davies (1987) set out one framework of different approaches to evaluation, which can be summarised as follows.

1   The experimental approach seeks to apply the principles of experimental science with the aim of producing generalisable conclusions about the outcome of a particular service through the control of variables and simplification of the question under scrutiny (Stecher and Davies 1987). Traditional approaches to educational evaluation have tended to follow experimental and psychometric traditions utilising pre- and post-intervention structured questionnaires as methods of data collection. However, these are considered to be artificial and limited in scope (Parlett and Hamilton 1987, p.57), as awareness of the instability and the complexity of individual and social interaction in education and social services has undermined the claims of the experimental model. Experimental evaluators have been criticised for over-emphasising outcome measurement and underestimating the importance of description and the relationship between inputs, process, context and outcome (Henkel 1998, p.286).

2   The goal-oriented approach aims to investigate the success of a service or programme in meeting specific goals and objectives that have been set (Stecher and Davies 1987). This approach reflects the above definition by Suchman, which focuses on the degree to which a planned programme achieves its objectives.

3   The decision-making approach focuses on the most relevant information that can be used for making decisions about the management and operation of services or programmes (Stecher and Davies 1987).

4   The user-oriented approach focuses on the participation of service providers in the evaluation to increase the likelihood that the evaluation studies' findings will be acted upon and used. This approach may be referred to as 'stakeholder' evaluation, and because the user is involved, study findings are more likely to be actioned. However, studies may be subject to manipulation and redirection (Stecher and Davies 1987).

5   The responsive approach to evaluation attempts to understand an issue from as many different viewpoints as possible using naturalistic methods (mainly observation and interviewing). The strengths of this approach lie in its capacity to identify problems, particularly those that had not been anticipated. Its weakness lies in the difficulty of simplifying information for decision-making purposes (Stecher and Davies 1987).

The framework by Stecher and Davies (1987) is helpful for revealing the different research approaches and methods of data collection which may be used for evaluation studies, and suggests that a range of ideologies, or sets of beliefs, may be accommodated when undertaking such studies. Researchers, it seems, need to ensure that the underlying beliefs and values of the model of evaluation should match those on which the programme was developed. However, as was highlighted above, the demands of stakeholders may also influence the evaluation approach adopted. With regard to palliative care education, educators may be particularly interested in goal-oriented and responsive approaches to evaluation, utilising qualitative methods of data collection to explore the experiences and outcomes of education from the participants' perspective. In contrast, external stakeholders may adopt a decision-making approach requiring methods of data collection that generate numerical data, thus raising questions about whether both sets of needs can be accommodated within one study or whether the needs of one group take priority.

In summary, the above definitions and discussion reveal the potential scope of educational evaluation, ranging from programme to policies and services. It appears that the need to adopt a systematic approach, interpret the findings and make a judgement to aid decision making emerge as key features for evaluators. Structured approaches to evaluation are regarded as more rigorous and more relevant to today's climate of accountability within higher education and clinical services, compared with incidental evidence brought together to confirm a hunch (Ashcroft and Palacio 1996, p.100). Nevertheless, the link between educational evaluation in terms of accountability and power, evaluators as gatekeepers, and their influence on decision making indicates the political, ethical and methodological problems inherent in evaluation studies. Such studies are considered to be intrinsically sensitive, with the possibility of revealing inadequacy or reporting findings that may be manipulated or ignored by stakeholders (Robson 1993, p.170).

Evaluating palliative care education

A search of the literature reveals a limited, although increasing number of evaluation studies focused on university-accredited modules and non-accredited study days and courses in palliative care. The majority of published studies appear to focus on education delivered by or within specialist palliative care services, with limited published research representing accredited modules delivered within higher education institutions. This may be due to the competitive nature of higher education, as institutions compete for contracts, funding and students. University departments may be reluctant to reveal information that could potentially affect their status or funding. In addition, this may reflect the possibility that the outcomes of university-delivered palliative care programmes are evaluated using standardised university evaluation questionnaires rather than specifically designed approaches.

An institutional approach to evaluation appears to have developed in order to meet the higher education institutions' processes for quality assurance and, in addition, to address some external stakeholders' needs. Typically, such standardised questionnaires combine a mixture of closed and open-ended questions covering subject content, administrative arrangements and resource issues. The use of open-ended questions provides students with the opportunity to comment on areas of individual importance. Nevertheless, the standardised questionnaire-based approach is considered to be subject to a number of problems. Brindley *et al.* (1998, p.98) identified that, although in-house questionnaires may be considered functional, their reliability remains unexplored. In addition, the process of analysis for open-ended questions can prove difficult (respondents rarely write elaborate answers, and analyser bias may be introduced as time constraints are often tight). Furthermore, response rates may be low and the timing of questionnaires may further bias responses. However, despite these limitations such questionnaires provide information for course and module teams, and therefore contribute to the quality assurance processes of the institution (Brindley *et al.* 1998; p.98). Although standardised evaluative systems may predominate within higher education institutions (Pateman and Jinks 1999, p.63), for palliative care educators these may appear to be at odds with the goal of palliative care and palliative care education.

The value system for palliative care education is described as acknowledging the self and subjectivity and, as an educational process, one that is *with* and *for* people rather than *on* people. Primary attention is given to the promotion of human welfare and being self-directed (Sheldon and Smith 1996, p.10). A tension may therefore arise between the underpinning philosophy of palliative care education and the generic strategies used to evaluate it within the higher education context, which may negate the whole student experience. However, published research is increasingly being reported that demonstrates the value of a range of methodologies in the evaluation of palliative care education (Macleod *et al.* 1994; Spall and Johnson 1997; Froggatt 2000; Arber 2001; Kenny 2001), as services delivering palliative care education seek to identify and refine effective teaching practices within this field and understand the impact of education on participants and care provision.

Macleod *et al.* (1994), as programme lecturers, utilised a triangulated methodology to evaluate the effects of a three-day workshop for general practitioners. The study attempted to discover the participants' self-perceptions of confidence both prior to and following the course using analogue scales to generate quantitative data in order to demonstrate any change attributable to the programme. In addition, by using open-ended questions it attempted to explore the impact of the course on participants' practice. The study is helpful in demonstrating that both quantitative and qualitative data collection methods may be combined when undertaking evaluation studies in this field, depending on the research questions being posed. In contrast, Froggatt (2000) adopted a responsive approach to evaluation (Stecher and Davies 1987), which enabled the process of development and the outcomes of a two-year education project to be explored from as many different points of view as possible. Using naturalistic methods, the aim was to portray the multi-dimensional and complex webs of interaction and relationship that characterised the organisation and delivery of the service in question (Robbins 1998, p.6). This paper reported the outcomes of the initiative and adopted a case study methodology, including participant observation and semi-structured interviews. In addition, a postal survey of participating and non-participating nursing homes was used. In contrast, Kenny (2001) utilised an action research approach including a variety of methods to collect qualitative data, with the aim of discovering whether accredited palliative care education was effective in developing competent, confident practitioners.

These studies reveal the range of methodologies and data-gathering methods which may be used to evaluate palliative care education. Nevertheless, a number of issues are raised by these evaluation studies which merit consideration by those planning to undertake education evaluation including the political dimension of evaluation research, the use of a neutral researcher or combined lecturer/researcher role, and the value of a longitudinal vs. a cross-sectional approach as well as consideration of the evaluation approach.

For example, the latter two studies highlight the ethical and political dimension that commissioners and evaluators may face with evaluation studies. Froggatt (2000) reported that the evaluation was undertaken by a researcher employed by the national cancer charity which was also a partner in the development, delivery and funding of the educational programme. This high-profile education project, and the potentially wide dissemination and influence of the evaluation findings, could lead to questions about the integrity of the researcher, the research and its findings. Similarly, Kenny (2001) discussed the issue of being an insider undertaking evaluation research. Cronbach (1982, p.6) emphasises that evaluators need to maintain their professionalism and not substitute their judgement. Equally, it may be argued that commissioners of evaluation studies need to maintain their integrity and professionalism by remaining impartial and not seeking to influence the research findings to serve their own political ends, if educational evaluation is to maintain its credibility. Although no impropriety is suggested in either of these studies, the potential exists for this to be raised and the influence of the study findings to be diminished.

The extent to which the combined roles of lecturer/researcher may influence participants' responses also merits exploration. Froggatt (2000) was an external researcher and not part of the teaching team. As an outsider undertaking participant observation, the amount of information elicited may depend on the researcher's ability to establish rapport and gain the trust of the informants as well as their observational skills (Field and Morse 1985, p.115). If trust is not present, then the setting will change when the researcher is present and participants will conceal facts from the researcher, thereby limiting the depth of data and interfering with the validity and reliability of the study. In contrast, Macleod *et al.* (1994) and Kenny (2001) adopted combined lecturer/researcher roles. The evaluator can be regarded as a stakeholder in the evaluation because they may represent a particular organisation or position, and also because decisions may be taken during the research process which will be idiosyncratic or reflect personal opinion. However, Kenny (2001) argues that being an insider was valuable in encouraging formal and informal sharing by students. In addition, Robbins (1998, p.128) asserts that there is little reason for a categorical preference for either internal or external evaluator. She suggests that evaluators are often diverse in their activities and working arrangements, and that what might be gained by impartiality and neutrality (outsider) might be offset by the lack of knowledge of processes and understanding of the context (insider). Crucially, Robbins (1998, p.128) argues that evaluators should have a clear understanding of their role in a given situation.

However, within palliative care education the use of a neutral (external) facilitator does appear to merit careful consideration, as students are encouraged to reflect on their personal experiences and beliefs with regard to death and dying or use examples from clinical practice. The need to maintain confidentiality within the group is usually established at the start of a programme and this may be difficult to overcome, particularly if the facilitator is unknown.

The design of an evaluation study using a cross-sectional or longitudinal approach also merits consideration by researchers. Macleod *et al.* (1994) and Kenny (2001) adopted a longitudinal approach in an attempt to demonstrate the changing confidence of participants over time and any resultant changes to their practice. In contrast, Froggatt (2000) adopted a cross-sectional approach. However, this is reported as having been due to circumstances rather than by design, and it is suggested that a longitudinal approach would have been preferred to substantiate claims that changes in practice were the result of the education programme. It appears that evaluators of palliative care education need to explore the relative merits of longitudinal studies, which reveal changes over time, in contrast to cross-sectional studies undertaken at the end of the programme, where any changes resulting from the programme may be difficult to substantiate.

Finally, the evaluation approach requires consideration. The naturalistic paradigm utilised by Froggatt (2000) is based on the ideas of humanism and subjectivism, and acknowledges the experiences and values underlying the different perceptions of students and teachers. The unexpected and evolving aspects of teaching and learning may be revealed (Melrose 1998, p.38). This model, it may be argued, is in sympathy with the philosophy of palliative care education. Indeed, Clark (1997) reports that the strengths of qualitative methods in palliative care research are seen in the flexibility and responsiveness of data collection, and also in their capacity to uncover meanings that are inaccessible by other means. Nevertheless, the aims and objectives of an evaluation will have a strong influence on the research strategy that will be most appropriate. Crucially, the evaluation question itself should determine the appropriate strategy or combination of strategies to use (Robbins 1998, p.12).

These studies represent a helpful beginning in the evaluation of palliative care education and the identification of issues for consideration for evaluators. However, there remains a need for further evaluation studies to be undertaken in order to understand more fully how to effectively plan and deliver uni- and inter-professional education events in palliative care and explore the outcome of these for participants and, ultimately, for patient care. In focusing on the evaluation of inter-professional education (IPE), Barr *et al.* (1999) helpfully suggested a hierarchy, modified from the work of Kirkpatrick, aimed at widening the overarching objective of discovering whether IPE works to more discrete objectives of the form 'What kind of IPE, under what circumstances, produces what kind of outcome type?'. The hierarchy includes the following:

- level 1 – learners' reactions
- level 2a – modification of attitudes/perceptions

- level 2b – acquisition of knowledge/skills
- level 3 – change in behaviour
- level 4a – change in organisational practice
- level 4b – benefits to patients/clients.

This hierarchy may also be helpful for uni-professional as well as inter-professional palliative care education by broadening the overarching objective to 'What kind of palliative care education, under what circumstances, produces what kind of outcome?'. This may encourage educators and evaluators in higher education institutions and specialist palliative care services to explore the structure and processes as well as the outcome of palliative care education, as these aspects of palliative care education also merit systematic evaluation. Table 11.1 offers a framework of

Table 11.1 Potential areas of investigation for evaluation studies in palliative care education

Stakeholder	Structure	Process	Outcomes
Student	Learning outcomes Content Methods of delivery	Teaching approaches Learning styles	Types of knowledge Problem-solving skills Lifelong-learning skills Academic credits/award
Lecturer	Curriculum Learning outcomes Method of delivery Student motivation	Teaching approaches Learning styles	Anticipated outcomes Unanticipated outcomes Academic credit/awards Impact on practice
Educational institution	Administration Marketing Resources (IT/library) Cost Training needs analysis (clinical settings)	Quality assurance processes	Awards Recruitment/retention Research funding
Health care provider education consortium	Quality assurance processes Method of delivery Cost Workforce planning Training needs analysis	Assessment and evaluation processes	Academic credit/awards Impact on practice Recruitment/retention
Patient			Competent and knowledgeable practitioner

potential areas of investigation for evaluation research in palliative care education viewed from a number of stakeholder perspectives and with consideration to the structure, process and outcome of education.

Cronbach (1982) writes that 'Evaluation is an art' and 'there is no single best plan for an evaluation, not even for an enquiry into a particular programme, at a particular time, with a particular budget'. Cronbach's conclusions suggest that there is little room for methodological dogmatism in the field of evaluation. Indeed, with regard to the evaluation of palliative care education, it appears that a wide range of research methodologies may be required.

In conclusion, this discussion has focused on the need for evaluation of palliative care education. A literature search revealed that research in this field is currently under-developed or under-reported. However, published studies do have lessons for the evaluation of palliative care education in demonstrating their feasibility and value as well as identifying issues for consideration. Although it may be argued that evaluating palliative care education from the students' perspective using a naturalistic paradigm is consistent with the philosophy of palliative care education and may offer an in-depth account of the impact of a programme, it is recognised that the naturalistic paradigm is not a panacea. There are limitations to the kind of research questions that may be answered by this approach, and indeed the demands of stakeholders may influence the type of data required. Above all, as Robson (1993, p.180) asserts, evaluators should ensure that studies are useful and feasible and can be undertaken with propriety and technical adequacy if they are to be influential in any decision-making processes.

Implications for the reader's own practice
1   What different approaches and methods of data collection for educational evaluation do you utilise at present? Identify the strengths and limitations of these approaches and methods.
2   How might you evaluate the process of learning of the student? What ethical and political considerations do you face and how might they be addressed?
3   How might you evaluate the outcome of learning of the student? What are the benefits and limitations of acting as an internal or external researcher?
4   How do you think you could evaluate the longitudinal learning of the student?
5   What would be your action plan for integrating educational evaluation into your practice?

References

Arber A (2001) Student nurses' knowledge of palliative care: evaluating an education module. *Int J Palliat Nurs.* 7: 597–603.

Ashcroft K and Palacio D (1996) *Researching into Assessment and Evaluation In Colleges and Universities.* Kogan Page Ltd, London.

Barr H, Hammick M, Koppel I and Reeves S (1999) Evaluating interprofessional education: two systematic reviews for health and social care. *Br Educ Res J.* **25**: 533–43.

Brindley C, Scoffield S and Cuthbert P (1998) Course quality assurance. Should we try qualitative methods? *Educ Manage Admin.* **26**: 97–104.

Clark D (1997) What is qualitative research and what can it contribute to palliative care? *Palliat Med.* **11**: 159–66.

Clark D, Malson H, Small N, Mallett K, Neale B and Heather P (1997) Half full or half empty? The impact of health reforms in palliative care services in the UK. In: D Clark, J Hockley and S Ahmedzai (eds) *New Themes in Palliative Care.* Open University Press, Buckingham.

Cronbach LJ (1982) *Designing Evaluations of Educational and Social Programs.* Jossey-Bass, San Francisco, CA.

Department of Health (1998) *A First-Class Service. Quality in the new NHS.* Department of Health, London.

Department of Health (2000) *The Cancer Plan.* Department of Health, London.

Department of Health (2001) *Investment and Reform for NHS staff. Taking forward the NHS Plan.* Department of Health, London.

Field P and Morse J (1985) *Nursing Research. The application of qualitative approaches.* Chapman and Hall, London.

Froggatt K (2000) Evaluating a palliative care education project in nursing homes. *Int J Palliat Nurs.* **6**: 140–46.

Henkel M (1998) Evaluation in higher education: conceptual and epistemological foundations. *Eur J Educ.* **33**: 285–97.

Holzemer W (1980) Research and evaluation: an overview. *Q Rev Bull.* **6**: 31–4.

House of Lords (1994) *Report of the Select Committee on Medical Ethics. Volume 1.* House of Lords, London.

Kenny LJ (2001) Education in palliative care: making a difference to practice? *Int J Palliat Nurs.* **7**: 401–7.

Kreuger R (1994) *Focus Groups: a practical guide for applied research* (2e). Sage Publications, London.

Langton H, Blunden G and Hek G (1999) *Cancer Nursing Education: literature review and documentary analysis.* English National Board, London.

Llamas KJ, Pickhaver AM and Pillar NB (2001) Mainstreaming palliative care for cancer patients in the acute hospital setting. *Palliat Med.* **15**: 207–12.

Lloyd-Williams M and Field D (2002) Are undergraduate nurses taught palliative care during their training? *Nurse Educ Today.* **22**: 589–92.

Macleod R, Nash A and Charny M (1994) Evaluating palliative care education. *Eur J Cancer Care.* **3**: 163–8.

Melrose M (1998) Exploring paradigms of curriculum evaluation and concepts of quality. *Qual Higher Educ.* **4**: 37–43.

National Council for Hospice and Specialist Palliative Care Services (NCHSPCS) (1996) *Education in Palliative Care.* Occasional paper 9. NCHSPCS, London.

National Council for Hospice and Specialist Palliative Care Services (NCHSPCS) (2002) *Definitions of Supportive and Palliative Care.* NCHSPCS, London.

Nisbet J (1987) The role of evaluators in accountability systems. In: R Murphy and H Torrance (eds.) *Evaluating Education: issues and methods.* Paul Chapman Publishing Ltd, London.

Parlett M and Hamilton D (1987) Evaluation as illumination: a new approach to the study of innovatory programmes. In: R Murphy and H Torrance (eds) *Evaluating Education: issues and methods.* Paul Chapman Publishing Ltd, London.

Pateman B and Jinks AM (1999) Stories or snapshots? A study directed at comparing qualitative and quantitative approaches to curriculum evaluation. *Nurse Educ Today.* **19**: 62–70.

Popham WJ (1988) *Educational Evaluation* (2e). Prentice Hall, New Jersey.

Robbins M (1998) *Evaluating Palliative Care. Establishing the evidence base.* Oxford University Press, Oxford.

Robson C (1993) *Real World Research. A resource for social scientists and practitioner-researchers.* Blackwell Publishers Ltd, Oxford.

Scriven M (1967) The methodology of evaluation. In: RE Stake (ed.) *Curriculum Evaluation.* Rand McNally, Chicago.

Sheldon F and Smith P (1996) The life so short, the craft so hard to learn: a model for post-basic education in palliative care. *Palliat Med.* **10**: 99–104.

Spall R and Johnson M (1997) Experiential exercises in palliative care training. *Int J Palliat Nurs.* **3**: 222–6.

Stecher BM and Davies WA (1987) *How to Focus an Evaluation.* Sage, San Francisco, CA.

Wolf R (1990) *Evaluation in Education. Foundations of competency assessment and program review* (3e). Praeger Publishers, New York.

CHAPTER 12

Life review: an educational perspective

Ian Trueman

I conceive of the life review as a naturally occurring, universal mental process characterised by the progressive return to consciousness of past experiences, and particularly the return of unresolved conflicts. Simultaneously, and normally, these conflicts can be surveyed and reintegrated. Presumably this process is prompted by the realisation of approaching dissolution and death, and the inability to maintain one's sense of personal invulnerability. It is further shaped by contemporaneous experiences, and its nature and outcome are affected by the lifelong unfolding of character.

(Butler 1963)

The aim of this chapter is to introduce readers to the concept of life review as a therapeutic intervention in palliative care. This will be achieved by discussing its similarities to and differences from reminiscence. Prior to exploring the potential of life review as a therapeutic intervention, it will be necessary to ascertain its psychological underpinnings utilising the work of Erikson. Finally, some suggestions with regard to the educational needs of individuals prior to undertaking the intervention will be considered, highlighting appropriate learning opportunities.

Learning outcomes
By the end of this chapter the reader should be able to:
- compare and contrast the differences between life review and reminiscence
- understand Erikson's psychoanalytical stage of *ego integrity vs. despair*
- discuss the rationale for offering life review to people with a life-threatening illness
- consider the educational requirements of healthcare professionals prior to implementing life review.

For some, the thought of dying may instil feelings of regret and loss of role and status, leading to a loss of self-esteem. In the writer's experience, nurses delivering palliative care in the community often use the palliative phase of a person's illness to 'get to know' the patient and their family and offer 'support' leading up to the terminal phase. Such visits can appear unstructured, with little direction or focus, and according to Seale (1992) they can often focus on the practical and physical aspects of care.

This chapter will explore the rationale for undertaking structured life review with people who have a life-threatening illness. To achieve this, it is necessary to differentiate between life review and reminiscence, and to consider the merits of both interventions in order to determine which would be the most appropriate for use in the context of cancer and palliative care. This chapter is not intended to focus on the process of each intervention or to offer a definitive guide to the implementation of life review in the clinical area.

Reminiscence

Borden (1989), Burnside and Haight (1994), Hitch (1994) and Lester (1995) suggest that life review is a distinctly separate process from that of reminiscence. They go on to suggest that reminiscence may be included in the life review process, although it is unusual for life review to be included in reminiscence. Haight and Burnside (1993) and Stevens-Ratchford (1992) suggest that many professionals use the terms interchangeably, and following the work of Butler (1963), which discussed reminiscence and life review in the same context, confusion has existed due to each intervention being misunderstood and nurses having misgivings about the effectiveness of either. Therefore it is of paramount importance that healthcare professionals have a clear understanding of the differences between the two interventions.

Haight and Burnside (1993) suggest that reminiscence and life review both use memory as the tool and recall as the process to enable a person to look at the past. They go on to suggest that, when used therapeutically, the facilitator taps into the memory and attempts to use guided recollections rather than it being a spontaneous process. This view is echoed by Wilkes (1981) and Gibson (1994), who add that this act may in turn lead a person to re-establish their identity.

Haight and Burnside are quite influential in this area, and have published extensively (Burnside and Haight 1991, 1994; Haight and Burnside 1992, 1993). They suggest that reminiscence tends to focus on positive or happy memories, is generally less structured, often occurs as a 'one-off' session and is often used to obtain information. They go on to suggest that reminiscence aims to improve self-confidence, and is commonly used to increase socialisation and communication skills. Furthermore, it is often carried out in groups and tends to be less probing. Thus reminiscence is used extensively in the elderly care setting, and is of value in patients with dementia and depression. This view is supported by several authors (Coleman 1986; Ashton 1992; Eagan 1996). Hitch (1994) adds that reminiscence tends not to be used for recent events, but rather for memorable events from the individual's past.

There appears to be an ongoing debate in which authors suggest that one-to-one reminiscence is more probing than group reminiscence (Stevens-Ratchford 1992; Soltys and Coats 1995; Puentes 1998). However, Burnside and Haight (1994) suggest that one-to-one reminiscence has similar aims and outcomes to group reminiscence. They warn that because there is no group coherence as is found in group reminiscence, facilitators need to be aware of the client's need to have feelings of a physical presence 'being there' and the psychological presence of 'being with' the person. The evidence suggests that reminiscence tends to be superficial in nature and may not assist the terminally ill patient to the degree intended. Such a rationale is based on the notion that a person with a life-threatening illness may harbour certain regrets about their life and wish to engage in a more profound discussion relating to painful memories. Moreover, it is suggested that people are likely to feel uncomfortable discussing such intimate details in a group setting. Therefore it could be potentially damaging to the patient if the session was less structured or occurred as a 'one-off', as they will be left having to deal with many psychological issues. The current literature also suggests that reminiscence (whether it is one to one or within a group) tends to focus on specific topics or incidents such as wartime memories or schooldays. It usually occurs in a less structured fashion and tends to be 'stand-alone' rather than a series of sessions.

Erikson's life-stage approach

Life review takes a more psychoanalytical approach (Stevens-Ratchford 1992; Wholihan 1992; Haight and Burnside 1993; Hitch 1994). The psychoanalyst Erikson moved away from Freud's biological and psychosexual approach and concentrated more on ego and social concerns. He was concerned with the development of identity, and expanded on Freud's theory by covering the entire lifespan using eight psychosocial stages which he called *the eight ages of man* (*see* Appendix 1, p.225). He considered life to be a series of 'crises' which a person has to overcome, thus enabling them to move on to the next stage and achieve maturation, including the development of personality (Crain 1992; Ewen 1993; Miller 1993).

With regard to cancer and palliative care, the stage of importance to the individual is Erikson's psychosocial stage *ego integrity vs despair* (Erikson 1982). Erikson believed this to be the final stage of a person's life, and as a result considered it to be of importance to elderly people. However, he refrained from defining when a person is considered to be elderly or in late adulthood, suggesting that factors other than age need to be considered when a person enters the ego integrity vs. despair stage. Indeed he suggested that the stages are not fixed and should only serve as a guide, allowing people the flexibility to move around the stages in any order.

Erikson was aware of the many physical and social adjustments that elderly people are often forced to make, suggesting that old age often relates to an accumulation of losses and adjustments. This view is supported by Havighurst (1972) and Miller (1999), who propose that old age can be associated with adjustment to decreasing physical strength and health, retirement and reduced income, and adapting to a slowing down of all social activities. Clearly such adjustments are also significant to a person who has a life-threatening illness. This view is supported by Lair (1996), Sheldon (1997) and Oliviere et al. (1998), who add that due to the nature of many life-threatening illnesses, such adjustments are often required within a short time span. Therefore it could be argued that the pressure on those who are dying to achieve ego integrity is enormous. Erikson (1982) identifies that individuals who are able to resolve the 'crisis' and achieve ego integrity are more likely to have a sense of meaning and order in their life, whereas those who do not may fear death. He goes on to suggest that life review reminiscence can be regarded as an important developmental task in older adulthood. Therefore, in the context of cancer and palliative care, it is proposed that older adulthood refers to where a person is situated along their lifespan, rather than to their age. Consequently, life review could be regarded as a useful tool to help those with a terminal illness to achieve ego integrity.

Life review

Stevens-Ratchford (1992), Gibson (1994), Hitch (1994) and Sheldon (1997) suggest that, like reminiscence, life review was initially developed in elderly care emanating from Butler's work and utilising Erikson's theoretical context, and includes elements of self-evaluation and coming to terms with life. However, life review can also be used to draw upon past experiences to help to find solutions. Burnside and Haight (1994) suggest that life review is the process of organising and evaluating the overall picture of an individual's life with the purpose of achieving integrity. They go on to suggest that, unlike reminiscence, life review must be performed on a one-to-one basis, cover the entire lifespan and address both positive/happy and painful/sad times, both recently and from the individual's past.

Leading a group in reminiscence is considered difficult for the client. However, Burnside and Haight (1994) suggest that life review is even harder for the client, given that they are required to recall, assess, evaluate, reframe and finally integrate the experience to gain wisdom and achieve integrity. The aim of this is to raise a person's self-esteem and satisfaction with life. In contrast to reminiscence, individuals who are engaged in life review are often offered the questions prior to the session, allowing them the opportunity to decide where they wish to take the life review. They may wish to examine their actions at a specific time, place or event, but will cover the entire lifespan over several planned sessions.

A key aspect of life review is the need for evaluation (Stevens-Ratchford 1992), a view that isechoed by Burnside and Haight (1994), who suggest that evaluation occurs when a person is able to review their life and accept it as the only way it could have been. One could argue that this might appear quite a simplistic view. However, to the client, accepting their life for what it *has* been is likely to mean that in order to achieve ego integrity they have been empowered to dispose of their regrets with regard to what *could have* been. With regard to cancer and palliative care, clients who are able to reach acceptance may develop a more peaceful attitude towards their own death.

The nurse's role in facilitating the two interventions differs. In reminiscence the sessions are less formal, and the facilitator acts as a supportive, non-probing listener. In life review the sessions are more formal, and the facilitator is required to be more probing and may encourage or ask for deeper insight (Haight and Burnside 1992).

A word of caution

This chapter has concentrated on the advantages of both reminiscence and life review. However, it is acknowledged that there can be a number of disadvantages with each of these interventions. Gibson (1994) suggested that, for some people, reminiscence may reinforce their inclination to avoid upsetting experiences, as the focus tends to relate to happy or positive memories. With regard to cancer and palliative care, it is suggested that this may allow people to remain (although sometimes appropriately) in denial rather than accepting the reality of their illness. The potential disadvantages of life review centre on its application, where poorly structured and undisciplined sessions may have limited success. Furthermore, the probing nature of life review has the potential to cause greater psychological distress. However, well-structured sessions where the patient is given the list of questions in advance should assist them in deciding which areas they wish to review, thus empowering them to feel in control. This view is supported by Sheldon (1997), who also suggests that such a structure is beneficial and highlights the seriousness of the process. Hitch (1993) suggests that life review is of less value for people with dementia because of their likely difficulties with adopting a lifespan approach. Therefore participants who are engaged in both interventions need to be fully informed about the purpose of the sessions, so it is essential that nurses are clear about the intervention they are facilitating and its desired aims.

The use of life review in cancer and palliative care

The probing nature of life review and the theoretical context of Erikson's work suggest that life review is more suitable for use in palliative care than is reminiscence. This view is supported by several authors who explain that life review is of value for people who are dying or who are in a crisis in which helplessness, despair or loss may be a factor (Burnside and Haight 1993, 1994; McDougall *et al.* 1997). While working as a community nurse, the author of this chapter discovered that many terminally ill patients felt the need to review their life and reflect upon their failures and achievements. This view is supported by Soltys and Coats (1995), who suggest that during this period many people feel the need to review their achievements and put their relationships in order. Therefore it is necessary to consider the impact that life review may have in cancer and palliative care and to determine whether it is a valuable intervention.

The majority of the literature pertaining to life review and reminiscence focuses on the benefits to the elderly, individuals who are depressed or those with dementia. However, Butler (1963) suggests that despite being a therapeutic tool with the abovementioned groups, life review could also benefit younger people who are dying. Much of the literature on life review in cancer and palliative care originates from America and uses the evidence put forward by Butler as the rationale for its use (Borden 1989; Pickrel 1989). However, such studies fail to suggest the desired point in an individual's illness at which to undertake life review. Some may argue that a person might wish to review their life upon diagnosis or during palliative treatment. However, those healthcare professionals who deliver palliative care may be unable to achieve this due to the eligibility criteria for accessing palliative care services. This view is postulated by the National Council for Hospice and Specialist Palliative Care Services (1995), who concur that in general people are eligible for palliative care services when medical opinion suggests that they are likely to be entering their final year of life. Consequently, in the context of this chapter, life review is likely to be undertaken during the final year of life, which may be too late for some individuals. However, it is acknowledged that many areas of the country have policies which enable a person to access palliative care services for up to three months if they are going through a 'crisis'. Therefore, if such a crisis relates to a difficulty in accepting their diagnosis or prognosis, it may be possible to undertake life review as a palliative care provider prior to the final year of life if this is considered appropriate or if the patient so wishes.

Several authors have suggested that the aims and benefits of life review in a terminally ill patient, irrespective of their age, are similar to those found in elderly people. These include reaffirmation of self-esteem and identity, a reduction in feelings of loss and isolation, and renewed emphasis on the positive aspects of their life (DeRamon 1983; Pickrel 1989; Wholihan 1992). In addition, they suggest that life review may offer the dying person the opportunity to anticipate and grieve for the end of their life, and thus has the potential to assist the patient in letting go. Furthermore, the terminally ill patient may feel alone and isolated due to the significant others in their life being preoccupied with their own anticipatory grief and consequently being unable to meet the patient's need for reflection and sharing of their anxieties or fears. Pickrel (1989) and Sheldon (1997) suggest that the prospect of approaching death may mean that there are no more chapters that can be added to the person's life story. Therefore life review can allow self-examination, reflection on past events and relationships, and an opportunity to complete unfinished business, and the act of repeating their story may have cathartic benefits. This view is echoed by Borden (1989), whose work with young adults dying of AIDS revealed that they all found an opportunity to reinforce their sense of identity and cohesiveness. Later, a small study conducted by Lester (1995) concluded that life review significantly improved emotional well-being and family relationships in distressed dying people.

However, it is acknowledged that in the same context as life review with elderly people, it would be inappropriate for healthcare professionals to assume that this intervention is right or indeed beneficial to all individuals who are undergoing cancer care or requiring palliative care. Many authors warn that healthcare professionals should be aware that a person might view their life as a waste and regard themselves as a failure. This in turn could lead to a negative outcome, where the dying patient is left with feelings of despair, anxiety, guilt or depression (DeRamon 1983; Pickrel 1989; O'Connor *et al.* 1990; Lester 1995). In such circumstances it is of paramount importance that healthcare professionals recognise both this and their own limitations, and refer the patient to the relevant specialist (a point that will be discussed later in this chapter).

Who should facilitate life review?

Concerns about the remote possibility of causing harm raise the question of which health/social care professional should facilitate life review. Haight and Olson (1989) found that following a short in-service training programme, American health aides (the equivalent of healthcare support workers) were able to facilitate structured life review for elderly clients in residential care homes. Their study illustrates that relatively junior staff can undertake life review. This view is supported by Burnside and Haight (1994), who suggest that even lay people or volunteers with little formal training can facilitate the process. However, it is of paramount importance that facilitators have effective communication and interpersonal skills. This view is echoed by DeRamon (1983), Burnside and Haight (1991), Haight and Burnside (1992) and Wholihan (1992), who go on to suggest that an understanding of verbal and non-verbal communication skills is essential, as the most important role of the healthcare professional is to be able to act as a therapeutic listener. However, there appears to be no literature available suggesting how people should be assessed with regard to the use of such skills in relation to life review. Hitch (1994) contends that it is vital that the facilitator is self-aware and is aware of their limitations. Therefore it could be argued that the professional who initiates life review as a therapeutic intervention has a professional and moral responsibility to ensure that an appropriate specialist is identified (e.g. a community psychiatric nurse, psychotherapist or clinical psychologist) prior to the commencement of such an intervention. Furthermore, it is vital that the patient is made aware that another professional may need to be involved, and to seek their permission, perhaps in the form of a contract.

Training requirements of facilitators

From a review of the literature it appears that life review can be facilitated by professionals from a variety of backgrounds, including nurses, social workers and occupational therapists (Borden 1989; Pickrel 1989; Burnside and Haight 1991, 1994; Stevens-Ratchford 1992). This view is supported by DeRamon (1983), Haight and Burnside (1992) and Wholihan (1992), who argue that the facilitators do not need to be specialists, because the promotion of self-expression through supportive listening is the goal, rather than in-depth psychic probing, analytical interpretation or psychotherapy.

Although this chapter has not focused on how the process of life review should be undertaken, extracts from the Life Review and Experiencing Form (LREF) developed by Haight (1988) have been included in Appendix 2 (*see* p.227) to illustrate the probing nature and lifespan approach of the life review. Such a form could be modified slightly if required, or indeed a form more pertinent to the reader's clinical area could be adopted. Therefore it may be prudent to consider activities to attempt to enhance the knowledge base of professionals in the facilitation of life review. Several authors have suggested that formal training in this area should enable all health/social care personnel to appreciate the benefits of facilitating such an intervention in the workplace and help to refine their listening and facilitation skills (Burnside and Haight 1994). Haight and Burnside (1993) suggest that healthcare professionals need to be taught the difference between reminiscence and life review, thus enabling them to be clear about their objectives. They go on to suggest that a sound understanding of communication and interpersonal skills is paramount, thus ensuring a client-centred approach which is based on acceptance of the patient's feelings and their interpretation of meanings within them. This view is echoed by Pickrel (1989), who adds that it is important for the listener to learn the value of silence and when to give feedback.

The successful completion of university-accredited oncology and palliative care courses often requires the student to complete a module on communication and interpersonal skills if they wish to obtain a recognised qualification in these specialties. However, Burnside and Haight (1991) argue that to enable professionals to have a clear understanding of life review, relevant literature in this area needs to be widely available. They point out that such literature is scarce, the majority of articles being published in less mainstream journals. This view is supported by the author of this chapter, who has experienced significant frustration when trying to obtain relevant literature (the majority of the papers used in the development of this chapter were specially requested from the British Library). Furthermore, the literature pertaining to life review specifically in relation to cancer and/or palliative care is even more scarce, indicating the need for further research to generate wider written evidence of the therapeutic value of life review in palliative care. Therefore it is suggested that the development of suitable programmes of training, education and mentorship in life review for professionals who are responsible for the delivery of palliative care could perhaps become a reality. It is suggested that the module leaders of current post-registration palliative care courses or pre-registration nursing training throughout the country could perhaps incorporate a session within their courses to serve as an introduction to this under-used intervention in palliative care.

Conclusion

This chapter has considered the potential benefits of the implementation of life review in the field of palliative care. To achieve this it has been necessary to explain the key differences between reminiscence and life review, thus helping healthcare professionals to determine the desired outcomes pertaining to each intervention.

Life review adopts a psychoanalytical approach that utilises Erikson's final stage of life, namely *ego integrity vs despair*. Arguments have been put forward which suggest that Erikson's ideas relating to this final stage can be applied to terminally ill patients, regardless of their age, by acknowledging that they are coming to the end of their lifespan. Life review has been considered in the context of cancer and palliative care, utilising appropriate evidence. Finally, the possible skills required by healthcare professionals who wish to incorporate life review into their current work area have been discussed, leading on to suggestions with regard to potential areas for training and education in the future.

This chapter has demonstrated that despite the fact that several authors advocated the use of life review within the context of palliative care during the late 1980s and early to mid-1990s, very little appears to have been taken forward in this respect. Since the success of life review is proven within the fields of elderly care and the management and treatment of dementia and depression, the time has perhaps come to explore further the potential benefits of life review in cancer and palliative care.

Key points to consider
- Life review and reminiscence are distinctly different interventions.
- Reminiscence tends to focus on positive/happy memories, occurs as a 'one-off' intervention and lacks structure.
- Life review focuses on the entire lifespan, including positive/happy and painful/sad memories, and is more structured and probing in nature.
- Erikson's psychoanalytical theory of ego integrity has become a common foundation for the use of life review in elderly people who are struggling to come to terms with the losses and adjustments associated with late adulthood.
- Such a rationale could also be applied to people who require palliative care.
- Professionals who facilitate life review may require further training in the intervention. However, communication and interpersonal skills with an understanding of one's limitations are just as important to the successful implementation of life review.
- Palliative care courses and pre-registration palliative care education could be a useful forum for introducing participants to the potential benefits of life review.

Implications for the reader's own practice

1   Is life review used in your clinical area? If so, how is it structured? If not, how could it be structured?

2   Do you see any potential problems with the implementation of life review in your clinical area? How might these be overcome?

3   What are the educational needs of the staff in your clinical area to undertake life review work?

4   What would you do to ensure that the staff in your clinical area have their clinical needs met?

5   Given that some areas have minimal patient contact, often over a short period of time, what are the implications for the successful implementation of life review?

6   How could you evaluate whether life review has been of benefit to your patients?

7   Would you know who to refer your patients to, and how, if major emotional or psychological issues were raised during the life review process?

References

Ashton D (1992) Therapeutic use of reminiscence with the elderly. *Br J Nurs.* **2**: 894–8.

Borden W (1989) Life review as a therapeutic frame in the treatment of young adults with AIDS. *Health Soc Work.* **14**(4): 253–9.

Burnside I and Haight BK (1991) Reminiscence and life review: analysing each concept. *J Adv Nurs.* **17**: 855–62.

Burnside I and Haight BK (1994) Reminiscence and life review: therapeutic intervention for older people. *Nurse Pract.* **19**: 55–61.

Butler RN (1963) The life review: an interpretation of reminiscence in the aged. *Psychiatry.* **26**: 65–76.

Coleman P (1986) *Issues in the Therapeutic Use of Reminiscence with Older People: a reader*. John Wiley & Sons, Chichester.

Crain W (1992) *Theories of Development: concepts and applications* (3e). Prentice Hall, Englewood Cliffs, NJ.

DeRamon PB (1983) The final task: life review for the dying patient. *Nursing.* **13**(2): 46–9.

Eagan DE (1996) The reminiscing game. *Penn Nurse.* **51**: 22–3.

Erikson EH (1982) *The Life Cycle Completed*. Norton, New York.

Ewen RB (1993) *An Introduction to Theories of Personality* (4e). Lawrence Erlbaum Associates, London.

Gibson F (1994) *Reminiscence and Recall: a guide to good practice*. Age Concern, London.

Haight BK (1988) The therapeutic role of a structured life review process in homebound elderly subjects, *J Gerontol.* **43**: 40–44.

Haight BK and Olson M (1989) Teaching home aides the use of life review. *J Nurs Staff Dev.* **5**(1): 11–16.

Haight BK and Burnside I (1992) Reminiscence and life review: conducting the processes. *J Gerontol Nurs.* **18**: 39–42.

Haight BK and Burnside I (1993) Reminiscence and life review: explaining the differences. *Arch Psychiatr Nurs.* **7**: 91–8.

Havighurst RJ (1972) *Developmental Tasks and Education.* (3e). David McKay, New York.

Hitch S (1994) Cognitive therapy as a tool for caring for the elderly confused person. *J Clin Nurs.* **3**: 49–55.

Lair GS (1996) *Counselling the Terminally Ill.* Taylor & Francis Ltd, London.

Lester J (1995) Life review with the terminally ill. Unpublished MSc thesis, University of Southampton, Southampton.

McDougall GJ, Blixen CE and Suen L (1997) The process and outcome of life review with depressed homebound older adults. *Nurs Res.* **46**: 277–83.

Miller C (1999) *Nursing Care of Older Adults* (3e). Lippincott, Philadelphia, PA.

Miller P (1993) *Theories of Developmental Psychology* (3e). WH Freeman & Co., New York.

National Council for Hospice and Specialist Palliative Care Services (1995) *Specialist Palliative Care: A Statement of Definitions.* Occasional paper 8. National Council for Hospice and Specialist Palliative Care Services, London.

O'Conner AP, Wicker CA and Germino BB (1990) Understanding the cancer patient's search for meaning. *Cancer Nurs.* **13**: 167–75.

Oliviere D, Hargreaves R and Monroe B (1998) *Good Practices in Palliative Care: a psychological perspective.* Ashgate Publishing Ltd, Aldershot.

Pickrel J (1989) Tell me your story: using life review in counselling the terminally ill. *Death Stud.* **13**: 127–35.

Puentes WJ (1998) Incorporating simple reminiscence techniques into acute care nursing practice. *J Gerontol Nurs.* **24**: 14–20.

Seale C (1992) Community nurses and the care of the dying, *Soc Sci Med.* **34**: 375–82.

Sheldon F (1997) *Psychosocial Palliative Care.* Stanley Thornes Ltd, Cheltenham.

Soltys FG and Coats L (1995) The SolCos model: facilitating reminiscence therapy. *J Psychosoc Nurs.* **33**: 21–6.

Stevens-Ratchford RG (1992) The effect of life review reminiscence activities on depression and self-esteem in older adults. *Am J Occup Ther.* **47**: 413–20.

Wholihan D (1992) The value of reminiscence in hospice care. *Am J Hospice Palliat Care.* **9**(2): 33–5.

Wilkes JW (1981) Remembering. *Theology.* **84**: 87–95.

Further reading

Borden W (1989) Life review as a therapeutic frame in the treatment of young adults with AIDS. *Health Soc Work.* **14**: 253–9.

Burnside I and Haight BK (1991) Reminiscence and life review: analysing each concept. *J Adv Nurs.* **17**: 855–62.

DeRamon PB (1983) The final task: life review for the dying patient. *Nursing.* **13**(2): 46–9.

Erikson EH (1982) *The Life Cycle Completed.* Norton, New York.

Haight BK and Olson M (1989) Teaching home aides the use of life review. *J Nurs Staff Dev.* **5**(1): 11–16.

O'Conner AP, Wicker CA and Germino BB (1990) Understanding the cancer patient's search for meaning. *Cancer Nurs.* **13**: 167–75.

Sheldon F (1997) *Psychosocial Palliative Care.* Stanley Thornes Ltd, Cheltenham.

CHAPTER 13

Humour in cancer and palliative care: an educational perspective

Steve Morris and Wendy Page

Life does not cease to be funny when people die, any more than it ceases to be serious when people laugh.

(George Bernard Shaw)

Introduction

The authors of this chapter have many years of nursing experience, and have both enjoyed and benefited from humour used within the workplace within cancer and palliative care settings and also within palliative/oncological educational settings. They have witnessed humour utilised between healthcare professionals, between professionals and patients, and among groups of patients. Their own experiences of situations where humour and laughter have made a significant difference to a patient's response to care, and many other anecdotal testimonials, demonstrate its usefulness. Consideration must be given to the establishment of rapport and the development of a relationship between healthcare professional and patient, and the impact that the use of humour might have upon this. Incorporating the use of humour in the building of a relationship with another person may have a positive or negative effect, and the abilities, skills and perceptions of the healthcare professional are paramount. Do they feel that having the ability to incorporate humour into practice enhances a relationship, and in doing so, does this boost their self-esteem? When patients initiate humour, what impact does this have on the relationship and do healthcare professionals feel equipped to respond to this appropriately? Humour may be an unobtrusive way of seeking help. It may be that the humour is an attempt on the patient's part to discuss a pertinent issue that is causing them concern. For example, dying patients have been heard to say that they are waiting in the Departure Lounge! This can therefore also work negatively. If humour is used by individuals to minimise their problems or concerns, then it may be erroneously assumed that nothing is wrong and no help is needed. Humour may also be used to defend or detract from issues, perhaps when the patient is not ready to discuss them just yet. So can we as professionals take humour at its face value and 'laugh it off', or are we skilled enough to be able to pursue, explore and discuss any fears or issues with the patient? Use of humour in our practice will impact on patients and professionals alike, and this will be discussed further later in this chapter.

Learning outcomes
By the end of this chapter the reader will be:
- aware of the underpinning theory relating to laughter and humour
- able to discuss the benefits and limitations of humour therapy
- able to apply humour in the context of cancer and palliative care
- able to analyse the merits of utilising humour in both formal and informal education.

What is humour?

Humour is an integral part of everyday life. It is a fascinating, complex, universal phenomenon that is unique and invaluable to every individual. Lawler (1991) described the sharing of humour between a patient and a nurse as being representative of care and concern for the patient's well-being.

The word 'humour' has many meanings, the root of the word being 'umor', meaning 'liquid' or 'fluid'. In the Middle Ages, humour referred to an energy that was thought to relate to a body fluid and an emotional state. This energy was believed to determine health and disposition (e.g. 'he's in a bad humour'). Wooten (1993) suggested that a sanguine humour was cheerful (and associated with blood), a choleric humour was angry (and associated with bile), a phlegmatic humour was apathetic (and associated with mucus) and a melancholic humour was depressed (and associated with black bile).

History of humour

Freud (1905) described humour as having subtle meanings, and he listed obscene or exposing jokes, hostile or aggressive jokes, cynical or critical jokes and sceptical jokes, all of which may be potentially destructive in nature. He also described humour as an 'ego' builder, and laughter as a potential 'triumph of the ego' when he stated that 'it is one of the great series of methods which the human mind has constructed in order to evade the compulsion to suffer'. However, consistent with his psychotherapeutic approach, he also represented humour as a control mechanism over aggression and sexual desires. His view was that sexual and aggressive impulses were hidden in the subconscious and repressed, because such behaviours were socially unacceptable. He viewed humour as a socially acceptable way of expressing these taboo feelings. Eichenbaum and Orbach (1985) criticise Freud's paternalistic stance, that stating 'the theory of female inadequacy, which is the starting point for Freudian theory on femininity, stems from his patriarchal bias'. Feinburg (1978) suggested seven humour categories, including word play, which may involve double meanings. The other six categories were obvious aggression, unexpected truth, sexual humour, scatological humour (from the term 'scatology', meaning the study of faeces, thereby implying obscene humour), nonsense and black humour. Kahn (1989) identified five primary functions that humour serves for individuals and groups. The first is that of 'coping', in which humour helps people to become detached from potentially threatening aspects of their situation. 'Reframing' allows a person to see things that they have previously taken for granted in a new light. 'Communication' allows a person to deliver messages with particular reference to taboo experiences such as death or bereavement. The fourth function of humour is 'expressing hostility' – it is not uncommon for racist, hostile or sexist feelings to be expressed via a joking medium. Framing the comment in such a way makes it difficult for the recipient to protest, and such humour can sometimes be vicious. The fifth and last identified function is 'constructing identities'. 'In-jokes' are often used to establish or maintain group cohesion and to provide evidence that the person speaking is a member of that specific social group. As such, they are often used to help members of a group to draw boundaries between their group and other people. Thus it is evident from the literature that humour can be both constructive and destructive in nature. Humour has been used from both perspectives throughout history, as can be seen in literature ranging from the works of Shakespeare to Charles Dickens, Oscar Wilde and George Bernard Shaw.

Humour therapy

One of the most influential proponents of humour and laughter therapy of modern times is Norman Cousins. His documented experiences as a patient undergoing treatment for ankylosing spondylitis first caught the attention of the medical community with regard to the potential therapeutic effects of humour and laughter, when he described his utilisation of laughter. Believing that negative emotions had an impact on his health, he postulated that the opposite was also true, and that positive emotions would have a positive effect. He believed that the experience of laughter could open him up to feelings of joy, hope, confidence and love. Since the behaviour of laughing tends to open one up to these positive emotions, he began watching amusing films to stimulate laughter. He reported that 'it worked, I made the joyous discovery that ten minutes of genuine belly-laughter had an anaesthetic effect and would give me at least two hours of pain-free sleep' Cousins (1979). Cousins spent the last 12 years of his life at the Department of Behavioural Medicine at UCLA Medical School, exploring the scientific proof of his belief. He established the Humour Research Task Force, which co-ordinated and supported his worldwide research on humour (Cousins 1976, 1979, 1989).

Benefits and limitations

The benefits of humour and laughter have long been recognised, and are even mentioned in the Bible. Proverbs 17:22 states that 'A cheerful heart does good like a medicine, but a broken spirit makes one sick'. Florence Nightingale (1859/1946) has also described the benefit of humour.

Physiologically, scientists have found that laughter is a form of internal jogging that exercises the body and stimulates the release of beneficial brain neurotransmitters and hormones. Laughter increases the levels of hormones such as endorphins and neurotransmitters, and decreases the levels of the stress hormones cortisol and adrenaline. Laughter is one of the body's safety valves, a counterbalance to tension. When we release that tension, the elevated levels of the body's stress hormones drop back to normal, thereby allowing our immune systems to work more effectively. Laughter boosts our emotional state, creating a feeling of well-being. Holden (1993) stated that 'a burst of happy, spontaneous laughter is one of the most delightful, wholesome and highly prized of all human experiences'. Cohen (1990) identified that 'stress is alleviated by humour because the joy and the sadness pathways are unable to operate simultaneously'. The therapeutic use of humour will allow many patients and their caregivers to deal with the sadness and stress in their lives by giving them the opportunity to smile or laugh, and the chance (even if only momentarily) to opt out of the stressful reality. 'A few moments of humour may in many instances help to sustain people through difficult life experiences, including terminal illness' (Kanninen 1998). Caregivers as well as patients are in need of the therapeutic effects of humour and laughter as borne out by Wooten (1993). While he was suffering from cancer, Freud (1905) claimed that humour had the potential to transform pain into pleasure, and he discussed the strength and beauty of humour allowing him to triumph over pain. Herth's study (1990) involving a small number of terminally ill patients showed that most of the subjects used humour and described it as fostering hope. Responses included descriptions such as the following:

- 'I feel more hopeful in general after I laugh'
- 'Humour makes me feel good all over'
- 'Humour helps me to realise what I am going through will pass'.

Use of humour in the delivery of information to patients and their families improves communication in three ways. It captures the attention of the learner, it enhances retention of the material and it helps to release the tension that blocks learning (Wooten 1993). If used appropriately, humour can be used to benefit patients and enhance both doctor–patient relationships and nursing practice (Fry 1992; Mathew 2003). Holden (1993) agreed with this when he wrote that 'humour can be a therapeutic tool for creating healthy relationships between patient and health professional'. It is recognised that humour improves communication. Black (1984) states that it is a culturally universal means of communication and that it is essential for uniting people, assisting in the building and maintenance of relationships. Shared laughter is a uniquely human bond, and serves as an equaliser and social lubricant (Wooten 1993). Martineau (1972) conceptualised humour as a 'type of social process and specific medium of communication'.

Humour in the context of cancer and palliative care

Humour, it is suggested, influences every stage of a group's life. Tuckman's classical model of *group forming, storming, norming and performing* describes how groups join together with a common purpose, negotiate how group goals may be achieved, establish and accept roles and behavioural norms for group members and eventually accomplish the tasks necessary to achieve the group goals (Tuckman 1965). Over time, members of the team leave and are replaced, ensuring that the team undergoes a process of reforming. Humour is seen as a creative activity within group dynamics and in general as a positive influence assisting in group promotion, and it may initiate the storming phase that leads to the group performing effectively. Humour helps people to bond by providing a commonality. However, it is important to consider that it requires only a small shift in perspective to assume that humour may sometimes be a potentially destructive or controlling influence on the group process. In cancer and palliative care, patients and carers may find themselves in a group situation and healthcare professionals should be mindful of the destructive and constructive aspects of humour. Similarly, cancer and palliative care educationalists should be aware of the strengths and limitations of humour in a group setting when delivering sensitive material.

Foot (1986) described the 'superiority theory' of humour, in which amusement is gained from the knowledge or observation of others' misfortune or problems. This view enshrines the notion that individuals believe they are in control of their lives when they are content or happy, and find amusement in the loss of control in others, which is aligned to a feeling of superiority. This can be linked to cancer and palliative care education in that we must first learn to laugh at ourselves, which is not always an easy thing to do.

Humour can also be used effectively among teams of healthcare professionals. Humour strategies offer managers innovative, inexpensive management tools for staff morale and people management (White and Howse 1993). Laughter promotes the development of confidence, and a good leader will recognise its use with regard to people management. For example, during times of conflict, the skilful use of humour will help to neutralise conflict, reduce tension and defuse a difficult situation. The deliberate use of properly chosen and well-timed humour could ultimately improve work relationships, with staff experiencing a reduction in strain and improvement in work conditions. Different types of shared humour, such as self-effacing humour, reveal one's own flaws and vulnerability, and can be used positively to create an environment in which participants feel safe to share, thereby promoting the establishment of relationships. Wooten (1996) noted that finding humour in a situation and laughing freely with others can be a powerful antidote to stress. In addition, Wooten (1997) stated that searching for humour – looking for something to laugh about – helps us to avoid focusing on the elements that are overwhelming or depressing.

Caring for cancer patients has frequently been described as stressful. Vachon (1986) stated that palliative care is considered to be a particularly stressful area for staff, as they must deal repeatedly with dying and death. However, Cooper and Mitchell (1990) found that nurses in intensive and coronary care units experienced higher levels of stress. Wilkinson (1994) concluded that 'cancer nursing appears to be no more of a stressful occupation than most other occupations'. In exploring these contradictory findings, Vachon (1995) confirmed that although stress was a problem in the earlier days of hospice care, this had been moderated by the effective intervention of staff support. The need for organisational and personal coping strategies to deal with stress is highlighted in Vachon's study, but the role that humour might play is given scant attention. Other factors such as education have been cited as stress buffers. Wilkinson (1986) found that nurses who had not undertaken a post basic course in cancer care reported being more stressed than those who had completed such a course. Mathew (2003) suggested that all professionals who have to deal with extremes of human emotion and suffering must use humour as a coping mechanism. Indeed, humour is used in all settings, and for healthcare professionals this includes both formal and informal education. This incorporates teambuilding, 'time out', supervision and all areas across the spectrum of healthcare. Humour can be seen to cause a positive therapeutic interaction between staff and can be very beneficial, motivating them and delivering a 'feel-good' factor.

Experience in the field of death and dying is also significant. Palliative care nurses experience decreased death anxiety and more positive attitudes towards death than those who encounter death less frequently (Brockup et al. 1991). This is discussed in detail by Graham Farley elsewhere in this book (see Chapter 6). There is increasing evidence suggest that humour might act as a stress buffer when used as a protective mechanism against potentially damaging effects of acute or chronic stress both in clinical areas (Coombs and Goldman 1973; Leiber 1986) and in educational settings (Leidy 1992). It has been reported that age shows a positive correlation with the use of humour. Sumners (1990) found that mature nurses tend to have a positive attitude towards humour, whereas younger nurses are more likely to be uncomfortable with its use. Therapeutic use of humour must be sensitive to the individual and their needs at that moment in time. Is it possible that more mature professionals feel more comfortable with this because they are more competent at recognising a client's needs due to their experience? Is that unique, personal exchange something that can be taught? Is it not used as effectively by younger nurses solely because they are not made aware of its potential value within their work? Sumners (1990) viewed humour as a spontaneous action or a natural resource of the individual nurse. Is it possible that the use of humour needs to be *taught* in order to enhance relationships between a patient and their care-giver? Or is this only likely to be successful with more mature students who have their own unique and individual experiences of life? Benner (1984) states that nurses must rely on their sensitivity and intuition, which develop with experience, becoming 'expert intuition', as both knowledge and experience are essential to the use of humour. Benner (1984) clearly distinguishes between the intuitive thinking of the expert and the concrete thinking of the novice, the period of time required to achieve expert functioning being five years. So is it unrealistic to expect that professionals with less experience will be able to use humour to its optimum potential in patient care? Astedt-Kurki and Luikkonen (1994) found that patients often regard a sense of humour as a characteristic of a good nurse, which reflects Benner's theory of novice to expert, as a sense of humour and effective use of humour with patients will develop with experience, as will other skills such as effective and skilful communication. However, it is important to recognise that this is not always the case. Experience does not always equate to effectiveness, and the authors of this chapter would suggest that not all healthcare professionals will be able to use humour effectively within their practice. The ability to do so effectively will require a great deal of self-confidence, self-awareness and competence in advanced communication skills.

The theme of black or gallows humour in healthcare is represented in the literature (Herth 1984; Perry 1996), where it has been viewed as a coping mechanism for healthcare professionals. Gallows humour was so named by Freud when he reported an incident of joking that occurred on the gallows by a man about to be hung. It is unique to caregivers and any other profession that deals directly with the gruesome reality of pain, suffering and death, and can be misunderstood and seen as hostile, inappropriate or 'sick' by people who are unfamiliar with those professions. Gallows humour acknowledges the disgusting or intolerable aspects of a situation and attempts to transform them into something light-hearted and amusing. An appreciation of this type of humour develops when the tension is so great that it must be released or one begins to feel crushed by the pressure. It is interesting to note that in Morris's unpublished study (Morris 2001) nurses felt more inclined to interact and share black or 'toilet' humour with other 'hands-on' professionals, perceiving that others would not understand or participate in such humour. In our stressful lives, dealing with sadness, loss and disappointment on a daily basis, humour allows us to take a step back and perhaps view a stressful situation from a broader and less personal perspective. It is important to recognise that stress in healthcare professionals may result not so much from an event itself but from the professional's perception of that event and the meaning that they give it (Selye 1956). Humour and laughter affect the way in which we perceive and respond to change, and provide a perceptual flexibility that can increase our sense of control.

Many nurses refrain from using humour, believing that it is unprofessional (Buxman 2002), although Crane (1987) stated that nurses worry that it is their colleagues who would equate the use of humour with being unprofessional. Holden (1993) looked at the art of living joyfully in relation to religion and pondered the question 'Does humour tarnish haloes or make them shine brighter?'. The authors of this chapter feel that a balanced use of humour in conjunction with good communication skills and an understanding of and relationship with another person will indeed make those haloes shine. The possession of a sense of humour seems to be considered an asset by many individuals, and although it is essential to retain high standards and to take work seriously, nurses and other healthcare professionals who cope daily with the reality of illness, suffering and death are advised that to avoid 'burnout', or more accurately 'compassion fatigue', it is important for them to be able to take themselves lightly. However, laughing at yourself is not always easy. There are adages such as 'Smile and the world smiles with you, cry and you cry alone', but it must be remembered that it is easy to be too immersed in a problem to find any humour in it.

Maslach (1982) describes burnout as depletion of the spirit, 'a syndrome of emotional exhaustion and cynicism that occurs frequently among individuals who do "people work" of some kind', as a result of which individuals feel that they have very little left to give. Finding humour in our work and in our life can be one way to lift the spirit's energy level and replenish us from compassion fatigue (Robinson 1991; Ritz 1995; Wooten 1995). Humour can be an effective self-care and coping tool that provides us with a detached perspective, facilitating disengagement from the suffering we witness and yet allowing us to remain sensitive. It is a survival tool for the healthcare professional who wishes to remain compassionate and caring (Wooten 1997).

Application to education

The nursing profession has come to view humour as beneficial within healthcare settings. The recognition of individual needs and holistic care facilitates our valuing the ability of humour to positively affect a patient's well-being. Many authors have written about the need for holistic care, and it seems to have become an accepted fact within healthcare that we must care for people and not just patients – whole people with emotional, psychological and spiritual needs as well as physical needs (Holden 1993). Affective elements of humour are integral to nursing's holistic framework (Ferguson and Campinha-Bacote 1989). Conversely, Ulloth (2003) states that nursing has remained stubbornly two-dimensional, addressing cognitive and psychomotor growth while generally neglecting effective learning. Some nurse educators, having recognised the value of humour as a viable teaching strategy, have learned to incorporate humour effectively into their classrooms. The benefits of humour also apply within the classroom, reducing anxiety and tension, making learning fun, aiding learners' focusing of their attention, increasing learning and memory, and strengthening social relationships (Ulloth 1998). Watson and Emerson (1988) stated that 'This [humour] reduces the authoritarian position of the teacher, allowing the teacher to be a facilitator of the learning process' in partnership with the learner. Humour can be 'integrated into instruction to facilitate learning' and thereby be considered a legitimate teaching tool (Berk 1998).

Mallet (1993, 1995) made the criticism that there is a lack of scientific research into humour. A large percentage of the literature on humour in healthcare considers the therapeutic value of humour when used within the nurse–patient relationship in clinical settings (e.g. Simon 1988; Bellert 1989; Schmitt 1990; Erdman 1993; Astedt-Kurki and Liukkonen 1994). It is clear that there is a need for further research into this area, but it is equally clear to experienced healthcare professionals that there is a role for humour within oncology and palliative care, and indeed within healthcare generally. In the literature on humour and palliative care, on the basis of findings from the only known research involving the palliative care population, Herth (1990) suggests that humour is 'as essential if not more essential in the terminal stage of the disease than at other times during illness and health.'

Yura-Petro (1991) listed humour as a need in nursing's *human need theory*, linking humour with cognitive and effective learning. Using a qualitative approach, Beck (1997) asked 21 registered nurses to describe in detail an experience they had had with humour while providing nursing care. The purpose of this study was to describe the meaning of the nurses' use of humour in their practice setting. Five themes emerged in which humour was found to:

- help nurses to deal effectively with difficult situations or difficult patients
- develop cohesion
- be an effective communication technique that helped to decrease patients' anxiety
- be either planned and routine or unexpected and spontaneous
- create lasting effects beyond the immediate moment for patients and nurses alike.

Bellert (1989) wrote that 'Humour during the (cancer) teaching process is helpful in allaying tensions and fears surrounding the learning experience'. The teacher must role model how humour might be applied with patients, and it must be used in a positive manner and not create negativity or tension within the classroom setting. Students will therefore learn from the teacher's example, and they should be actively encouraged to think about how they would apply humour in the clinical setting.

Certainly the nursing education curriculum will need to increase awareness of the appropriate use of humour and the opportunities to use it in practice (Watson and Emerson 1988). If it was incorporated into the learning process in a structured manner, humour could enhance the students' communication skills and be used effectively as part of the nursing process. This could also help to reverse the more negative attitudes of younger nurses with regard to the use of humour (Sumners 1990).

It is clear that much work is still needed regarding the use of humour in cancer and palliative care. It is also felt that the application of humour and the education of staff is very much an untapped issue within professional education. Although it would be difficult to teach humour and its use – after all in UK culture it is felt that it cannot be likened to a clown and juggling act – healthcare professionals need to be aware of the appropriate use of humour and its impact on individuals, and not just the use of humour in an academic situation, but also its use in day-to-day opportunities working alongside our colleagues. There are many opportunities that we shall encounter in everyday situations where humour may be utilised to relieve tension, promote learning, reduce anxiety and diffuse anger (among other things) with a broad spectrum of different people, from vastly different backgrounds, each with their own unique individuality.

In practice, the use of humour can be included within both formal and informal education, its value being considerable when the situation has been assessed correctly and humour has been used skilfully. It can be used within all settings, with all individuals, and will help teambuilding, bonding and the promotion of learning by the 'students' as they have fun. It is used by many to aid maintenance of interest, and as a relief to tension and stress. Who has not attended a lecture where the speaker used humour within their presentation, either verbally or through the use of cartoons and humorous pictures/slides? Those are the lectures that we remember and often learn from most. Humour is also a valuable tool to use at the bedside when teaching learners or patients themselves within the clinical setting. This promotes integration of students and patients in the learning process, assisting in the maintenance of control for the patient, as they too will learn from the situation and be able to contribute their ideas, feelings and opinions. Who could be a better teacher of patient care than the patients themselves? This also gives the novice healthcare professional the opportunity to view the experienced professional in practice, witnessing advanced skills in communication, care and compassion. Humour with patients must be led by them, must be sensitive to their needs and must acknowledge where they are within their disease process at any given moment, as was discussed earlier in the chapter. It has been known for patients themselves to initiate gallows humour, even when they are seriously or terminally ill, but our response to and acknowledgement of this must be appropriate and well timed. The use of humour as a therapy seems to depend on the skill of the healthcare professionals involved with individual patients. In some countries, the use of 'humour carts' and 'humour rooms' has become common practice. In the UK, Holden runs humour workshops for healthcare professionals, but perhaps this is something that we should expand on in the field of cancer and palliative care. Due consideration would have to be given to culture and to the British sense of humour, as certain forms of slapstick comedy may not be appropriate. Patients could have access to comedy videos/audiotapes, whoopee cushions, games, practical jokes and so on, should they choose to use these. Therefore the use of humour as a therapy, so long as the relevant equipment and environment are provided, could well be patient-led.

Summary

It seems almost intuitive that humour and laughter can make one feel better in terms of stress reduction and self-healing.

It is evident from the literature that patients will not consider humour to be unprofessional if it is used appropriately. After all, how many of your patients have initiated humour with you? We must be selective and considerate in the use of humour, but recognise that it enhances the rapport and relationship that a professional has with the individual, and reassures them that someone has come to understand their needs and is beginning to understand their uniqueness. Matching our humour interventions with the patient's preferred style of humour is essential in order to stimulate laughter and its therapeutic potential. Be aware that the patient may disguise a serious concern in the form of a joke, and be perceptive and sensitive about this. We must understand that humour has the power to wound, torment and ridicule (Sullivan and Deane 1988), and that there is a fine line between constructive and destructive humour. Humour is not innately good or bad – it is the use of it that takes it one way or the other (Holden 1993). Rapport must first be established with a client before humour can be safely incorporated into patient care. This enables the patient to understand that shared humour does not replace concern, care or respect, but adds to it. A sense of humour allows us all, patients and healthcare professionals alike, to perceive and appreciate the incongruities of life, and it also provides moments of joy and delight.

You are invited to incorporate humour into your life, for yourself as much as for those for whom you care. The social activist Patch Adams, who was once a patient and a doctor at a mental institute, has dedicated his life to changing America's healthcare system. He has formed the Gesundheit Institute, which is dedicated to a more connected, personalised, holistic approach to medicine. There patient care incorporates laughter, joy and creativity as part of the integral healing process. Adams' care of his patients is very much driven by humour, and he promotes and practises unorthodox techniques such as dressing up as a clown or other humorous characters, filling rooms with balloons, etc., all with the aim of eliciting a smile, a spiritual connection or a simple moment of pleasure for a patient. For those who desire a closer and speedy insight into Adams' work, there is a film dedicated to his approach, entitled *Patch Adams*. Each person's sense of humour is unique, and the techniques used to create humour need to be individualised so that you and your patients will reap the rewards.

Key points to consider
- If all those working within cancer and palliative care were to focus on the ways and means of integrating humour into their working practice, the financial implications of this would need to be considered.
- Pursue the possibility of devising teaching packs to educate healthcare professionals in the use of humour with both colleagues and patients. Look at the content of these packs and consider the theory and practice of humour therapy.
- Incorporate the use of humour into other training and education (e.g. communications skills packages).

- Further investigate the use of humour therapy in different settings and integrate it into practice across organisational and care boundaries.
- Measure the impact of the use of humour with healthcare professionals, taking into consideration the potential reduction in stress and the impact on levels of staff sickness and retention.
- Consider researching the use of humour therapy both in the clinical setting and in educational environments.

As we have researched and observed within our own and our patients' lives, humour is integral to life – it is a universally recognised commonality and bond. There is no doubt that some day we shall all succumb to death – that is the only certainty. However, on life's pathway the development of self-awareness and the ability to use humour in a skilful manner will improve the quality of life both for ourselves and for those around us. This is demonstrated in the closing quotes, depending on your own unique sense of humour, of course.

> The human race has only one really effective weapon, and that's laughter. The moment it arises, all our hardnesses yield, all our irritations and resentments slip away, and a sunny spirit takes their place.
>
> (Mark Twain)

> Life was a funny thing that occurred on the way to the grave.
>
> (Quentin Crisp)

Implications for the reader's own practice

1 With how many of your patients have you initiated humour? And how many have initiated it with you?
2 Is it different depending on who initiates the interaction? If it is, in what way is it different, and why do you think this might be?
3 In what ways do you utilise humour in your present practice? How could you expand this in the future?
4 What could you include in a teaching session on humour therapy?
5 How might you utilise humour more effectively in a teaching/learning environment?
6 What research could you undertake which might provide useful evidence to demonstrate the advantages and disadvantages of utilising humour in cancer and palliative care?

References

Astedt-Kurki P and Luikkonen A (1994) Humour in nursing care. *J Adv Nurs.* **20**: 183–8.

Beck CT (1997) Humour in nursing practice: a phenomenological study. *Int J Nurs Stud.* **34**: 346–52.

Bellert JL (1989) Humour: a therapeutic approach in oncology nursing. *Cancer Nurs.* **12**: 65–70.

Benner P (1984) *From Novice to Expert.* Addison Wesley, Wokingham.

Berk RA (1998) Professors are from Mars, Students are from Snickers. Mendota Press, Madison, WI.

Black D (1984) Laughter. *JAMA* **252**: 2995–8.

Brockup DY, King DB and Hamilton JE (1991) The dying patient: a comparative study of nurse caregiver characteristics. *Death Stud.* **15**: 245–58.

Buxman K (2002) Burnout: nothing to laugh at. *J Geront Nurs.* **28**: 3.

Cohen M (1990) Caring for ourselves can be funny business. *Holistic Nurs Pract.* **4**: 4.

Coombs RH and Goldman LJ (1973) Maintenance and discontinuity of coping mechanisms in an intensive care unit. *Soc Prob.* **20**: 342–55.

Cooper CL and Mitchell S (1990) Nursing the critically ill and dying. *Hum Relations.* **43**: 297–311.

Cousins N (1976) Anatomy of an illness (as perceived by the patient). NEJM **295**: 1458–63.

Cousins N (1979) *Anatomy of an Illness.* Bantam, New York.

Cousins N (1989) *Head First: the biology of hope.* EP Dulton, New York.

Crane A (1987) Why sickness can be a laughing matter. *Regist Nurse.* **50**(2): 41–2.

Eichenbaum L and Orbach S (1985) Understanding Women. Penguin Books, Harmondworth.

Erdman L (1993) Laughter therapy for patients with cancer. *J Psychosoc Oncol.* **11**: 55–67.

Feinburg L (1978) The secret of humour. *Maledicta.* **2**: 87–110.

Ferguson S and Campinha-Bacote J (1989) Humour in nursing. *J Psychosoc Nurs Ment Health Serv.* **27**: 29–34.

Foot H (1986) *Humour and laughter.* Croom-Helm, London.

Freud S (1905) *Jokes and their Relationship to the Unconscious.* Volume 6. Penguin Books, London.

Fry WF Jr (1992) The physiological effects of humour, mirth and laughter. *JAMA.* **267**: 1857–8.

Herth K (1984) Laughter: a nursing prescription. *Am J Nurs.* **00**: 991–2.

Herth K (1990) Contributions of humour as perceived by the terminally ill. *Am J Hospice Care.* **7**: 36–40.

Holden R (1993) *Laughter: the best medicine.* Harper Collins, London.

Kahn WA (1989) Towards a sense of organisational humour: implications for organisational diagnosis and change. *J Appli Behav Sci.* **25**: 45–63.

Kanninen M (1998) Humour in palliative care: a review of the literature. *Int J Palliat Nurs.* **4**:(3) 110–14.

Lawler J (1991) *Behind the Screens.* Churchill Livingstone, Edinburgh.

Leiber D (1986) Laughter and humour in critical care. *Dimens Crit Care Nurs.* **5**: 162–70.

Leidy K (1992) Enjoyable learning experiences – an aid to retention? *J Contin Educ Nurs.* **23**: 206–8.

Mallet J (1993) Use of humour and laughter in patient care. *Br J Nurs.* **2**: 172–5.

Mallet J (1995) Humour and laughter therapy. *Compl Ther Nurs Midwifery*. **1**: 73–6.

Martineau H (1972) A model of the social functions of humour. In: J Goldstein and P McGhee. *The Psychology of Humour: theoretical perspectives and empirical issues*. Academic Press, New York.

Maslach C (1982) *Burnout: The cost of caring*. Prentice-Hall, Englewood Cliffs, NJ.

Mathew FM (2003) Laughter is the best medicine: the value of humour in current nursing practice. *Nurs J India*. **94**: 146–7.

Morris S (2001) *Humour in palliative care: a study of the occurrence, usage and meaning of humour in a palliative nursing context as described and experienced by professional nurses*. Unpublished MSc dissertation, The University of Hull, Hull.

Nightingale F (1859/1946) *Notes on Nursing: what it is, and what it is not*. Edward Stern & Co., Philadelphia, PA.

Perry B (1996) Influence of nurse gender on the use of silence, touch and humour. *Int J Palliat Nurs*. **2**: 7–14.

Ritz S (1995) Survivor humour and disaster nursing. In: K Buxman. *Perspectives on Humour*. Springer, New York.

Robinson V (1991) *Humour and the Health Professions* (2e). CB Slack, Thorofare, NJ.

Schmitt N (1990) Patients' perceptions of laughter in a rehabilitation hospital. *Rehabil Nurse*. **15**: 143–6.

Selye H (1956) *The Stress of Life*. McGraw-Hill, New York.

Simon JM (1988) Humour and the older adult: implications for nursing. *J Adv Nurs*. **13**: 441–6.

Sullivan JL and Deane DM (1988) Humour and health. *J Gerontol Nurs*. **14**: 20–24.

Sumners AD (1990) Professional nurses' attitudes toward humour. *J Adv Nurs*. **15**: 196–200.

Tuckman BW (1965) Development sequence in small groups. *Psychol Bull*. **63**: 284–99.

Ulloth JK (1998) *Intentional classroom humour in nursing: a multiple case study*. Unpublished doctoral dissertation, St. Andrews University, Berrien Springs, MI.

Ulloth JK (2003) A qualitative view of humour in nursing classrooms. *J Nurs Educ*. **42**: 125–30.

Vachon MLS (1986) A comparison of the impact of breast cancer and bereavement: personality, social support and adaptation. In: Hobfoll (ed.) *Stress, Social Support and Women*. Hemisphere, New York.

Vachon MLS (1995) Staff stress in hospital palliative care: a review. *Palliat Med*. **9**: 91–122.

Watson M and Emerson S (1988) Facilitate learning with humour. *J Nurs Educ*. **27**: 89–90.

White C and Howse E (1993) Managing humour: when is it funny – and when is it not? *Nurs Manage*. **24**: 80.

Wilkinson SM (1986) *The satisfactions and stresses of nursing cancer patients*. Unpublished MSc thesis, University of Manchester, Manchester.

Wilkinson SM (1994) Stress in cancer nursing: does it really exist? *J Adv Nurs*. **20**: 1079–84.

Wooten P (1993) Laughter as a therapy for patient and caregiver. In: J Hodgkin, G Connors and C Bell (eds) *Pulmonary Rehabilitation*. Lippincott, Philadelphia, PA.

Wooten P (1995) Interview with Sandy Ritz. *J Nurs Jocularity*. **5**: 46–7.

Wooten P (1996) Humour: an antidote for stress. *Holistic Nurs*. **10**: 49–55.

Wooten P (1997) Humour skills for surviving managed care. *Dermatol Nurs.* **9**: 423–9.

Yura-Petro H (1991) Humour: a research and practice tool for nurse scholar-supervisors, practitioners and educators. *Health Care Supervisor.* **9**: 1–8.

Further reading

Adams P (2002) Humour and love: the origination of clown therapy. *Postgrad Med J.* **78**: 447–8.

Bain L (1997) The place of humour in chronic or terminal illness. *Prof Nurse.* **12**: 713–15.

Bennett M (2003) The effect of mirthful laughter on stress and natural killer cell activity. *Altern Ther Health Med.* **9**: 38–44.

Dean R (1997) Humor and laughter in palliative care. *J Palliat Care.* **13**: 34–9.

Mooney N (2000) The therapeutic use of humour. *Orthop Nurs.* **19**: 88–92.

Useful websites

www.corexcel.com

www.jesthealth.com

www.jocularity.com

www.laughterremedy.com

www.patchadams.org/flash.htm

www.worldlaughtertour.com

CHAPTER 14

Education in cancer and palliative care: an international perspective

Robert Becker

When we speak of challenges we must not forget that of teaching and enthusing our professional colleagues and students. I suspect we have got it wrong. We are filling the syllabus with doses and data when we should be trying to change attitudes. Wherever I travel in the world I find palliative care workers who feel they must justify their existence, particularly if they have specialist status, and they do so by parading facts and figures rather than sharing some of the profound insights which so characterise palliative care.

... we will not be judged by the number of people we have treated or the number of services we have established. We will not be remembered by the number of papers we have had published or the books we have edited. We shall be judged by our willingness, indeed our eagerness, to share our facts and figures and sensitive insights about Man and how he reacts to suffering and loss with our students and colleagues in other disciplines and specialities.

(Derek Doyle 1999, Farewell Address, Geneva)

The aim of this chapter is to give the reader an overview of the diversity of issues and the constantly challenging nature of education in cancer and palliative care throughout the world today.

Learning outcomes
By the end of this chapter the reader should be able to:
- understand the need for a flexible and creative approach to cancer and palliative care education, which embraces both the art and the science of good clinical practice
- reflect on the challenging social, economic, religious and political condi-

tions in different countries which impact on the development of cancer
and palliative care education
- appreciate the need for continuity in the education process that is sensitive to cultural norms and yet prepared to challenge those norms in the
best interests of the patient.

Introduction

This will be a chapter of contrasts, paradoxes and sometimes challenges to the
status quo, which I hope will be thought-provoking to the reader. The opening
quote from Derek Doyle is in itself provocative and worthy of debate, which is
exactly why it was chosen. The sentiments expressed are in part indicative of the
global need for education that is founded on the acknowledged principles of good
practice, and are patient and family focused in the truest sense. The chapter also
poses a series of important questions about healthcare politics, provision and priorities which influence the education process in different cultures.

It is important to remember that *how* we learn is as relevant as *what* we learn,
because teaching and learning is a complex issue that is certainly not confined to
the classroom or conference platform. If healthcare professionals are to influence
attitudes as Derek Doyle suggests, and arguably this is the cornerstone of successful
education, then the caring professions need to learn how to pass on effectively the
important messages learned from clinical experience, discussion and debate with
colleagues, research and the very people who are perhaps the most influential and
important teachers of all – the patients.

Evolution of the issues

Unfortunately, it is beyond the scope of this chapter to mention the huge range of
successful and often inspirational initiatives that have taken place around the world
over the last few decades in the field of cancer and palliative care education.
However, it is appropriate at this point to pay tribute to the many teachers and clinicians who work tirelessly within their own teams across the world against sometimes enormous social, economic and political odds to train and educate their
colleagues.

It is so important to recognise that it is not only the notable names and high-
profile conferences that have contributed their vast expertise and helped to shape
policy, standards and practice, but also the small but significant army of volunteer
professionals of all disciplines from many countries, who often give up their own
time and money to travel to developing countries and work in sometimes
harrowing and difficult circumstances at the 'sharp end' with patients, families and
colleagues. It is perhaps these individuals who influence attitudes and clinical
practice more in the long term, because they invariably teach by example, and put

themselves forward as exemplar role models. It is a daunting responsibility, but the learning that results can make an enduring difference to people's lives.

There are a number of significant factors that influence the education agenda in cancer and palliative care around the world today and which will be discussed in the main body of this chapter. These include:

- the development of integrated healthcare systems for the general population of a country
- the ethical value of life within the country itself
- cultural norms with regard to:
  - acceptable treatment regimes
  - expression of grief and hope
  - pain and symptom control
  - truth telling
- media representations of health, youth and death
- political priorities (i.e. funding)
- medical attitudes.

The first part of this list relates to the developing countries of the world that struggle to develop a functional healthcare system which can deal with the major life-threatening diseases that kill the majority of the population. It is these countries that have rising death rates from all of the major cancers, and where the ageing population is likely to double by 2030 (Aranda 1999). Death in these countries is a frequent event at all ages, and dealing with it remains a major part of family life. Traditional rituals passed down over many centuries dominate the grieving process, and medicine has little to offer in curative terms.

Most palliative care in the developed world is provided in expensive specialist units, and is therefore by its very nature selective. This may be acceptable in western countries, where social and professional status is gained by being associated with the units, but it is of little use in the developing world.

In western countries, scientific, interventionist medicine predominates when it comes to government funding. However, in eastern and Third World countries there is little or no health infrastructure that is actively curative. Ironically, these are often the very countries without the healthcare infrastructures to support the knowledge gained, yet they see the western model of healthcare as the right one to aspire to. It is a 'best of the west' perception, which is frequently entirely inappropriate for the population's needs at the time. Palliative care in these countries is not a luxury. With around 80% of all cancers that present to medical services already in advanced stages, and no curative or preventive medicine available, palliative care becomes the only feasible option to ease suffering (Sembhi 1995). Educational awareness of what palliative care can offer should therefore be a priority, and the models that are adopted should be encouraged to be strongly community team oriented rather than specialist units.

The *ethical value of life* as perceived by a country's government, its people and most importantly its medical practitioners is a highly complex and sensitive issue, and one on which it is difficult to comment objectively. No self-respecting government around the world will openly admit to contraventions of human rights, either during or at the end of life, for fear of international sanctions. However, it is clear that there is abundant anecdotal evidence of huge contradictions between official policy and acknowledged practice in many countries. The education of both the public and professionals in the guiding principles of cancer and palliative care in these circumstances becomes a potential moral and ethical minefield. This must be addressed at a local level in the context of what is acceptable within that culture, balanced against a real need at times to challenge accepted conventions where it is in the patient's best interest to do so.

Cultural issues

Here we have a tension between modern western-style care and traditions with different values and ethical norms. Family structures may differ and the social support networks may simply not exist to help ill people at home, and there is often a need for family carers to remain in employment in order to meet the basic survival needs of the family (Jones 1997). In Hong Kong, for example, communities will rally round a family. However, in the west there are varying values with regard to support. In the Middle East the religious beliefs of Islam make it difficult to apply palliative concepts of any degree, and access to morphine-related drugs is severely limited (Stjernsward and Joranson (1995). Conversely, in the oil-rich Middle Eastern economies provision of cancer treatment facilities may be excellent.

Holistic family-centred care that emphasises choice, dignity and individuality is unacceptable to many cultures because it is loaded with western values, and even if it is desirable it may not be achievable due to resource limitations. There are few if any care choices in many countries, and the concept of dignity for the individual is a culture-bound value which may not be acceptable.

Norms with regard to pain control, expression of grief and truth telling vary enormously across the world. For example, in Southeast-Asian societies the open expression of grief is uncommon, whereas in Mediterranean cultures and Puerto Rica, the expression of grief is dramatic by comparison (Trill and Holland 1993). To take another example, it is common in a number of cultures for physical pain to be experienced as an acceptable and essential part of the dying process. To alleviate that pain would therefore contradict cultural norms, and this needs to be recognised in education programmes.

Interestingly, even with regard to the almost universal recognition of a 'need for hope', there are many differences in the understanding of what nurtures and what discourages hope. Such differences affect cultural attitudes and education concerning the disclosure of a cancer diagnosis (Gordon 1990).

In terms of education, therefore, palliative care services and healthcare professionals have to be flexible in their interpretation of palliative and cancer philosophy and responsive to the norms of each community. This is an enormous challenge, but it is important to remember that the well-developed, university-validated, academic, formal model of education based on western ethical values does not hold the moral high ground.

Truth telling

Doctors in many cultures believe that it is right not to tell the patient the diagnosis and prognosis. For example, it is accepted practice in Japan for the patient's family to be told the diagnosis first, and this is accepted by the patients themselves as normal practice. The doctor will inform the relatives and leave the decision to them, or actively collude in not telling the patient. This is done in the firm belief that it is the right thing to do, and may culturally be the only acceptable path to follow. Equally, in Italy and Egypt, being truthful about a patient's grave diagnosis is viewed by many as a cruel and untactful act (Dodd *et al.* 1985; Ali *et al.* 1993).

However, many countries are now beginning to acknowledge that it is a good thing to inform patients honestly and sensitively, but they do not know how to do this. Therefore it can become an 'all-or-nothing' situation, where education in culturally appropriate communication skills is a real necessity (Becker 1999).

Inadequacy of public and professional education

False beliefs and myths about the causation and development of cancer are rife. Some beliefs revolve around cancer being infectious or contagious, or possibly developing from a physical injury that has failed to heal properly. These beliefs can result in people either becoming ostracised from the family home through fear, or not revealing serious symptomatology until it is far too late (Navon 1999).

The influence of the media

In most western countries the rapid growth and availability of information technology have undoubtedly played a significant part in the shaping of attitudes towards death and dying. We now live in a complex and pluralistic society that views death as essentially a failure of medical treatment, and that values youth and good health above all else (Corner and Dunlop 1997). Changing family structures and lifestyles coupled with the instant availability of information have raised expectations of quality and length of life, yet have removed the experience of death to the bevy of professionals that we represent (Neale 1993).

Palliative and cancer care professionals have effectively become the surrogate families for the 60–80% of individuals who die in institutions in Europe, and we have professionalised death in a way that emphasises the technical skills of the service at the expense of empowering the family and the individual. (Beck-Friis 1997). This begs the question, in terms of education, of whether we as health professionals are part of the solution or whether we are in fact contributing to the problem.

Medical attitudes

The prevalence of stereotypes, ignorance and myths with regard to cancer and palliative care practice is perhaps the most intractable and yet potentially the most useful tool available with regard to good education. In most western societies medicine has a dominant social and political position that imbues its practitioners with considerable power and responsibility. If doctors are convinced of the value of palliative care provision, their influence can be huge and can fundamentally change the attitudes both of the public and of the government. However, if palliative care is perceived by doctors to be a waste of resources and a threat to the development of curative services, education will be held back for many years.

Physicians and even oncologists in some countries have an ambivalent attitude towards pain and education in pain management, and see it as a low priority in care (Takeda 1993; Van Roenn 1993; Larue 1995). There are suspicions surrounding the Christian foundations of hospice-based palliative care, particularly in the Middle East and indeed anywhere where the predominant religious philosophy is fundamentally different (Aranda 1999).

Evidence of good education practice

- Over the last decade the European Association of Palliative Care has been instrumental in developing and promoting both education and research into all aspects of palliative care. It has drafted curricular content for both undergraduate and postgraduate courses, produced many informative documents in multiple languages for professionals, and actively works towards unification of national organisations. Its biannual conference has established itself as without doubt the foremost event for professionals working in the field across the world, as well as in Europe.
- In the USA, education in palliative care for nurses has been taken on board and developed by their professional organisation, namely the Hospice and Palliative Nurses Association. It sets formal multiple-choice-style examinations for registered nurses working within the field, and issues successful candidates with a nationally recognised certificate. The examinations themselves are carefully structured and rigorously tested for reliability and validity and cover a huge range of topic areas, but with a noticeable bias towards pain and symptom management. Re-examination is essential every four years, with the option of providing professional evidence as in the UK for alternate four-year cycles. In this litigation-conscious society this method of education is perhaps the only realistic way forward, but it contains no element of interaction, discussion or debate.
- There are ever increasing numbers of good-quality Internet websites that support both cancer and palliative care education available to the computer user. Most of them provide information about books, journals, multimedia

resources and sometimes teaching resources which can be either bought or downloaded direct to a computer. A few websites enable the professional to join discussion forums on topical issues. However, a good selection are put together specifically for patients and their relatives to enable them to access up-to-date information about cancer in what is generally a user-friendly format.

- The Open Society Institute in New York, which is a US-based charitable trust and part of the Soros Foundation, provides funding opportunities for health professionals working in cancer and palliative care, particularly those from Eastern European countries, to travel and gain working experience and education.

- The Socrates exchange scheme aims to provide Europe-wide funding opportunities for universities and other institutions to link together and exchange ideas and staff in topic areas where each has a perceived need. This scheme allows healthcare professionals in particular, linked to universities, to actively build long-term relationships with a like-minded organisation to the mutual benefit of all concerned, and could have a significant impact on education in cancer and palliative care (Becker 2003).

- Hospice twinning is an informal idea that has been around for some years, and a small but growing number of hospices have taken it up. It simply involves one hospice making contact with another overseas, and the two institutions agreeing to help each other in small but realistic ways. This usually involves an exchange of ideas, literature and sometimes staff in areas such as commissioning and development of services, documentation of care and in particular education.

- The UK Forum for Hospice and Palliative Care Overseas is a new initiative supported and developed jointly between Help the Hospices and the Hospice Information Service, attached to St Christopher's Hospice in London. Its aims are broad and encompass policy development, liaising with governments, promoting hospice twinning, supporting existing international services and producing a database of individuals willing to work overseas, but more significantly it hopes to promote information exchange and establish a training and education programme. Key national and international leaders in palliative care from a range of disciplines are directly involved in running the forum, including experienced educators. It is to be hoped that it will receive the support that it rightly deserves.

Contentious issues

The formal, lecture-style, rigid approach to education in cancer and palliative care is still predominant in most countries around the world, even those with a developed and integrated university system that has close links to the education of healthcare professionals. Where this methodology exists there is little audience interaction and discussion and even less debate and skills instruction. It is not that certain elements of cancer and palliative care cannot be taught by lectures, but rather that the unique nature of some of the subject matter is better taught by the sharing of personal knowledge in a variety of ways, which conveys real meaning through the participants' interpretation of what is said and which has a moral and spiritual dimension (James and MacLeod 1993). No one country can hold its head up high and say that it has now 'got it right' in this area.

There are many complex reasons for this, which revolve around issues such as professional politics (see the quote at the beginning of this chapter) and cultural tradition, but one thing is certain. The ability of people to actively learn and translate this learning into changed behaviour and practice in their work, when exposed to this rigid, didactic style of teaching, is severely limited and handicaps the education process enormously.

Perhaps the key reason for maintaining such an approach is the competence and confidence of those doing the teaching. Few if any countries outside the UK and North America are developed enough in terms of their cancer and palliative care education infrastructure to employ on a full-time basis experienced clinicians who have undergone additional courses in the theory and practice of education at a recognised academic level, who can develop and implement a wide range of initiatives that are not only founded on the underlying values of quality care for cancer and palliative patients, but also embody educational principles that are tried and tested. At present only the UK, the USA, Canada, Australia and New Zealand employ full-time educators in cancer and palliative care.

In many countries it is not yet possible to aspire to such developments. The education that does take place is therefore frequently ad hoc, and it is in the hands of willing clinicians who in many respects do an excellent job, but lack the knowledge of curriculum development and perhaps the confidence to use a variety of teaching styles to enhance learning.

One of the other most contentious issues worldwide is that alluded to by Derek Doyle in the opening quote. Many countries in the world value the scientific and technical aspects of palliative care very highly, and the acquisition of knowledge and skills in these areas is a priority for them. The danger is that the only acceptable education from a palliative perspective is therefore oriented towards the control of physical pain and symptoms and the skilled use of pharmacology at the expense of the other equally important elements, such as truth telling, spiritual care, dealing with ethical issues, understanding grief and loss as a lived experience and family care.

Within cancer care specifically there is an aspiration towards expensive and often unrealistic treatment options in countries that have few resources to deal with even the basic issues of population growth or rising poverty (Hilton 1999). Therefore education with regard to the prevention and early detection of cancer represents the only realistic hope of controlling cancer spread in the decades ahead. Compared with treatment, preventive education requires far fewer human resources, less technology and less money to implement, so it makes good economic sense (Magrath and Litvah 1993).

Possible future developments

There is clearly no panacea for the successful embodiment of the principles and practice of cancer and palliative care within healthcare education. It can be argued that each country should develop its own methodologies in the context of its own needs, and few would disagree with those sentiments. Indeed history shows us only too well how imposing differing value systems, however well meaning, on to a society creates confusion and can actively undermine that society's own efforts to respond to the presenting issues.

Someone once said to me 'When teaching abroad it is important not to become a palliative care tourist ... stepping in and delivering, basking in the reflected glory and then going home, never to return. Continuity is the only way to make a real difference'. My own experience of teaching in a number of countries has verified for me just how true that is. I do believe, therefore, that there are a number of objectives that can be achieved over the next decade, which will make it much easier for the developing nations in particular to access practical help and advice when they request it, and which will help to provide that much needed continuity. Some of these goals are listed below.

- Much better and wider use of technology such as the Internet as an education resource, not only to build up accurate and regularly updated data on educational developments that are taking place, but also to produce and publish free teaching materials that are culturally sensitive, academically and clinically robust, adaptable and easy to download, in multiple languages, for use in many more countries around the world.
- Setting and maintaining realistic and workable core standards for education services in both developed and developing countries.
- Helping government departments to devise and implement curricula that are workable, realistic and sensitive to cultural norms.
- Asking governments to identify leading clinicians from a range of professions, who are willing to be seconded, perhaps even to another country, to train as educators and to become leaders back in their own country, working in both education and clinical practice. Such individuals would need to receive full financial support to make this happen.
- Selecting potential educators with great care, as the unique nature of education in cancer and palliative care demands a reflective maturity from the individual that is arguably above and beyond that expected within other healthcare fields.
- Maintaining an international database of experienced educators and their field of expertise, who on request could take time out from their jobs, to travel abroad to help to develop educational programmes, with an ongoing commitment to see them through to the point of evaluation and beyond, or who could perhaps provide consultancy advice.
- The wider establishment of cancer and palliative care chairs of medicine in universities, coupled with the recognition of cancer and palliative care as

distinct medical specialties in their own right. Experience has shown that where this occurs, education and training become a much higher priority and recognition acts as a springboard for formal education developments at both undergraduate and postgraduate levels for medicine, and thereafter often for nursing and other professions.

- The development of means by which the unique nature of cancer and palliative care education can be assessed and evaluated more accurately to attempt to demonstrate not just knowledge and skills, but also changes in attitude in clinical practice over time.

Cancer treatment and palliative care: a cultural comparison

In order to help you to gain a clearer sense of perspective about the reality of the challenges faced by educators in cancer and palliative care across the globe, the following two clinical scenarios are offered as a catalyst for reflection and perhaps discussion. These two cases have not been exaggerated in any way to increase their impact. The names have been changed because the situations described are representative of real individuals.

> Mary is a 60-year-old woman from a suburb of London. A small breast tumour was detected six years ago by a routine mammogram. Mary was referred to a specialist cancer unit where she saw the professor of surgery. She underwent a lumpectomy followed by radiotherapy, and was subsequently prescribed tamoxifen. With the encouragement of her family, she also received regular counselling and joined a local breast cancer support group. Mary had frequent check-ups at the specialist centre and remained disease-free until six months ago, when she presented with rib pain. On examination she was found to have multiple bony secondaries. She received palliative radiotherapy, and her family rallied round. She was referred to her local hospice as an outpatient and she attends the day centre there three days a week. Mary knows that she can be admitted in the future if she requires this. She has told her palliative care consultant that she would prefer to remain at home until she dies. In addition to the primary healthcare team she has a Macmillan nurse assigned to her, and if she requires it a Marie Curie nurse will be available.

> Ludmilla is a 60-year-old woman from a small suburb just outside Moscow. Six years ago she noticed a lump in her breast, but she was frightened to tell anyone about it. She continually lived with the fear that it was cancer, and she felt that she was being punished for events in her younger life. Ludmilla

concealed the lump from her family even when it began to fungate, dressing the wound with lilac or cabbage leaves and strips of old bed-linen tied around her body. She did this because she knew that neither she nor her family could afford proper dressings. When the wound became malodorous she avoided social contact as much as possible and drank herbal teas to try to ease the pain in her body. Her granddaughter Svetlana, a medical student, went to visit her recently and, realising that something was wrong, persuaded her to see a doctor. He examined Ludmilla and told Svetlana in private that it was advanced cancer. Svetlana thought it best not to tell her grandmother, preferring to tell her that it was a bad infection. Ludmilla remained terrified, went back to her home and refused to see anyone, even her granddaughter. One month later when the neighbours complained about the smell from her flat, the door was forced open and she was found dead in bed. By her side was a half-full bottle of vodka, an empty packet of rat poison and a carefully written note for her granddaughter.

Both Mary and Ludmilla are the same age and suffer from breast cancer which presented itself six years ago, but there the similarity ends. Their vastly different experiences of cancer treatment and palliation highlight and encapsulate the multiple factors discussed in this chapter, which influence the education agenda across the world.

Key points to consider
- Globally, palliative care and cancer education is neglected. The size of the problem must be made clear to politicians, policy makers and healthcare professionals.
- Relatively few resources are allocated to primary prevention of cancer and palliative care services, while most go to curative therapy, which is both expensive and often inappropriate for the needs of the population.
- Political vision and leadership are needed to consider ethical, social and socio-economic factors in education priorities.
- Remember the maxim that 'more medical care does not necessarily equal better health'. It is the behaviour of individuals and the attitudes and habits of society that are likely to have a greater impact on education, rather than the technical advances which at present are inaccessible to so many of the world's population.

Implications for the reader's own practice
Consider the cases of Mary and Ludmilla.
1   What are the physical, social and emotional issues that are common to both of these women?

2 What are the key points that stand out for you as the main differences between the experiences of Mary and Ludmilla?

3 How do you feel you could realistically help the Russian healthcare professionals to improve the lot of people like Ludmilla who live in a very different cultural climate?

4 What connections, if any, do you have in your work area or locality with the healthcare services of developing countries and how do you feel that you could perhaps contribute towards helping out?

5 Consider and explore how you could integrate the rich vein of clinical, anecdotal, intuitive human experience from cancer and palliative care situations into your teaching.

References

Ali NS, Khalil HZ and Yousef W (1993) A comparison of American and Egyptian cancer patients' attitudes and unmet needs. *Cancer Nurs.* **16**: 193–203.

Aranda S (1999) Global perspectives on palliative care. *Cancer Nurs.* **22**: 33–9.

Becker R (1999) Teaching communication skills with the dying across cultural boundaries. *Br J Nurs.* **8**: 938–42

Becker R (2003) Bridging the gap: European collaboration in palliative care education. *Eur J Palliat Care.* **10**(6): 244–6.

Beck-Friis B (1997) A Swedish model of home care. In: D Clark, J Hockley and S Ahmedzai (eds) (1997) *New Themes in Palliative Care.* Open University Press, Buckingham.

Corner J and Dunlop R (1997) New approaches to care. In: D Clark, J Hockley and S Ahmedzai (eds) (1997) *New Themes in Palliative Care.* Open University Press, Buckingham.

Dodd MJ, Ahmed NT, Lindsey AM and Piper BF (1985) Attitudes of patients in Egypt about cancer and its treatment. *Cancer Nurs.* **8**: 278–84.

Doyle D (1999) Upon reflection: a farewell address. *Support Care Cancer.* **8**(2): 77–9.

Gordon DR (1990) Embodying illness, embodying cancer. *Cult Med Psychiatry.* **14**: 275–97

Hilton LW (1999) Vital signs at the Millennium: becoming more than we are. *Cancer Nurs.* **22**: 6–16

James CR and Macleod RD (1993) The problematic nature of education in palliative care. *J Palliat Care.* **9**: 5–11.

Jones W (1997) Issues affecting the delivery of palliative care in Russia. *Int J Palliat Nurs.* **3**: 82–6.

Larue F (1995) Oncologists' and primary care physicians' attitudes towards pain control and morphine prescribing in France. *Cancer.* **75**: 2375–82.

Magrath I and Litvah J (1993) Cancer in developing countries: opportunity and challenge. *J Natl Cancer Inst.* **85**: 862–74.

Navon L (1999) Cultural views of cancer around the world. *Cancer Nurs.* **22**: 39–45.

Neale B (1993) Informal care and community care. In: D Clark (ed.) *The Future of Palliative Care.* Open University Press, Buckingham.

Sembhi K (1995) Palliative care in developing countries: luxury or necessity? *Int J Palliat Nurs.* **1**: 48–52.

Stjernsward J and Joranson D (1995) Opioid availability and cancer pain: an unnecessary tragedy. *Support Cancer Care.* **3**: 164–7.

Takeda F (1993) Assessment of physicians' attitudes to cancer pain management in Japan. In: GF Gebhart and TS Jenson (eds) *Proceedings of the Seventh World Congress on Pain.* IASP Press, Seattle. WA.

Trill MD and Holland J (1993) Cross-cultural differences in the care of patients with cancer: a review. *Gen Hosp Psychiatry.* **15**: 21–30.

Van Roenn JJ (1993) Physicians' attitude and practice in cancer pain management: a survey from the Eastern Co-operative Oncology Group. *Ann Intern Med.* **119**: 121–6.

Further reading

Jeffrey D (2000) *Teaching Palliative Care: a toolbox.* Midwives Press, London.

Jeffrey D (ed.) (2001) *Teaching Palliative Care.* Radcliffe Medical Press, Oxford.

MacLeod RD and James C (eds) (1994) *Teaching Palliative Care: issues and implications.* Patten Press, Oxford.

Websites that may be of interest

European Association of Palliative Care: www.eapcnet.org/

The Hospice and Palliative Nurses Association: www.hpna.org

The Socrates Erasmus Programme: www.erasmus.ac.uk/

The Hospice Information Service based at St Christopher's Hospice in London, UK: www.hospiceinformation.info/

The Soros Foundation: www.soros.org/netprog.html
This site provides links to the Open Society Institute.

Hospice Care: www.hospicecare.com/
This site sets out to promote communication and to provide an education resource for patients, professionals, healthcare providers and policy makers around the world.

The Edmonton Regional Palliative Care Programme: www.palliative.org/
This Canadian site provides a comprehensive range of education information for the healthcare professional, including online courses.

The End-of-Life Physician Education Resource Centre (EPERC): www.eperc.mcw.edu/
This site is aimed at doctors but contains much of relevance for other disciplines. Users can contribute their own teaching materials and obtain those contributed by others.

The End-of-Life Nursing Education Consortium (ELNEC) Project: www.aacn.nche.edu/elnec/
This site is produced by the American Association of Colleges of Nursing and has a wide remit for professional education and support.

The Australia and New Zealand Society for Palliative Medicine: www.anzspm.org.au/education/ugc/index.html
This site gives a synopsis of the complete undergraduate curriculum in palliative care for doctors.

Cancer Education; www.cancereducation.com/cancersyspagesnb/splash.cfm
  This site has a wide range of high-quality material on cancer education for both patients and professionals.

Cancer Nursing; www.cancernursing.org
  This site has a rapidly developing range of high-quality education resources and online courses on cancer topics available for study.

CHAPTER 15

An overview of hospice education

Janis Hostad

The principles, the standards, the whole approach in hospice care are of a quality which could be of fundamental service to health provision as a whole. This can only be achieved by the best teachers and the right training, reaching out widely to benefit those in need of it. So, caring and teaching with equal emphasis should be the aim on which hospices in the future concentrate.

(Duchess of Norfolk, Chairman of Help the Hospices 1996)

It is the supreme art of a teacher to awaken joy in creative expression and knowledge.

(Albert Einstein)

This chapter will outline the history, development, complexity, politics and contemporary issues related to hospice education. The aim is to focus on the diversity and creativity offered in such establishments, as well as the challenges to be faced by hospices and their educators in the future.

Learning outcomes

By the end of this chapter the reader should be able to:

- reflect on the history of the hospice movement and how this has impacted on the development of hospice education
- consider the different paradigms, models and approaches to hospice education, and the constraints or the freedom that these may provide
- understand the need for a holistic, creative and flexible approach to hospice education
- appreciate the qualities and skills needed by the educator in providing effective education that will influence attitudes and values and change practice.

Introduction

This chapter aims to provoke the reader to re-examine their ideas and educational approach to hospice education in some small way. By highlighting the advantages and disadvantages of this specific type of education, it enables hospices to consider ways of improving and developing this vital element of their service. Recent years have seen a proliferation in the number of books, journal articles and seminars dealing with the needs of patients with life-limiting diseases. However, there is still a dearth of information with regard to palliative care, cancer and, specifically, hospice education.

History of the development of hospice education

It is important to acknowledge the eminent leaders of the hospice movement, and the effect that they have had on the development of hospice education. The evolution of the hospice movement is not discussed here, as it is expected that the reader is already familiar with these developments, which have been documented in detail by other authors.

However, we do need to remind ourselves that when Dame Cicely Saunders opened St Christopher's Hospice in 1967 and founded the hospice movement, education was an important and vital component.

As hospices were established, staff began to recognise the need to share the skills and knowledge that they were acquiring. The first accredited Joint Board for Nursing Studies on Caring for the Dying commenced at St Christopher's Hospice in London (Hill 1988).

Another major development consisted of the landmark studies by Quint (1967), who undertook extensive research into how nurses were being educated in the care of terminally ill patients, and found the provision to be grossly inadequate. As a result of her work in the USA, Quint argued strongly for systematic death education to be introduced into nurse education and training. The developments in the UK were also influenced by some of the death education programmes that were initiated in the USA in the 1950s and 1960s.

Since then, many studies have been conducted that emphasise the need for education within this field. Some have emphasised the inadequacies in pain education, while others have highlighted deficiencies in the preparation of healthcare professionals for the task of caring for patients with life-limiting illnesses (McCaffery and Ferrell 1995; Doyle 1996; Twycross 1997; Kindlen *et al.* 2000). Some studies have focused on education relating to communication (Crute *et al.* 1989; Heaven and Maguire 1996; Maguire *et al.* 1996; Wilkinson *et al.* 1998, 1999; Krujver *et al.* 2000; Ladouceur 2003).

Many of these studies were conducted in medical schools, colleges and universities (Howells and Field 1982; Field 1984; Field and Kitson 1986; Hockley 1998; Corner 1993; Mills *et al.* 1994; Field 1995; Field and Wee 2002; Dowling and

Bloomfield 2003) rather than in hospices, where such educational research has been sparse. Saunders has continued to advocate the importance of palliative care education. The Wilkes Report published in 1970 also emphasised the importance of this component of hospice care, recommending that there should not be a continued proliferation of hospices, but rather that the emphasis should be on education. Little heed was paid to this advice, with only a minority of hospices investing in this aspect of their service. Sadly, it would appear that some hospices view educational activities as potential income generators rather than a means of improving the quality of patient care. Nevertheless, this educational provision would ultimately be for the benefit both of those within the hospice and of the wider community.

As the hospice movement evolves and the provision of palliative care has widened, the need for effective and appropriate education is increasing.

The *Hospice Directory*, sponsored by Macmillan Cancer Relief and produced annually by the Hospice Information Service, provides very valuable information about the different services around the country, as well as international links. This encourages the sharing of initiatives and reciprocity across the whole of the hospice movement (as illustrated in the previous chapter). Interestingly, although a number of hospice departments and specific manpower resources are listed, no mention is made of educational posts and departments! However, *Hospice Information* does publish regular updated information to help to identify education and training opportunities across the UK.

The nature of hospice education, as already mentioned, implicitly informs the reader that it requires a flexible, creative approach and, consistent with the thinking in many of the other chapters, the central tenet must be that of holism. In order to continue to deliver high-quality 'whole-person' care as healthcare professionals, we aspire to meet the diverse needs of the whole person (Doyle 1996; Sheldon 1996). This is just as true in the educational setting.

Through the education experience, the educator can role model the principles of palliative care (i.e. physical, psychological, spiritual and social needs), thus endeavouring not only to teach these principles, but also to address these needs where relevant with the student. As Albert Einstein said 'Example isn't another way to teach, it is the only way to teach'.

Educators learn to tap into the student's inner resources to improve their learning experience, and ultimately to improve patient care. In other words, this approach aims not just to teach relevant subjects, but also to truly empower the individual to make a difference. Throughout the whole learning experience, encouraging the student to become more self-aware and encouraging personal growth can have a positive impact on care provision (Redman *et al.* 1995; Coles 1996; Sheldon 1996; Loftus and Thompson 2002).

> It is the self-aware palliative care nurse who, with a blend of expertise, intuition, creativity and compassion, can make the experience as bearable as possible for the patient and his or her family.
>
> (Buckley 2002)

Government policies (Department of Health 1996, 2000a, 2000b, 2000c) continue to direct the broadening of the palliative care approach and encourage further education in both cancer and palliative care.

The first document to focus exclusively on education, entitled *Education in Pallia-tive Care* (National Council for Hospice and Specialist Palliative Care Services 1996), provided a foundation on which those teaching palliative care could build. These developments have subsequently led to a need, and indeed a demand, for more education at all levels and in many different formats.

Hospices are ideally placed to provide this necessary service.

Hospice educational provision

Hospices range from those with no specific education department or named respon-sible individual, to large academic departments linked to one or more universities. The number of individuals and types of roles seem in most cases to distinguish the type of education provided. For example, some hospices have a staff development officer who provides career development and support, appraisal training, training needs analysis, health and safety training, etc., with less time spent on academic courses. Hospices that employ lecturers tend to have less input with regard to appraisal training and staff development, and more with regard to accredited academic courses. There are some hospices that have both of these types of roles and approaches in place.

There are also some hospices that have a lecturer/practitioner role, where the lecturer also works alongside the healthcare professionals in their workplace. Often, in such cases, both staff development and academic activities are integrated into this one role.

The provision of education responds to national and local needs and demands, resulting in hospice education in the UK being both similar and diverse. In general, the following areas are encompassed within such educational provision:

- staff development
- professional development
- public education
- research
- academic education.

Before we consider each of these individually, it is perhaps pertinent to look at the job, role and qualifications of the staff. The provision and the staff are intrinsi-cally linked, and therefore when setting up a new education department, the type of person required needs to be considered alongside ideas of how the provision will develop. For example, if the workforce consists mainly of healthcare profes-sionals, should the educator have a similar background? If most of the staff are nurses, should he or she be a nurse? As palliative care is multi-professional, should this be a consideration? Does the educator need to have a background in cancer and palliative care? What academic qualifications would you expect? Is being an academic more important than having the right experience? These are only a few of the considerations necessary to ensure that the right person is appointed to take forward the education provision of the hospice. So what about the qualities of this individual, and what makes a good teacher in this specialised field of care?

Qualities of a good cancer and palliative care educationalist

Perhaps the previous chapters begin to answer this question. As a new field of care, anyone who joins the educators in this specialty becomes something of a pioneer themselves, as Kwa Kwa said in Chapter 2, using Star Trek jargon, 'boldly going where no one has gone before!'.

Most of the authors of previous chapters are working (or have in the past worked) in hospice education in some form or another. Many of these authors fit all of the above criteria (i.e. experience in palliative or cancer care, academic qualifications and relevant healthcare backgrounds). However, the author of this chapter would suggest that many of them also have the qualities which allow them to excel in their roles.

Perhaps this manifests itself in creativity, determination, a humanistic approach, great tenacity, a subtle blend of kindness and courage, an ability to embrace change and to innovate, and of course a sense of humour. Becker, the author of Chapter 14, suggests that cancer and palliative care education demands a reflective maturity which is, he argues, above and beyond that expected within other healthcare fields. This chapter also supports that viewpoint, endorsing the need to choose educators with great care.

Prior (2001) espouses the importance of caring, promoting both the art and the science of caring within cancer and palliative care. Perhaps a missing component of her article is the effect that the teacher might have on caring. Roach's (1987) model of caring characteristics could just as easily be transferred to palliative care and cancer education. Compassion, competence, confidence, conscience and commitment are all important characteristics of a teacher, ensuring that the student knows they are supported throughout the learning process with their particular concerns.

Teaching such sensitive topics requires the teacher to have excellent communication skills so that he or she can pick up the more subtle verbal and non-verbal cues related not only to the students' knowledge and skills, but also to how these topics affect them personally.

It is perhaps this 'connection' between teacher and student, which Campbell (1984) referred to as 'skilled companionship', that sets the good teacher apart from the rest. In terms of Benner's book, *From Novice to Expert* (Benner 1984), this may be starting to describe an 'expert' teacher. As the well-known quote by Carl Jung quote states, 'one looks back with appreciation to the brilliant teachers, but with gratitude to those who touched our human feelings'. In his book, *Mortally Wounded*, Kearney (1996) talks of the importance of working with patients at a deeper psychological level to help to heal their soul pain. He describes the soul as the lining between the surface and the unfathomable and meaning-rich depths of who we are. In one of his stories, he describes the connection he has with the patient: 'She in her turn gave me the incredible experience of soul-to-soul communication at a level I will always treasure.'

Perhaps we can emulate this approach or 'way of being' as educators, by role modelling it with our students so that they may share their feelings, emotions and experiences. This leads to deeper understanding and acceptance of one another's humanity.

The emphasis on this connectivity of teaching and student relationship is shown in Box 15.1, which offers a guide to the specific qualities, attributes and skills of an effective cancer and palliative care teacher. This connectivity hopefully leads to the formulation of this special catalytic relationship and developing as a skilled companion. The caring philosophy and ethos inherent in a hospice environment lend themselves to the formulation of a supportive educational approach.

The list of qualities and skills in Box 15.1 makes an attempt to 'unpick' or deconstruct the connectivity and humanistic nature of this student and teacher relationship and focus on the individual qualities and skills that together formulate this holistic and caring approach.

Benner (1984) claimed that caring cannot be coerced, suggesting that it is embedded in the personal and cultural meaning and in particular the commitment of individuals. This caring ethos is a vital component of cancer and palliative care education in hospices.

The hospices that have invested more significantly in education are in the best position to provide this type of caring, effective and comprehensive service. If they have more than one individual working in a hospice education department, they can provide the most appropriate education as well as the necessary diversity. This means that the educators do not need to have the same background, profession or qualifications as each other, and in fact it may be more desirable to have different knowledge bases and skills.

This diversity adds to the variety of courses and educational events, approaches and expertise available (however, having a number of core competencies common to all educators means that they could provide cover for one another). The hospice would then benefit from having a very highly qualified, trained and experienced team to provide not only academic courses and study days, but also the potential to organise, co-ordinate and develop the organisation's induction, training needs analysis, research, in-service training, staff development (involving appraisals), staff support systems, statutory training, etc. The relevant topics and methods for delivering effective hospice education, although extremely important, are beyond the scope of this chapter.

Box 15.1 Qualities and skills of an effective cancer and palliative care teacher

Core qualities
Empathy
Genuineness
Warmth
Creativity
Passion
Positivity

Attributes
Compassion
Sensitivity
Charisma
Enthusiasm
Reflexivity
Tenacity
Sense of humour

Key skills
Advanced communications
- Listening with acceptance
- Ability to tune in to emotions
- Ability to enable and facilitate emotional expression and recovery
- Increased sensory accuity
- High level of non-verbal skills
- Advanced feedback techniques
- Counselling skills
- Visionary and innovative skills
- Ability to effectively link theory to practice
- Extensive knowledge base
- Relevant clinical experience
- Motivational skills

Ability to constructively challenge students' behaviours, beliefs, attitudes, values and horizons
Research awareness and expertise
Leadership skills
Ability to act as an agent of change
Ability to facilitate individualised, holistic, student-centred learning

Plus
All the usual skills related to teaching/presentation and facilitation

Administrative support

Administrative support is often overlooked, but is an essential part of hospice education. By the very nature of their roles, educators are not often in an office, and it is therefore invaluable to have an office-based assistant who is responsible for the day-to-day smooth running of the department.

These administrative duties may include dealing with telephone calls and enquiries, dealing with visitors, taking bookings for courses, negotiating dates for in-service training, booking any rooms and resources which may be available, and sending out information to prospective students and service users. Further tasks may involve producing posters and programmes, undertaking mail shots, setting up databases of enquirers (either individuals or organisations), implementing the department's marketing strategy, day-to-day running of the library (recording book issues and returns), setting up and testing audiovisual equipment, provision of handouts and teaching packs, producing data for reports, and administering budget spend against agreed expenditure and income targets. (This extensive list is not an exhaustive account of possible duties.)

These administrative support tasks are important, so it is essential to secure multi-skilled individuals. In universities there are equipment technicians, librarians and IT co-ordinators, as well as administrators and secretaries, available to support lecturers. Within a hospice, due to financial constraints, these support services are often incorporated into the role of one individual. The right person, chosen carefully, could oversee volunteer librarian rotas and volunteer educational receptionists and secretaries, and could also support students if he or she has basic IT skills and Internet awareness, in addition to all of the abovementioned roles and skills.

When hospices link with local universities, they are keen to see such support in place to help students, especially the provision of IT assistance on the hospice site.

This role also facilitates good customer care with the provision of continuity and consistency – the same friendly face or voice who can solve simple problems and, if necessary, pass on the specific issue to the relevant educator.

The administrator, in this author's opinion, has a pivotal role that allows the educator to utilise their time more effectively in working with and developing staff and students. A hospice that is determined to improve and develop their educational facilities would do well to invest in such a role!

Staff development

The staff development function of the department can incorporate activities such as career advice and planning clinics, including interview preparation. A full organisation-wide training needs analysis linked to appraisal training is often integrated into this function (this involves developing appraisal strategies and systems, and organising and facilitating all appraisal training). Staff support systems and other statutory and mandatory training may be organised from this department, together with supervision and health and safety training. This usually also incorporates volunteers' induction and training.

Educators need to take into account the Knowledge and Skills Framework (Department of Health 2003b) and the Skills Escalator (Department of Health 2000b, 2000d), mapping them appropriately to skilfully identify each staff member's deficits, and identifying how to develop them to their true potential. The National Cancer Nursing Competencies have now been mapped with the Knowledge and Skills Framework (KSF Mapped Version 2004), which makes the educational role much easier. Their role is then one of extending the Framework and Competencies to palliative care, and matching them to training needs analysis and job descriptions. Evidence needs to be formulated and agreed for each level and competency, to provide a robust system that ensures equity, consistency and quality across the organisation. This evidence could be incorporated into the staff member's professional portfolio so that it can also provide evidence for PREP (United Kingdom Central Council for Nurses, Midwives and Health Visitors 1990). All of this will also be working towards the *Agenda for Change* (Department of Health 2003a).

Competencies are often perceived as the ability to transfer underlying cognitive abilities such as decision making and problem solving to new situations (MacDonald and Taylor 2002).

Safe, effective patient care requires an amalgamation of knowledge, skills and attitude, and is therefore more than a competence (Hager and Gory 1996). Notions of competence have in the past been confusing and easily misconstrued (White 1994). This problem has been addressed, and this is exemplified by the National Competencies that are being developed for different professionals. They perhaps do not go far enough (i.e. producing specific evidence). Clearly there is still much work to be done in clarifying conceptual and theoretical definitions of competence, and in identifying competencies for practice (Flanagan 2000). This is undoubtedly an important area for consideration and action for hospice educators in the future.

Professional development

A thriving education department can offer a variety of professional development opportunities. These may include in-depth training, study days, evening courses, portfolio development, IT skills, study skills, presentation skills, book and journal clubs, clinical governance, quality assurance and benchmarking groups. All of these activities can be used to develop individuals' skills and knowledge, and to change their attitudes.

Another useful approach is to organise secondments and exchanges with local hospitals and the community. Each individual has a learning contract and a reflective journal to accompany them. This method has been utilised by the author of this chapter using Steineker and Bell's (1979) *Taxonomy* to plot and evaluate the learning, and has proved to be most successful. Leach and Scott (2000) suggest that this approach could be utilised effectively as an evaluation tool to measure the learning of students. Evaluation is obviously essential, too, and is covered in depth in Chapter 11.

In a number of establishments the educationalist works alongside the individuals in the clinical setting, or observes their skills in practice. The essence of this work-based learning is for the learner to manage the process, while at the same time bringing together self-knowledge, expertise in the clinical setting and university knowledge to maximise opportunities for learning and staff development (Flanagan 2000).

Some hospices employ lecturer/practitioner or practice development posts in order to achieve this holistic approach. The time split is often difficult to maintain, and many postholders find that such roles require both great dedication and detailed organisation. However, it does allow the staff to be supported and encouraged in applying theory to practice.

Educationalists on the 'work floor' can be very effective, but are not always the complete answer. The staff require help from experienced and knowledgeable practitioners to relate this knowledge to their practice.

It is hoped that in a hospice senior practitioners will have been trained to a high standard, with training and coaching skills to mentor or supervise junior staff and students. They will use their expert skills to help, support and assist the learning process. Mentorship has been found to be particularly successful in assisting role transition when qualified nurses move into hospice nursing (Rosser 2003). This is another teaching opportunity to enhance the practitioners' skills in supporting the learning of junior staff.

Working closely with the clinical managers and charge nurses is imperative. Their support is essential to close the loop in marrying theory to practice. For example, they should make sure that teaching, coaching, mentoring and supervision are written into key job roles. Equally, it is essential to agree on the training needs, competencies and skills required for each role. Ensuring that the managers are aware of the content of the courses and the activities available from the education department will enhance care at the bedside – the theory continues to keep pace with the practice, and conversely that practice is married to the theory. Educationalists need to be aware of planned strategies and developments, such as nurse-led clinics, 24-hour telephone information services, etc., which allow programme planning in collaboration with management to meet the educational and training needs of the service for the future.

All of these unique characteristics and patient care needs will determine the nature and content of the educational programmes which the hospice can offer.

Public education

Many organisations are now developing this key aspect of hospice education. It is an area which possibly has the greatest potential for the greatest expansion. Most hospices are engaged in some form of public education, whether it be public awareness raising, or patient and carer information and educational sessions.

Patient education brings with it different challenges to the usual student groups. There are a number of specific variables that affect patient learning (Redman 1988). Blumburg (1990) mentions factors which are specific to the cancer patient's ability and willingness to learn. These include physical condition, stage of life, means of social support, information preferences and emotional response to the disease. Fredette (1990) supports this view, suggesting that failure to attend to the variable of emotional response to the disease can prevent learning. Fredette presented a model in which teaching strategies are based on the patient's behavioural responses, and she suggested that this improves teaching effectiveness in clinical practice. These are important issues to consider when embarking on patient education. Although the variables might be complex, they cannot be ignored if such education is to truly benefit the patient.

One excellent example of this is the Doncaster Hospice Education Department, where a purpose-built information centre dovetails education with patient and carer information. The aim of the centre is 'to bring together the people of Doncaster affected by, and able to affect the experience of, life-threatening illness in a place designed to offer contact, direction and hope'.

Public education has many other dimensions. These are covered in depth in Chapter 3.

Research

Research is a very important aspect of palliative and cancer education. Unfortunately, research carried out within hospices remains limited. The gaps between theory, practice and research have widened as the specialty has developed (Dowell 2002).

Benner (1984) suggested that the practitioner needs to be able to gain 'know-how' knowledge, and that this is in fact essential for the development of theory. Mulhall (2001) claims that if this is the case, then the theory–practice gap can be reconceptualised as a problem with academia rather than a problem with practice.

An education department within a hospice is uniquely placed to work closely with the staff in their clinical settings, to bridge the theory–practice gap. This could enable a framework to be developed as follows, providing practitioner-centred research as coined by Rolfe (1998).

- *Replicative research*. This tests the findings from traditional research. The educational staff could work with the clinicians and practitioners in the inpatient unit or day hospice, and work with patients to check out the findings of such research in these specific groups.
- *Reflective research*. This helps to produce new personal and experiential knowledge. This could be developed by educationalists working with individuals, or within small group tutorials, with staff collecting information related to a case study or a critical incident. This encourages critical evaluation of and reflection on their own practice, and could perhaps be linked to clinical supervision.

- *Reflexive research.* This is where research and change in practice go hand in hand. It is also often referred to as action research, where the process of research works simultaneously with the change that it creates. In a hospice situation, this is a good way of linking research to continuing professional development, particularly looking at developing healthcare professionals in preparation for promotion. It also allows hospice staff to be involved in the research process, and to see the immediate benefits both to the patient and to the service.

The above discussion illustrates the need for more education, requiring the staff to understand both the research process and change management theory.

Hospices must have all of the relevant mechanisms in place to ensure that the required ethical issues are given due consideration. Some hospices have their own ethical committees, while others link with one of the local NHS trusts.

The only way to move forward with regard to this dimension of hospice care is to ensure that everyone is aware of its importance, as well as making sure that all members of the multi-professional team – managers, educationalists and clinical staff – are aware of how it could improve practice in the future.

The educators can assist in empowering the staff to become involved in research. This could involve running basic research awareness-raising sessions, helping individuals to put together research proposals, and developing a directory of research activity carried out by staff, including their results and conclusions. Staff should also be assisted and encouraged to publish their findings.

Another approach that is increasingly utilised is multi-centre research involving a number of hospice sites, so that the data produced reach the level of statistical significance. This may be useful when looking at improving educational evaluative techniques in the future.

Academic education

This involves the hospice being linked to a university, not necessarily locally. However, if the university is local, this will help the student in terms of career pathways.

Some hospices link together to offer what used to be the ENB 931 Care of the Dying courses. Others offer an extensive range of courses related to cancer, palliative care, bereavement, communication and complementary therapies, some providing courses from certificate level to masters level.

To a certain extent the link with an academic institution, and the way in which it was established, may fashion the approach and development of the education that is offered by the hospice (*see* Figure 15.1).

These appear to be the most common models. However, they are not exhaustive. Some hospices that do not have education departments may have a financial agreement with a university, which can include some form of reciprocity. For example, hospice staff may teach on specific university courses in return for a number of places on relevant courses.

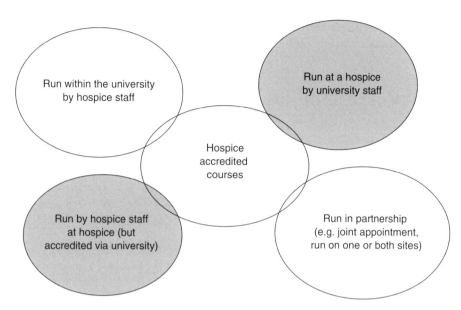

Figure 15.1   Common models of hospice and university workings

There are many benefits to a hospice in having their courses accredited, as the following list suggests.

1   It provides the necessary qualifications for internal staff.
2   Most hospice mission statements state that they 'share specialist palliative care knowledge and skills with others'. Accreditation suggests a research base, and this gives the credence and recognition that the course requires.
3   Accredited courses attract confederation funding, whereas many non-accredited courses do not (i.e. they are free at source).
4   Managers are more likely to release staff for accredited courses which fulfil the growing need for continuing professional development and accrual of academic credits, leading to a specific qualification as well as improved quality of care.
5   Staff are more likely to attend accredited courses, as they fulfil continuing professional development requirements as well as enhancing their skills and career development opportunities.

Some hospices work with more than one university, having different courses or levels of courses accredited by different institutions. For example, sometimes the local university does not accredit courses at level one, so this may necessitate looking further afield. The disadvantage of not working with the local university may be failure to secure confederation funding. It may also mean that students are unable to use their academic points on a locally chosen degree pathway.

The establishment of links between the hospice and the local university can only be beneficial, working towards cross-fertilisation of ideas, knowledge and skills. This leads to a common purpose and a shared goal of improved patient care.

Multi-professional and inter-professional education

Education in palliative care should reflect the principles and practices of palliative care. It should be multi-professional and, better still, 'inter-professional', but also linked to improving the whole process and outcomes of care (Dowell 2002). The National Council for Hospice and Specialist Palliative Care Services (NCHSPCS) recommends that the five principles based on the hospice philosophy should be part of any palliative care education programme. These are to include all disciplines (National Council for Hospice and Specialist Palliative Care Services 1996).

There is some literature which suggests that multi-professional and inter-professional education are interchangeable. However, the term 'multi-professional education' tends to suggest different professionals working together in a formal setting, having a mutual respect and understanding for all of the contributions of the team, whereas 'inter-professional education' suggests professionals from different disciplines learning with, from and about each other in a more dynamic and interactive process.

There are a number of topics which this NCHSPCS document suggests may be taught in a multi-disciplinary arena. Many creative approaches are being utilised. For example, in a hospice in the north of England, a number of clinical and non-clinical staff from general practitioners' surgeries (multi-professional) are brought together for workshops on communication issues, and then again to focus on clinical challenges. This format has been found to be most successful (Gamlin 2001). A major study conducted some time ago in Oxford supported this approach, suggesting that the establishment of multi-professional improvement teams in general practices increased collaboration and focus on planning and strategy within practices (Lawrence and Packwood 1996).

Another excellent example of hospice inter-professional education is found in the regular workshops run by the education team at Countess Moutbatten House in Southampton (Wee *et al.* 2001). The first part of the workshop explores each professional's background, courses and working environment. The second part of the session encourages the students to work together in small groups, while listening to an individual who is at present a carer. The account of their relative's journey is told while the students take notes.

They then discuss the 'story' further and report back, and the plenary session continues their discussions with regard to possible inter-professional teamworking issues. The evaluation of these workshops has been very positive (although research is still ongoing).

Part of its success is surely not only due to the powerful effects of utilising patients and carers in the educational process, but also due to the fact that they ensure facilitators also reflect the different professional backgrounds of the students.

As Wee (2001) states, 'this ability to blur yet respect boundaries between each other's roles is more likely to result in effective and efficient care'.

As yet there is insufficient research to suggest whether these topics are best taught in a multi-professional environment. Most studies have tended to focus only on nursing and medical staff, usually in hospital and community settings rather than in hospices (Jeffrey 1994; Macleod and Nash 1994). Where knowledge and attitudes improved (Breitbart *et al.* 1998), it was not stated whether or not this had influenced everyday practice. There seems to be little examination of pre-baseline knowledge and attitudes, which raises the question of how robust some of these studies were, and how much we can interpret from them.

Considering the inter-professional working environment of a hospice, and the teamworking requirements of cancer and palliative care, it seems well suited to specific inter-professional educational research by hospice educationalists in the future. If this is indeed the best way to teach students, what are the implications? Should the teaching also reflect this and be taught by different professionals, or should there be team teaching with input from a number of different disciplines? How should the courses be marketed to ensure that members of the group are drawn from a number of different professions?

As professionals we have a tendency to polarise towards our own disciplines. Yet within palliative care the hospice movement has always been commended for its multi-professional nature. Within a hospice educational setting there is an excellent opportunity to build on this even further.

This is a challenging area of work, in which imaginative methods of research, planning, delivery and evaluation will undoubtedly provide exciting approaches for the future.

Cost and control

Finances and politics are intrinsically linked within a hospice, particularly within educational departments. Some hospices know little about the educational philosophy of the hospice movement, and as a result do not see education as a priority. They prefer their budget to be spent on clinical services (e.g. inpatient units), not realising the long-term effects of such an approach. This brings to mind the saying 'If you think education is expensive, you should try ignorance.'

It is essential that all education departments work within strict budgetary constraints. However, many such departments have very limited budgets, if any (Chippendale 2001). Chippendale warns of the real risk to some of the independent hospice education units caused by lack of support and finances. The author of this chapter has personal experience of a thriving hospice education department in the north of England being drastically reduced in this way.

It is important that training needs analysis (both internally and externally) is carried out together with business and marketing plans, so that realistic educational budgets within the hospice can be identified. Funding needs to be secured in conjunction with the local NHS trust's workforce confederations, etc., which take into account the national and local cancer and palliative care strategies and policies. However, such funding should only be provided to hospices if they have competed fairly, by tendering.

Most hospice education departments levy a charge for their courses to external participants. However, in order to ensure that healthcare professionals both in the NHS and in the private sector can attend, there is a need to keep costs low. Until cancer and palliative care is recognised as a priority, many healthcare professionals will have to continue to self-fund.

Hospices need to see education as one of their key objectives in providing high-quality care for those with cancer and other life-limiting illnesses. Perhaps this is where educationalists can be of value as an integral part of the hospice senior management team. Their influence can assist in strategic developments, ensuring that education, training, research and staff development are always central tenets. Roache and Baldwin's (1995) conceptual model is consistent with the above approach, with practice and education as an equal partnership involving personal, professional and political influences.

The induction and training of hospice trustees and governors with regard to the true philosophy of the hospice movement may also help to promote understanding about education. Many educationalists also maintain a high profile working with network leads, universities, NHS working groups, etc.

Working in hospice education means being imaginative in obtaining funding from other sources (e.g. from local charities and trusts, national lotteries, etc.). Such funding could be for books, IT, equipment, furniture, buildings, etc. One hospice received £250 000 for a public education project, and another received £1.25 million for an information and education centre.

Key points to consider

- If multi-professional and inter-professional education is to be the way forward, hospice educationalists are well placed to explore the most effective ways of facilitating this. They can carry out research and evaluation so that this form of education may become more effective in the future.
- Each local hospice education department needs to consider how it will interface with the National Health Service University, now that it has come onstream this year (2004).
- Hospice educators need to keep abreast of all new healthcare-related Government policies. The document entitled *Improving Supportive and Palliative Care for Adults with Cancer* (National Institute for Clinical Excellence 2004) has now been published, and this is bound to affect educational provision. The implications of this need to be considered.
- Research activities could be increased and improved by collaboration with other hospices. The data would be more acceptable, and the approach and processes would be more robust. Directories of research projects are kept

at some hospices, and this good practice could be disseminated so that ideas, tools and methods are shared. Nationally, this notion of reciprocity would be a good foundation leading to more comprehensive collaborative research in the future.

- Hospices must ensure that they have developed an effective appraisal system, interfacing with the Knowledge and Skills Framework (Department of Health 2003b), the Skills Escalator (Department of Health 2000b, 2000d), detailed training needs analysis and the *Agenda For Change* (Department of Health 2003a). All of these must be mapped together in order to produce more competent practitioners who can truly make a difference in practice. This will increase educational effectiveness for the future.
- Hospices must evaluate their own mission statement, philosophy, business plan and hospice strategy. In what way does education feature? Is it an important and integral element of the hospice provision? It is often at this level that education is not given the credibility that it deserves and requires. It may need much effort to ensure that the basic foundations are put in place from which education can grow.
- Strong leadership in hospice education departments is vital for the future, when competing with the other important aspects of hospice care, to ensure that this element is not merely being paid lip-service.
- Proactive business planning by hospice education departments will bode well for the future (interviewing various stakeholders who are likely to require this education, both internally and externally).
- Appropriate, creative and effective methods of teaching need to be explored, developed, evaluated and shared.

Conclusion

In conclusion, this chapter has focused on how education is axiomatic to the whole operation of a hospice, and indeed the whole of the hospice movement. Educationalists in hospices are publishing increasingly frequently. However, the creative work that they undertake in their workplace tends to be under-reported.

There are a number of palliative care and cancer teachers' professional groups and forums across the UK which do proactively share their good practice. These groups support and encourage the development of cancer and palliative care education.

Perhaps now is the time to unite in order to influence the development of cancer and palliative care education for the future. Use of this dynamic workforce could produce in-depth research studies with a wide range of research methodology – to find out what works best, where, by whom and at what level – in order to ultimately change practice and improve care. Hospice educators in the current financial climate need to become increasingly politically active, and have a collective approach and therefore a stronger voice to lobby the Government to secure funding for hospice education. As Chippendale (2001) stated, 'Palliative care education has achieved a lot with minimum resources – it could achieve even more with a little more funding.'

Finally, hospice education should be given the recognition that it deserves. The lack of funding has undoubtedly limited the delivery of this education both within hospices and to a wider audience. On the other hand, there is still much that can be achieved on a limited budget with imagination, determination and creativity. This is consistent with the original goals of Dame Cicely Saunders (1972), namely that 'effective education is essential to support the development of effective palliative care'.

Education in cancer and palliative care is becoming a dynamic area of health-care, and the need for education in these topics will continue to grow. Therefore in this culture of educational competition and politics, educationalists must continue to strive to find ways of auditing and evaluating, ultimately working together, to cross boundaries, enhancing care through more effective education. To achieve this requires, as stated in the opening quote by the Duchess of Norfolk, 'the best teacher and the right training'. Also of vital importance, as she says, is that 'caring and teaching, with equal emphasis, should be the aim on which hospices in the future concentrate.'

Good clinical practice in cancer and palliative care is therefore inexorably bound to education, and one cannot be developed without the other (Kenny 2001).

The future is boundless so long as hospices are willing to rise to the challenge.

Implications for the reader's own practice

1   What kind of education is provided in your local hospice? Will any of this meet your own educational and professional development needs?
2   Do you develop programmes and study days in collaboration with your local hospice? If not, how would you undertake this in the future?
3   What qualities does the teacher that you most admire have that you would like to role model?
4   In what ways is the educational experience in a hospice setting different to that which you have encountered before?
5   What educational activities do you think hospices should embark on in the future?

References

Benner P (1984) *From Novice to Expert*. Addison-Wesley, Menlo Park, CA.

Blumburg B (1990) *Adult Patient Education in Cancer*. United States Department of Health and Human Services. National Institute of Health, Bethesda, MD.

Breitbart W, Rosenfield B and Passik SD (1998) The Network Project: a multidisciplinary cancer education and training program in pain management, rehabilitation and psychosocial issues. *J Pain Symptom Manage.* **15**: 18–26.

Buckley J (2002) Holism and a health-promoting approach to palliative care. *Int J Palliat Nurs.* **8**: 505–8.

Campbell AV (1984) *Moderate Love: A theology of professional Care Society for the Propagation of Christian Knowledge.* SPCK, London.

Chippendale S (2001) The importance of funding palliative care education: a look to the future. *Int J Palliat Nurs.* **7**: 298-300.

Coles C (1996) Undergraduate education and palliative care. *Palliat Med.* **10**: 93–8.

Corner J (1993) Education and training in palliative care: the nursing perspective. In: D Doyle, G Hanks and N MacDonald (eds) *Oxford Textbook of Palliative Medicine.* Oxford Medical Publications, Oxford.

Crute VC, Hurgie ODW and Ellis RAF (1989) An evaluation of a communication skills course for health visitor students. *J Adv Nurs.* **14**: 546–52.

Department of Health (1996) *A Policy Framework for Commissioning Cancer Services: palliative care services.* HMSO, London.

Department of Health (2000a) *Nursing Contribution to Cancer Care.* The Stationery Office, London.

Department of Health (2000b) *The NHS Plan.* The Stationery Office, London.

Department of Health (2000c) *The Cancer Plan.* London: The Stationery Office, London.

Department of Health (2000d) *Work Force for All Talents.* The Stationery Office, London.

Department of Health (2003a) *Agenda for Change: proposed agreement.* The Stationery Office, London.

Department of Health (2003b) *Knowledge and Skills Framework.* The Stationery Office, London.

Dowell L (2002) Multiprofessional palliative care in general hospital: education and training needs. *Int J Palliat Nurs.* **8**: 294–303.

Dowling S and Bloomfield D (2003) Undergraduate teaching in palliative care in Irish medical schools: a questionnaire survey. *Med Educ.* **37**: 455–7

Doyle D (1996) Education in palliative medicine. *Palliat Med.* **10**: 91–2.

Field D (1984) Formal instruction in United Kingdom medical schools about death and dying. *Med Educ.* **18**: 429–34.

Field D (1995) Education for palliative care: formal education about death, dying and bereavement in UK medical schools in 1983 and 1994. *Med Educ.* **29**: 414–19

Field D and Kitson A (1986) Formal teaching about death and dying in UK schools of nursing. *Nurse Educ Today.* **6**: 270–76.

Field D and Wee B (2002) Preparation for palliative care: teaching about death, dying and bereavement in UK medical schools, 2000–2001. *Med Teacher.* **36**: 561–7.

Flanagan J (2000) Work-based learning as a means of developing and assessing nursing competencies. *J Clin Nurs.* **9**: 360–68.

Fredette S (1990) A model for improving cancer patient education. *Cancer Nurs.* **13**: 207–15.

Gamlin R (2001) Palliative nursing: past, present and future. In: S Kingham and R Gamlin (eds) *Palliative Nursing Bringing Comfort and Hope.* Bailliere-Tindall, London.

Jeffrey D (1994) Education in Palliative Care: a qualitative evaluation of the present state and the needs of general practitioners and community nurses. *Eur J Cancer Care.* **3**(2): 67–74.

Hager A and Gory P (1996) What is competence? *Teacher.* **18**: 15–18.

Heaven CM and Maguire P (1996) Training hospice nurses to elicit patient concerns *J Adv Nurs.* **23**: 280–86.

Hill R (1988) The future development of specialist nurse education. *Contact.* **5**: 2–3.

Hockley J (1998) Specialist proactive – at what cost? *Palliat Med.* **12**: 217–18.

Howells K and Field D (1982) Fear of death and dying among medical students. *Soc Sci Med.* **16**(15): 1421–4.

Kearney M (1996) *Mortally Wounded: stories of soul pain, death and healing.* Marino Books, Dublin.

Kenny LJ (2001) An evaluation-based model for palliative care education: making a difference to practice. *Int J Palliat Nurs.* **9**: 189–94.

Kindlen M, Smith V and Smith M (2000) Loss, grief and bereavement. In: J Lugton and M Kindlen (eds) *Palliative Care: the nurse's role.* Churchill Livingstone, Edinburgh.

Krujver I, Karkstra A, Bersing J and Van de Wiel HJ (2000) Nurse–patient communication in cancer care. A review of the literature. *Cancer Nurs.* **23**: 20–31.

KSF Mapped Version (2004) *Core Competency Framework for Cancer Nursing: delivering effective patient care.* Lead Cancer Network Nurses Forum, London.

Ladouceur R (2003) Breaking bad news: impact of a continuing medical education workshop. *J Palliat Care.* **19**: 238.

Lawrence M and Packwood T (1996) Adapting total quality management for general practice: evaluation of a programme. *Qual Health Care.* **5**: 151–8.

Leach A and Scott G (2000) *Measuring education in palliative care.* Paper presented at National Conference on Dimensions in Palliative Care Education, Scarborough. 3–4 June.

Loftus LA and Thompson E (2002) An evaluation of a palliative care course for generic. *Int J Palliat Nurs.* **8**: 354–60.

MacDonald R and Taylor R (2002) Postgraduate Medical Education for Modern Cancer Services. In: M Baker (ed.) *Modernising Cancer Services.* Radcliffe Medical Press, Oxford.

Maguire P, Booth K, Elliot C and Jane B (1996) Helping health professionals involved in cancer care acquire key interviewing skills – the impact of workshops. *Eur J Cancer.* **32**: 1486–9.

McCaffery M and Ferrell BR (1995) Opioid analgesia. Nurses' knowledge about cancer pain: a survey of five countries. *J Pain Symptom Manage.* **5**: 356–69.

Macleod RD and Nash A (1994) Multi-disciplinary education in palliative care. *J Interprof Care.* **8**: 283–8.

Mills M, Davies HTO and Macrae WAI (1994) Care of dying patients in hospital. *BMJ.* **209**: 583–5.

Mulhall A (2001) Bridging the research–practice gap: breaking new ground in health care. *Int J Palliat Nurs.* **2**: 389–94.

National Council for Hospice and Specialist Palliative Care Services (1996) *Education in Palliative Care.* Occasional paper 9.

National Council for Hospice and Specialist Palliative Care Services (2004) *Improving Supportive and Palliative Care for Adults with Cancer.* National Institute for Clinical Excellence, London.

Prior D (2001) Caring in palliative nursing: competency or complacency? *Int J Palliat Nurs.* **7**: 339–44.

Quint JC (1967) *The Nurse and the Dying Patient.* Macmillan, New York.

Redman B (1988) *The Process of Patient Education.* CV Mosby, St Louis, MO.

Redman S, White K, Ryan F and Hemnikus D (1995) Professional needs of palliative care nurses in New South Wales. *Palliat Med.* **9**: 36–44.

Roach M (1987) *The Human Act of Caring: a blueprint for the health professions.* Canadian Hospital Association, Ottawa.

Roache J and Baldwin MA (1995) Quality through partnership. *Int J Palliat Nurs.* **1**: 96–100.

Rolfe G (1998) *Expanding Nursing Knowledge.* Butterworth-Heinemann, Oxford.

Rosser M (2003) Experience before and throughout the nursing career: transition experiences of qualified nurses moving into hospice nursing. *J Adv Nurs.* **43**: 206.

Sheldon F (1996) The life so short, the craft so hard to learn: a model for post basic education in palliative care. *Palliat Med.* **10**: 99–104.

Steineker N and Bell M (1979) *The Experiential Taxonomy – A New Appraisal to Teaching and Learning.* Academic Press, New York.

Twycross R (1997) *Symptom Management in Advanced Cancer* (2e). Radcliffe Medical Press, Oxford.

United Kingdom Central Council for Nurses, Midwives and Health Visitors (1990) *Report on Professional Registration Education and Practice.* United Kingdom Central Council for Nurses, Midwives and Health Visitors, London.

Wee B, Hillier R, Coles C, Mountford B, Sheldon F and Turner P (2001) Palliative care: a suitable setting for undergraduate interprofessional education. *Palliat Med.* **15**: 487–92.

White A (1994) Competence versus performance – which is more important? *J Adv Nurs.* **20**: 525–31.

Wilkes E (1970) *Terminal Care: report of a working party standing advisory committee.* Wilkes Report. HMSO, London.

Wilkinson S, Roberts A and Aldridge J (1998) Nurse–patient communication in palliative care: an evaluation of a communication skills programme. *Palliat Med.* **12**: 13–22.

Wilkinson S, Bailey K, Aldridge J and Roberts A (1999) A longitudinal evaluation of a communications skills programme. *Palliat Med.* **13**: 341–8.

Appendix 1

Below is a table that illustrates Erikson's *eight ages of man*. Within the table are Freud's psychosexual stages, to indicate where these would relate within Erikson's work. The table demonstrates the *crisis* life stage and the desired resolution. Also indicated are the three further stages which Erikson developed to cover the entire lifespan.

Life stage	Crisis	Resolution	Psycho-sexual stage
Infancy	Trust vs. mistrust	Hope	Oral
Early childhood	Autonomy vs. shame	Will	Anal
Play age	Initiative vs. guilt	Purpose	Genital
School age	Industry vs. inferiority	Competence	Latency
Adolescence	Identity vs. role confusion	Fidelity	Puberty
Young adulthood	**Intimacy vs. isolation**	**Love**	
Maturity	**Generativity vs. stagnation**	**Care**	
Old age	Integrity vs. despair	Wisdom	

Appendix 2

Extracts from Haight's Life Review and Experiencing Form (LREF) (Haight 1988)

Childhood

What were your parents like? What were their weaknesses and strengths?

Adolescence

Do you remember feeling left alone, abandoned, or not having enough love or care as an adolescent?

Family and home

Who in your family were you most like? In what way?

Adulthood

Tell me about your work. Did you enjoy your work? Did you earn an adequate living? Did you work hard during those years? Were you appreciated?

Summary

What was the happiest period of your life? What was it about it that made it the happiest period? Why is your life less happy now?

Index